T0303385

SUPER *Vegan* SCOOPS!

Plant-Based **Ice Cream** for Everyone

By Hannah Kaminsky

Skyhorse Publishing

Copyright © 2021 by Hannah Kaminsky

All rights reserved. No part of this book may be reproduced in any manner without the express written consent of the publisher, except in the case of brief excerpts in critical reviews or articles. All inquiries should be addressed to Skyhorse Publishing, 307 West 36th Street, 11th Floor, New York, NY 10018.

Skyhorse Publishing books may be purchased in bulk at special discounts for sales promotion, corporate gifts, fund-raising, or educational purposes. Special editions can also be created to specifications. For details, contact the Special Sales Department, Skyhorse Publishing, 307 West 36th Street, 11th Floor, New York, NY 10018 or info@skyhorsepublishing.com.

Skyhorse® and Skyhorse Publishing® are registered trademarks of Skyhorse Publishing, Inc.®, a Delaware corporation.

Visit our website at www.skyhorsepublishing.com.

10 9 8 7 6 5 4 3 2 1

Library of Congress Cataloging-in-Publication Data

Names: Kaminsky, Hannah, 1989- author.
Title: Super vegan scoops!: plant-based ice cream for everyone / Hannah Kaminsky.
Description: New York, NY: Skyhorse Publishing, [2021] | Includes index. |
Identifiers: LCCN 2020056124 (print) | LCCN 2020056125 (ebook) | ISBN 9781510757974 (print) | ISBN 9781510757981 (Ebook)
Subjects: LCSH: Ice cream, ices, etc. | Vegan cooking. | LCGFT: Cookbooks.
Classification: LCC TX795 .K36 2021 (print) | LCC TX795 (ebook) | DDC 641.86/2—dc23
LC record available at https://lccn.loc.gov/2020056124
LC ebook record available at https://lccn.loc.gov/2020056125

Cover design by Daniel Brount
Cover photo by Hannah Kaminsky

Print ISBN: 978-1-5107-5797-4
Ebook ISBN: 978-1-5107-5798-1

Printed in China

Contents

Introduction

Digging myself out of the icy tundra previously known as my freezer, I knew I had a problem.

Long gone were the bulky ice cube trays, evicted without advance notice. Previously neat stacks of leftovers lay in ruin, wedged into the farthest corners, largely out of reach. Basic staples like peas and corn now resided in the fridge below, thawing, dripping through zippered bags unceremoniously tossed into the vegetable bin. Ice cream of every color, scooped and stashed in containers big and small, lined the shelves there now, and yet there still wasn't enough room for my latest creation. Layered with mountainous tiers of cake and billowing frosting with a softly set ice cream core, it simply would not fit. Pressing the plate more firmly at the base, hoping some container in back might simply bend and not break, every passing second felt like an hour in which previously perfect pints began to melt back into sugary puddles. When the door finally, agonizingly clicked closed, I sighed with deep relief . . . Until moments later when the magnetic seal failed and it popped back open, yawning wide with icy breath that felt like splinters down the back of my neck.

This is the struggle of the humble ice cream fiend. Surely you can relate, on some level, for always wanting more but finding it just beyond reach. One more scoop on top, one more spoonful before bed; ice cream consumption should have no limit. Those who get it understand how profound this yearning is, encompassing quantity and quality alike. Burnt by icy textures, bland flavors, and boring treats overall, the array of packaged nondairy desserts still has a long way to come.

Making ice cream at home unleashes the full potential of the frozen art form. Anything you can dream, you can create, without the need to rely on animal products as a crutch. Embrace the true, full flavors of peak seasonal fruits, or untainted 100 percent cacao, or whole, fragrant vanilla beans instead of masking them with eggs and dairy. It's a difference you can taste right away.

Beyond simple bases, there's a wide world of frozen desserts completely out of reach for the compassionate consumer. It's impossible to merely pop into the local parlor and pick up a birthday cake, and even more frustratingly, few promising recipes exist to fill that void. Even smaller format novelties are reserved for specialty stores or high-end grocers that command ungodly prices for a few melting mouthfuls.

You and I, true ice cream connoisseurs no doubt, are going to put an end to this. We have the tools, the patience, and (hopefully) the freezer capacity to churn out frozen desserts far greater than the world has ever seen before.

And, in case you were wondering, duct tape does wonders to keep a tricky freezer shut, in a pinch.

What's in a Name?

Ice cream, gelato, frozen custard, ice milk, sherbet, sorbet—deep down in the core of their frozen hearts, what is it that separates these distinct varieties of frozen desserts? At the end of the day, it all comes down to butterfat percentages, at least according to the FDA. The greater portion of fat found in the concoction, the richer the end results, beginning with frozen custard and moving down to the lightest of the batch, sorbet, which excludes dairy products entirely.

Those minute differences become far more difficult to define when talking about vegan frozen treats, containing none of the tell-tale dairy component. For the purposes of keeping things nice and simple, I refer to anything made with nondairy milk as "ice cream," and anything with a fruit or vegetable base as "sorbet." More decadent creamy bases with a truly luxurious mouthfeel might earn the designation of "frozen custard," to signify an elevated level of indulgence above your everyday sort of scoop. Likewise, "sherbet" is appropriate for a halfway blend of ice cream and sorbet; a very fruit-forward treat that still has a bit of a milky foundation. Granted, these titles are largely arbitrary, which means you're more than welcome to rename your creations as you see fit.

As long as you don't call me cold-blooded about these naming conventions, this sugar-coated ice queen will be happy as can be!

Ingredients Glossary

Acai Puree

Finding fresh acai berries in the United States is still somewhat of an impossible dream, but packages of pureed berries are frozen into convenient single-serve packages, readily available in most specialty and natural foods markets. Be careful to select unsweetened varieties to avoid syrupy, sugary blends, or other mixes that incorporate greens or other fruits. In a pinch, humble blueberry puree can also fit the bill, but the results will be sweeter, without the same tart-tangy punch.

Agar

Known also as agar agar or kanten, agar is a gelatinous substance made of seaweed. It's an ideal substitute for traditional gelatin, which is extracted from the collagen of animals' connective tissues. Agar comes in powder, flakes, and sticks. I prefer powder because it is easier to incorporate smoothly into puddings, thickens faster, and measures gram for gram like standard gelatin. If you can only find flakes or larger chunks, just blitz them in a spice grinder for a few minutes to create instant agar powder. Agar can be found in Asian markets and some health food stores, often in the supplement section.

Agave Nectar

Derived from the same plant as tequila but far less potent, agave is the sweet syrup at the core of cacti. It is available in both light and dark varieties; the dark possesses a more nuanced, complex, and somewhat floral flavor, while the light tends to provide only a clean sweetness. Unrefined, agave nectar has a much lower glycemic index than many traditional granulated sweeteners and is therefore consumed by some diabetics in moderation. Any health food or natural food store worth its stuff should stock agave nectar.

All-Purpose Flour

While wonderful flours can be made from all sorts of grains, beans, nuts, and seeds, the gold standard in everyday baking would be all-purpose. Falling somewhere between cake flour and bread flour, all-purpose flour has the ability to create light desserts which still have substance. It is therefore used most often in my recipes and stocked as one of my pantry staples. All-purpose flour may be labeled in stores as unbleached (naturally aged, rather than chemically treated) white flour or simply "plain flour."

All-Purpose Gluten-Free Flour Blend

Standard sorbet and ice cream bases are naturally gluten-free, but some of the fancier recipes call for baked goods to be mixed or blended in. It's easy enough to switch out the wheat flour for a more allergy-friendly mix, though. Many ready-made combinations of gluten-free flours exist in the marketplace now, and though there are varying results based on the brand and the exact blend, most can replicate the texture of standard flour very well. I've had good results with Bob's Red Mill® and King Arthur® gluten-free flour blends, which can all be substituted 1:1 for all-purpose flour. If you'd like to whip up your own mix, that's also a snap if you have a well-stocked pantry.

All-Purpose Gluten-Free Flour Blend

- 6 cups white rice flour
- 2 cups potato starch or cornstarch
- 1 cup tapioca flour
- 2 tablespoons xanthan gum

Simply whisk all the dry goods together until thoroughly mixed. Store in an airtight container and measure out as needed. If the recipe you're following already calls for xanthan gum, you can omit it from this blend.

Almond Meal/Flour

Almond flour is simply the end result of grinding down raw almonds into a fine powder; almond meal is generally just a bit coarser. To make your own, throw a pound or so of raw, unsalted almonds into your food processor, and let the machine work its magic. If you opt to stock up and save some for later, be sure to store the freshly ground almond flour in an airtight container in the refrigerator or freezer. Due to their high oil content, ground nuts can go rancid quickly. To cut down on labor and save a little time, almond flour or meal can be purchased in bulk from natural food grocers.

Apple Cider Vinegar

As with oil, vinegar can be made from all sorts of fruit, grains, and roots, which all create unique flavor profiles and chemical compositions in the finished product. Thinking along these lines, apple cider vinegar could be considered the olive oil of vinegars—flavorful, useful, and an all-around great thing to have on hand. Regular white wine vinegar or the other standard options would certainly *work,* but the distinctive "twang" of apple cider vinegar rounds out baked goods so perfectly, and it is so easy to find . . . why wouldn't you use it? Hunt around the oil and salad dressing aisles in your local supermarket, where you should have no problem securing a bottle.

Aquafaba

It's the not-so-secret ingredient taking the world by storm, dubbed a "miracle" by some and a food science breakthrough by others. In case you're not already a fervent fan, aquafaba is the excess liquid found in any ordinary can of chickpeas. Technically, any bean can produce aquafaba, but the unique ratios of protein and starch found in garbanzo beans has been found to best mimic the unique binding and whipping properties previously only seen in egg whites. Different brands will yield slightly different results, but I've never found any that are complete duds. For more delicate applications like meringues or marshmallow creme, you can always concentrate your aquafaba to create a stronger foam matrix by cooking it gently over the stove and reducing some of the water.

Arrowroot Powder/Flour

Thanks to arrowroot, you can thicken sauces, puddings, and mousses with ease. This white powder is very similar to kudzu and is often compared to other starchy flours. However, arrowroot is so fine that it produces much smoother, creamier results, and is less likely to stick together and form large, glutinous lumps. It freezes very nicely, which is why it's one of my favorite thickeners when making ice cream. Compared to cornstarch, it generally has a silkier texture, is translucent, and holds up to acidic ingredients better as well. Most mega-marts have one or two brands to choose from tucked in among the flours in the baking aisle.

Black Cocoa Powder

What do you get when you oxidize Dutch-processed cocoa powder to the extreme? Black cocoa, of course! Dark as coal, it certainly lives up to its name and produces an amazing, jet-black color in baked goods. However, it has a much lower fat content than standard cocoa, and should therefore be used sparingly to avoid altering the texture of your baked goods. I rarely use black cocoa, because it is difficult to find and more expensive than the alternative. Nonetheless, if you wish to create breath-taking chocolate desserts, black cocoa will never fail to impress. You can hunt it down at some tea or spice specialty shops, but if all else fails, a search online should prove fruitful. Feel free to substitute regular Dutch-processed cocoa for an equally tasty, if comparatively pale, dessert.

Black Salt (Kala Namak)

Lovingly if crudely nicknamed "fart salt" around these parts, the sulfurous odor released by a big bagful really does smell like . . . well, you can probably guess. Despite that unpromising introduction, it does taste far better, and eerily similar to eggs. Enhancing everything from tofu scrambles to loaves of challah, it's one of those secret ingredients that every vegan should have in their arsenal. Don't let the name confuse you though; the fine grains are actually mottled pink in appearance, not black.

Butter

It's a basic kitchen staple, but good dairy-free butter can be quite elusive if you don't know what to look for. Some name brands contain whey or other milk-derivatives, while others conceal the elusive, animal-derived vitamin D_3, so be alert when scanning ingredient labels. For ease, I prefer to use it in stick format, such as Earth Balance® Buttery Sticks or Miyoko's® European Style Cultured VeganButter. Never try to substitute spreadable butter from a tub! These varieties have much more water to allow them to spread while cold, and will thus bake and cook differently. I always use unsalted butter unless otherwise noted, but you are welcome to use salted as long as you remove about ¼ teaspoon of salt per ¼ cup of butter from the recipe. Overly salted food is one of the first flaws that diners notice, so take care with your seasoning and always adjust to taste.

Cacao Nibs

Also known as raw chocolate, cacao nibs are unprocessed cacao nuts, simply broken up into smaller pieces. Much more bitter and harsh than the sweet, mellow chocolate found in bars or chips, it is often used for texture and accent flavor in most desserts. Sometimes it can be found coated in sugar to soften its inherent acidity, but for baking, you want the plain, raw version if possible. Seek out bags of cacao nibs in health food stores; if you're really lucky, you may be able to find them in the bulk bins of well-stocked specialty stores.

Cheese Shreds

Depending on the brand, vegan cheese shreds are generally made from either pea or soy protein, vegetable oils like coconut, palm, or safflower, starches and gums, and yeast. They're a bit different from the artisan nut-based cheeses you'd want to eat plain, with crackers and fruit, but they're designed to melt down to a smooth and creamy consistency, which is exactly what you want for sauces or custards. Daiya® is the most commonly found brand, right alongside Follow Your Heart®, which are both solid choices. They're packaged in hanging bags, nestled into the standard selection of processed dairy options in mainstream supermarkets.

Chia Seeds

Yes, this is the same stuff that makes Chia Pets so green and fuzzy, and yes, the seeds are edible! Tiny but mighty, what makes these particular seeds so special is that they form a gel when mixed with liquid. This makes them a powerful binder when trying to replace eggs, or should flaxseeds be in short supply. Store in the freezer for a longer lifespan, and grind them before using in baked goods to maintain an even crumb texture.

Chocolate

Chocolate is chocolate, right? One would assume so, but many name brands that prefer quantity to quality would beg to differ. Obviously milk chocolate is out of the picture, yet some dark and semi-sweet chocolates still don't make the vegan cut. Even those that claim to be "70% cacao solids, extra-special dark" may have milk solids or butterfat lurking within. Don't buy the hype or the filler! Stay vigilant and check labels for milk-based ingredients, as unadulterated chocolate is far superior. Semi-sweet has approximately half as much sugar as cocoa solids, and bittersweet tends to have even less.

Chocolate Crème-Filled Sandwich Cookies

As America's favorite cookie, it is no surprise that the Oreo® would come up sooner or later on this list. While the original Oreo is now changing its ways to take out the trans-fats and animal products, there are many other options that are even more ethically acceptable. Newman's Own makes an excellent organic version that tastes just like the cookies you might remember from your childhood. Plus, along with some exciting flavor variations, Newman's® Newman-O's (as they are called) can even be found in a wheat-free format! Any Oreo-like cocoa wafers with a vegan crème filling will do, so it is up to your own discretion as to which brand you would like to endorse.

Cocoa Butter

Chocolate is comprised of two key elements: the cocoa solids, which give it that distinct cocoa flavor, and the cocoa butter, which is the fat that provides the body. Cocoa butter is solid at room temperate like all tropical oils, so it's best to always measure it after melting, as the firm chunks can appear deceptively voluminous. For authentic white chocolate flavor, it's really important to pick up high-quality, food-grade cocoa butter, since that's the main ingredient that you're going to taste. As a popular ingredient in body lotions and lip balms, some offerings come with fillers and undesirable additives, so shop carefully if you search locally. Also avoid deodorized cocoa butter, unless you prefer taste-free food.

Coconut Cream

This is the thick, solidified portion of canned coconut milk that forms when chilled. Like dairy-based cream, the high fat content allows it to whip into a fluffy topping all by itself, no additives or sweeteners needed. It can be purchased canned all by itself, without the need to skim it off the top of more watery liquid, allowing for less waste and less fuss. Just make sure it's plain coconut cream, with no sugar, stabilizers, or additives in the mix. You'll still have the best results for whipping when it's thoroughly chilled.

Coconut Milk

When called for in this book, I'm referring to regular, full-fat coconut milk. In the case of ice cream, light coconut milk cannot be substituted without detrimental effects to the final texture. That fat is necessary for a smooth, creamy mouthfeel, and of course a richer taste. Plain coconut milk is found canned in the ethnic foods aisle of the grocery store. You can make it yourself from fresh coconut meat, but in most baking and general dessert-making cases, when it's not the featured flavor, the added hassle honestly isn't worth the expense or effort.

If using coconut milk to extract coconut cream (see above) the brand does, unfortunately, make a big difference in quality. Some have a higher percentage of water, leaving less of the good stuff, and others won't blend as smoothly, or whip quite as high. My favorite is Thai Kitchen®, followed closely by Aroy-D®. Whole Foods®' house brand 365 also makes a highly competent option.

Coconut Oil

Once demonized as artery-clogging sludge not fit to grease a doorframe, nutritionists now can't recommend this tropical fat highly enough. Touted for its benefits when consumed or used on the skin or hair, it's readily available just about anywhere you turn. Two varieties populate store shelves: Virgin (or raw/unrefined) coconut oil and refined coconut oil. Virgin gets the best press from the health experts since it's less processed, and it bears the subtle aroma of the coconut flesh. Refined is wonderful for baked goods, however, since it has been deodorized and is essentially flavorless, allowing it to blend seamlessly with any other flavors. They both solidify below 76°F., but virgin oil reaches its smoke point at 350°F. while refined is at 450°F. Either works fine for raw or unbaked treats, but I would recommend refined for baked applications.

Coconut Sugar

Dark brown granules finer than turbinado sugar but coarser than the standard white powder, this natural sweetener derived from the infinitely versatile coconut palm has a deep, molasses-like flavor more akin to brown sugar. It takes a bit more agitation and heat to dissolve smoothly, but with enough patience, can be used as an equally capable substitute in most recipes.

Confectioners' Sugar

Otherwise known as powdered sugar, icing sugar, or 10x sugar, confectioners' sugar is a very finely ground version of standard white sugar, often with a touch of starch included to prevent clumping. There are many vegan options on the market, so just keep your eyes open and you will likely find a good supply. You can make your own confectioners' sugar by powdering 1 cup of granulated sugar with 1 tablespoon of cornstarch in your food processor or spice grinder. Simply blend the sugar and cornstarch on the highest speed for about two minutes, and allow the dust to settle before opening your machine up to avoid inhaling a cloud of sugar.

Cream Cheese

Many innovative companies now make dairy-free products that will give you the most authentic shmears and cream cheese frostings imaginable. These soft spreads also hold up beautifully in cookie dough and piecrusts, contributing a great tangy flavor and excellent structure. My favorite brands are Tofutti®, Kite Hill®, Treeline®, and Miyoko's®, but there are even more options in ample supply at well-stocked natural foods markets.

Cream of Tartar

Don't let the name fool you; cream of tartar has absolutely nothing to do with either cream or tartar sauce. It's actually created through the fermentation process that grapes undergo in the production of wine. Thus, it can contribute a good deal of acid to recipes in very small doses. Sometimes used as a stabilizer, it can create flavors similar to buttermilk, or be used to create baking powder: For a small batch, sift together 2 tablespoons cream of tartar with 1 tablespoon baking soda and 1 teaspoon cornstarch.

Flavor Extracts

In most cases, I try to stay as far away from extracts as possible, because they are all too often artificial, insipid, and a poor replacement for the real thing. However, real vanilla and almond are my two main exceptions, as high-quality extracts from the actual sources are readily available in most markets. Just make sure to avoid any bottles that contain sugar, corn syrup, colors, or chemical stabilizers in addition to your flavor of choice. For some of the more unusual extracts, if your supermarket searches end up unsuccessful, the Internet will never let you down.

Flaxseeds

Ground flaxseeds make an excellent vegan egg-replacer when combined with water. One tablespoon of the whole seeds produces approximately 1½ tablespoons of the ground powder. While you can purchase pre-ground flax meal in many stores, I prefer to grind the flaxseeds fresh for each recipe, as they tend to go rancid rather quickly once broken down. Not to mention, it takes mere seconds to powder your own flaxseeds in a spice grinder! If you do opt to purchase flax meal instead, be sure to store the powder in your refrigerator or freezer until you are ready to use it. These tiny seeds can be found in bulk bins and prepackaged in the baking aisle of natural food stores.

Food Coloring

Paint the town red—or yellow, green, or blue, if your heart desires, by tinting your treats with a variety of edible coloring agents. Traditional food dyes are of course nontoxic, but full of unsavory ingredients that read more like the contents of a chemistry set than something meant for consumption. Natural food coloring eschews synthetic hues by using the power of plants instead. The results can be more subtle, so it might take larger doses to reach the same intensity. Coloring gels, such as those made by ChefMaster®, are preferable for use in ice cream since they contain less water and thus won't throw off the ratios in the recipe. When it comes to liquid, Color Garden® provides the greatest range of hues with the best clarity, although Color Kitchen® shouldn't disappoint, either.

Garbanzo (Chickpea) Flour

Gaining popularity as a versatile, gluten-free flour, garbanzo flour is just as you might imagine; nothing but dried, ground chickpeas! Although it is now used primarily in baking to substitute for wheat flours and to add a certain density to cakes or cookies, it can also be cooked with water like polenta, and eaten either as a hot porridge or let set overnight in a baking dish, sliced, and then fried to make what is called chickpea panisse. Just be warned that eaten raw (if, say, someone decided to sample raw cookie batter that contains garbanzo flour) it is very bitter and unpleasant.

Garbanzo flour should be readily available in most grocery stores in the baking or natural foods section, but if you have a powerful blender like a VitaMix® (see Kitchen Toys and Tools) with a dry grinding container, you can make your own from dried, split chickpeas (also known as chana dal). Process 2 cups of legumes at a time, and use the plunger to keep things moving. Once finely ground, let the mixture sit for a few minutes before removing the lid of the container, so that the dust can settle.

Graham Crackers and Graham Cracker Crumbs

When I first went searching for vegan graham crackers, I was appalled by my lack of options. Why every brand in sight needed to include honey was beyond me. So, what is a hungry vegan baker to do in a tight situation like this? Keep on looking, of course. Concealed amongst the rest, and often in natural foods stores, there are a few brands that exclude all animal products. Surprisingly, store brands are often your best bets. Once you secure your crackers, you have two options to turn them into crumbs. For a coarse, more varied crumb, toss them into a sturdy plastic bag and just go at it with a rubber mallet or rolling pin. To achieve a fine, even crumb, grind them down in your food processor or spice grinder in batches, and you will have a perfect powder in no time.

Granulated Sugar

Yes, plain old, regular white sugar. Surprised to see this basic sweetener here? It's true that all sugar (beet or cane) is derived from plant sources and therefore vegan by nature. However, there are some sneaky things going on behind the scenes in big corporations these days. Some cane sugar is filtered using bone char, a very non-vegan process, but it will never be specified on any labels. If you're not sure about the brand that you typically buy, your best bet is to contact the manufacturer directly and ask.

To bypass this problem, many vegans purchase unbleached cane sugar. While it is a suitable substitute, unbleached cane sugar does have a higher molasses content than white sugar, so it has more of a brown sugar–like flavor, and tends to produce desserts that are denser. Luckily, there are a few caring companies that go through great pains to ensure the purity of their sugar products, such as Florida Crystals®, Zulka®, Wholesome Sweeteners®, Now Foods®, Trader Joe's®, Woodstock Farms®, and Sugar in the Raw®, among others. I typically opt for one of these vegan sugar brands to get the best results. You can often find appropriate sugar in health food store bulk bins these days to save some money, but as always, verify the source before forking over the cash. As sugar can be a touchy vegan subject, it is best to use your own judgment when considering which brand to purchase.

Hemp Seeds

Yes, these are edible seeds from cannabis sativa, but unlike the leaves, they won't get you high. Instead, they're a concentrated source of omega-3 fatty acids and many other vital nutrients, which has bolstered their public profile in recent years. Dubbed a "superfood" by many, what I find most attractive about these tiny kernels is their deeply savory, nutty flavor that blends nicely into both sweet and savory applications. Most hemp seeds are sold hulled, to make them a bit easier on the digestion, and are often squirreled away amongst the dietary supplements or in bulk bins.

Instant Coffee Powder or Granules

Though completely unfit for drinking as intended, instant coffee powder is an ideal way to add those crave-worthy roasted, smoky notes to any dessert without also incorporating a lot of extra liquid. This is especially important when keeping ratios intact for ice cream. Stored in the fridge, a small jar should last a long time. You can even find decaf versions, in case you're more sensitive to caffeine but still want that flavor in your recipes. I prefer powder to granules because it dissolves more easily, but both can work interchangeably with a bit of vigorous mixing.

Luster Dust

All that glitters is not gold . . . Sometimes it's silver, copper, and pearlescent, too! They get their gleam from minute amounts of mica. Add an extra shimmer or sparkle to your desserts with these shining powders. Brush on dry or dissolve in a drop of vodka to paint on smoothly. Additionally, you can create shimmery cocktails, champagne, beer, or any drink by adding a little edible luster or super pearl dust to your beverage. You can find them at specialty cake supply stores and many craft stores, in the cake decorating department.

Maple Syrup

One of my absolute favorite sweeteners, there is simply no substitute for real, 100 percent maple syrup. The flavor is like nothing else out there, and I have yet to meet a single brand of pancake syrup that could even come close. Of course, this incredible indulgence does come at a hefty price, and the costs only continue to rise as the years go by. Though it would be absolute sacrilege to use anything but authentic grade-B maple syrup on pancakes or waffles in my house, I will sometimes bend the rules in recipes where it isn't such a prominent flavor, in order to save some money. In these instances, I'll substitute with a maple-agave blend, which still carries the flavor from the actual source, but bulks it up with an equal dose of agave for sweetening power.

Maraschino Cherries

Lurid red marbles that bear only a passing resemblance to the fresh fruits they once were, maraschino cherries are generally an ingredient I avoid at all costs. However, for the sake of nostalgia and preserving the integrity of certain classic flavor combinations, I have been known to make a few exceptions. What I take issue with most is the intense (and vaguely bitter) artificial coloring and syrupy sweetness, typically contributed by high-fructose corn syrup. Thankfully, with a bit of hunting, you can find natural alternatives out there. Versions produced by Luxardo®, Silver Palate®, and Tillen Farms®, for example, contain no preservatives and are colored solely by fruit and vegetable extracts. They can be found in specialty grocery stores and online.

Marshmallows

Snow-white, fluffy pillows of sugar, it's no secret that these simple treats are one of my favorite confections. Most hold a dirty little secret of their own though; the average mallow is made from gelatin, which is made from the collagen in animals' skin and bones. Truly gruesome stuff for such innocent candy! Luckily, Dandies by Chicago Soy Dairy® source kinder gelling agents and are even better than the old-school jet-puffed variety. Found in both mini and regular sizes, keep an eye out for seasonal specialty flavors like pumpkin spice and peppermint, too. Trader Joe's also stocks their own house brand of vegan marshmallows that are eerily similar . . . and at a lower price!

Matcha Powder

Perhaps one of my all-time favorite flavorings, matcha is a very high-quality, powdered green tea. It is used primarily in Japanese tea ceremonies and can have an intense, complex, and bitter taste when used in large amounts. Contrary to what many new bakers think, this is *not* the same as the green tea leaves you'll find in mega mart tea bags! Those are vastly inferior in the flavor department, and real matcha is ground much finer. There are many levels of quality, with each step up in grade carrying a higher price tag. Because it can become quite pricey, I would suggest buying a medium grade, which should be readily available at any specialty tea store. When translated directly from Japanese, the spelling is "maccha," but the typical English spelling is matcha. Whichever way the package is labeled, you will still find green tea powder within.

Miso Paste

Fermented soybeans coarsely ground and mixed with water sounds like a sad excuse for soup, yet it's the single most celebrated starter for any Japanese meal, be it breakfast, lunch, or dinner. The length of time that the beans are fermented determines the color and flavor of the finished paste; traditional miso is aged for at least 3 to 5 years, yielding a very dark, robust, and salty base. Lighter, gentler miso is often called "sweet" miso, which is delicious used as a condiment as well, spread very thinly on an ear of roasted corn, for example. Those sensitive to soy can now find many alternatives, the most common being chickpea miso, which more closely mimics the flavor of a light or white miso paste. Though all types can be substituted with more or less success, no two misos are exactly alike, and any changes can drastically change the end results.

Nondairy Milk

The foundation of all ice cream recipes, I kept this critical ingredient somewhat ambiguous for a reason. Most types of nondairy milk will work in these recipes, and I wouldn't want to limit anyone with specific allergies. The only type that I absolutely *do not* recommend using is rice milk, as it tends to be much thinner, often gritty, and completely lacking in the body necessary to make rich, satisfying frozen desserts. Unless explicitly specified, any other type of vegan milk-substitute will work. My top pick for ice cream making is unsweetened almond milk because it tends to be a bit thicker, richer, and still has a neutral flavor. The best brands include Three Trees® and Elmhurst®, because they use just whole nuts and water, nothing else. Ripple® makes a pea protein milk that tastes the most like cow's milk, and I've got to give a shout-out to Planet Oat® for their "Extra Creamy" variety that churns like a dream. Don't be afraid to experiment, though; there's a lot to choose from!

If a craving strikes when there's nothing creamy in the fridge, in a pinch, you can make your own nondairy milk almost instantly.

Instant Nondairy Milk

- ½ cup smooth raw nut or seed butter
- 4 cups water
- ⅛ teaspoon xanthan gum

Place the nut or seed butter or your choice in the blender along with the water. Puree on high speed, and while the motor is running, slowly sprinkle in the xanthan gum. Although you could technically make milk without this, it keeps the mixture homogenous and a bit more stable, so it won't separate when it sits, and freezes more smoothly.

Keep quick vegan milk in the fridge in an airtight container and consume within 5 days.

Nutritional Yeast

Unlike active yeast, nutritional yeast is not used to leaven baked goods, but to flavor all sorts of dishes. Prized for its distinctly savory, cheesy flavor, it's a staple in most vegan pantries and is finally starting to gain recognition in mainstream cooking as well. Though almost always found in savory recipes, I sometimes like to add a tiny pinch to particular desserts, to bring out more subtle buttery characteristics. There is no substitute for nutritional yeast, so if you can't find it, your best bet here is to simply leave it out.

Orange Blossom Water

Distilled from bitter-orange flowers, this delicately perfumed extract isn't citrus-flavored as it might sound, but floral. A little bit goes a long way, so even a small bottle should last you a good long time. Middle Eastern markets are your best bet for reasonably priced options. In a pinch, rose water can work instead.

Phyllo Dough

Alternately spelled "fillo" or "filo" dough, this gossamer-thin pastry is not something for the average cook (or even most highly skilled ones) to attempt at home. Rather, it's much more sensible to buy it frozen at the grocery store, where most brands should be vegan. Just double-check labels for any sneaky dairy derivatives that may be lurking, and all the rest should be good.

Salt

The importance of salt in desserts cannot be overstated, especially when it comes to ice cream. It's that spark that makes flavors pop and balances out a bit of the sweetness that might otherwise overwhelm the palate. It also acts like sugar, helping to prevent large ice crystals and keeping your frozen treats at a scoopable consistency. In short, you do not want to leave this unassuming but critical ingredient out! Unless otherwise noted, I use regular old table salt (finely ground) in baking. Kosher salt can be fun to sprinkle directly over finished scoops before serving for an extra punch of flavor, but be careful not to overdo it; there's a fine line between salted and downright salty.

Sour Cream

Another creative alternative comes to the rescue of vegan bakers everywhere! Vegan sour cream provides an amazingly similar yet dairy-free version of the original tangy spread. In a pinch, you might be able to get away with using "Greek" style vegan yogurt instead, but it doesn't have the same richness and body, so the resulting desserts may be a bit less decadent. Vegan sour cream can often be found neatly tucked in among its dairy-based rivals in the grocery store, or with the other refrigerated dairy alternatives. The soy-based Sour Supreme from Tofutti® remains my favorite, even after a decade of baking experiences.

Speculoos

Crisp like gingersnaps but redolent of cinnamon rather than ginger, these brown sugar cookies can be spiced heavily or lightly, rolled thick or thin, and used as an ingredient or finished treat by themselves. No two bakers' speculoos will taste the same, but Biscoff by Lotus® brand has set the standard with a mild, universally beloved cookie that is perfectly engineered for dipping into a cup of steaming coffee or hot chocolate. Lacking access to this crisp Belgian treat, graham crackers sprinkled with a bit of cinnamon can suffice.

Sprinkles

What's an ice cream sundae without a generous handful of sprinkles on top? Though these colorful toppers are made primarily of edible wax, they are often coated in confectioner's glaze, which is code for mashed-up insects, to give them their lustrous shine. Happily, you can now find specifically vegan sprinkles (sold as "sprinkelz") produced by the Let's Do...® company, in both chocolate and colored versions, which can be found at just about any natural food store. When you want to go all out and paint the town in rainbow colors, however, you cannot beat the selection on BakingTimeClub.com. Everything in their online catalog is certified vegan, gluten-free, and gorgeous! They make the most stunning blends of every shape, color, and size of sprinkles imaginable. You can also make your own; see page 280.

In addition, you can also make a healthier, sugar-free version with . . . amaranth! That's right; just plain old amaranth soaked in plant-based dyes and dehydrated will do the trick, since these toppers should be applied sparingly and don't contribute any discernable flavor. All you need to do is soak amaranth in a colorful liquid for 4 hours, drain, and bake for 50 to 60 minutes at 200°F., stirring every 10 minutes or so, until dry to the touch.

Use just enough liquid to cover the grains and ratios as desired to reach the shade you'd like, but bear in mind they won't be as brilliant as anything store-bought or chemically enhanced. Variations on these colors are easily blended, but this mix tends to do just fine for that extra touch of whimsy. Bake the grains in separate batches until completely dry to prevent the colors from bleeding. Store in an airtight container until ready to sprinkle in some fun!

Your dyeing guide is as follows:

- Beet juice for red/pink
- Turmeric with water for yellow
- Matcha with water for green

Tahini

An irreplaceable staple in Middle Eastern cuisine, most regular grocery stores should be able to accommodate your tahini requests. Tahini is a paste very much like peanut butter but made from sesame seeds rather than nuts. If you don't have any on hand and a trip to the market is not in your immediate plans, any other nut butter will provide exactly the same texture within a recipe, though it will impart a different overall taste. You can also make your own just as you would make nut butter, but a high-speed blender is highly recommended to achieve a smooth texture.

Tamarind Paste or Concentrate

Tangy, tart, and often downright sour, tamarind possesses a powerful, sometimes polarizing flavor that's best used sparingly to balance out a dish, rather than dominate. Harvesting the edible fruit from the pod can be a taxing proposition, thanks to its tough outer shell, fibrous interior, and hard, sticky seeds. Head straight for the prepared paste, a smooth, soft puree, to bypass the labor without sacrificing the taste. It's readily available anywhere that exotic fruits are sold, either in the fresh produce section or canned goods aisle. Stored in an airtight container in the fridge, I've found that it's pretty much indestructible.

Tofu

Yes, I make desserts with tofu and I'm not ashamed to admit it! When I use tofu for baked goods and ice creams, I always reach for the aseptic, shelf-stable packs. Not only do they seem to last forever when unopened, but they also blend down into a perfectly smooth liquid when processed thoroughly, with not a trace of grit or off-flavors to be found. The most common brand is Mori-Nu®, which is found all over the place, especially in Japanese and natural food stores.

Turbinado Sugar

Coarse, light brown granulated sugar, I just love the sparkle that this edible glitter lends when applied to the outside of cookies. Though it's not the best choice for actually baking with since the large crystals make for an uneven distribution of sweetness, it adds a satisfying crunch and eye-appeal when used as decoration. Turbinado sugar is very easy to find in the baking department of any typical grocery store or mega-mart.

Vanilla (Extract, Paste, and Beans)

One of the most important ingredients in a baker's arsenal, vanilla is found in countless forms and qualities. It goes without saying that artificial flavorings pale in comparison to the real thing. Madagascar vanilla is the traditional full-bodied vanilla that most people tend to appreciate in desserts, so stick with that and you can't go wrong. Happily, it's also the most common and moderately-priced variety. To take your desserts up a step, vanilla paste brings in the same amount of flavor, but includes those lovely little vanilla bean flecks that make everyone think you busted out the good stuff and used whole beans. Vanilla paste can be substituted 1:1 for vanilla extract. Like whole vanilla beans, save the paste for things where you'll really see those specks of vanilla goodness, like ice creams, custards, and frostings. Vanilla beans, the most costly but flavorful and authentic option, can be used instead, at about 1 bean per 2 teaspoons of extract or paste.

Once you've split and scraped out the insides, don't toss that vanilla pod! Get the most for your money by stashing it in a container of granulated sugar, to slowly infuse the sugar with delicious vanilla flavor. Alternately, just store the pod in a container until it dries out, and then grind it up very finely in a high-speed blender and use it to augment a good vanilla extract. The flavor won't be nearly as strong as the seeds, but it does contribute to the illusion that you've used the good stuff.

Wafer Cookie Crumbs

Essentially just flat, crunchy cookies, available in a wide variety of shapes and flavors, there are quite a few vegan options on the market. Just be sure to check the ingredient and allergen statement, and stay away from those that look soft or chewy. For a thrifty endeavor, you could also try baking your own at home! See page 311 for a recipe. With your cookies at the ready, pulverize them into crumbs using a food processor, spice grinder, or a good old-fashioned rubber mallet, depending upon your mood. I prefer to crush mine fairly finely, so that it resembles something like almond meal, but a rough crumble can lend a rustic charm, too.

Wasabi Paste and Powder

Just like the mounds of green paste served with sushi, the prepared wasabi paste found in tubes is almost certainly not made of wasabi root. Strange but true, it's typically colored horseradish instead, due to the rarity and expense of real wasabi. Read labels carefully, because it's one of those things that seems guaranteed to be vegan-friendly, but can give you a nasty surprise if you're not careful. Milk derivatives are often added, for reasons I couldn't begin to explain. Wasabi powder can be potent stuff indeed, but only if it's extremely fresh. The flavor dissipates over time, so be sure to toss any that has been sitting in your pantry well past its prime. If quality paste is nowhere to be found, opt for prepared horseradish (blended only with a dash of vinegar) instead. In some cases, mustard powder can lend a similar flavor instead of wasabi powder, but only in very small doses.

Whipped Cream

Still something of a novelty, big mainstream brands are becoming hip to the plant-based movement and have begun to offer ready-to-use aerosol cans of vegan whipped cream. Reddi-wip® is the latest to enter the fray with both almond and coconut versions. Unfortunately, these toppings are very expensive and often difficult to dispense, so it's much more practical, and nearly as easy, to make your own whipped topping from scratch. My standard formula is as follows.

Coconut Whipped Cream

- 1 (14-ounce) can full-fat coconut milk, thoroughly chilled
- 3 tablespoons confectioners' sugar
- 1 teaspoon vanilla extract

Do not shake the can of coconut milk, and open it carefully so as not to disturb the contents. Skim off the top layer of thick coconut cream, placing it in the bowl of your stand mixer. Save the remaining thin coconut milk for another use.

Start the mixer on low and let it begin to create large bubbles before gradually increasing the speed, until it's all full tilt. Sprinkle in the confectioners' sugar 1 tablespoon at a time until it's all incorporated. Whip the coconut cream for a full 5 to 10 minutes, until thick and fluffy. Add in the vanilla last and beat to incorporate. Serve immediately.

White Whole Wheat Flour

Look out, whole wheat pastry flour, healthy bakers everywhere have a new best friend! It may look and taste like regular white flour, but is instead milled from the whole grain. Simply made from hard white wheat berries instead of red, the color and flavor is much lighter, making it the perfect addition to nearly every sort of baking application you can think of. If you're concerned about getting more fiber into your diet, feel free to switch out the all-purpose flour in any recipe in this book for white whole wheat.

Whole Wheat Pastry Flour

I love using whole wheat flour whenever possible, to add in some extra fiber and nutrients, but all too often it can make desserts dense and unpalatable. This is where whole wheat pastry flour steps in! It has a lower gluten content and is therefore less likely to create that tough, heavy texture typically associated with the wholesome grain. White whole wheat flour can also be used for the same applications.

Wine

While I rarely drink the fruit of the vine, I can tell you that if your wine isn't something you'd want in a glass, it's not something you'd want in a cake or sorbet, either. Avoid so-called "cooking wines" and just go with something moderately priced, and on the sweeter side to complement the dessert that it's going into. Don't be afraid to ask for help when you go shopping; the people who work at wine stores tend to have good advice about these things! Be vigilant and do your homework though, because not all wines are vegan. Shockingly, some are filtered through isinglass, which is actually fish bladders! So, to avoid a fishy brew, double check brands on barnivore.com/wine.

Yogurt

Readily available just about everywhere, there are several great brands with numerous flavors to choose from. No longer just soy, but coconut, almond, cashew, and beyond, there's a nut or a grain for everyone! Unless specified, opt for plain yogurt, rather than "Greek" style which will be considerably thicker. I prefer to purchase larger containers and weigh or measure out the requisite amount, since single serving cups can vary in size. I'm quite partial to the almond-based version made by Kite Hill® but the "cashewgurt" from Forager® is a close second.

Kitchen Tools and Toys

The specific demands of ice cream making require some specialized tools that might not be considered standard kitchen equipment by everyone. Fear not—most are simple and inexpensive implements that are readily available at stores that sell kitchenware, and exhaustive searches of specialty stores shouldn't be necessary. Since the process of creating ice creams is so simple, attention to detail is key, which includes proper collection and care of your appliances, both big and small.

Blender

Having enough horsepower behind your blade can make the difference between silky-smooth custard and a grainy, chunky mess. A basic model can certainly work, as long as you give your mixtures plenty of time to puree, stopping to check the consistency frequently and scrape down the sides of the container to ensure that everything is getting to the blade. Always plan on straining your purees afterward, since there will inevitably be something left behind.

Given an unlimited budget, a high-speed blender is definitely what you want to buy, and I'm a big fan of my Vitamix®. Nothing breaks down food faster or smoother at that price point, and they're a snap to clean. The Blend Tec® is also a highly worthy option to investigate, for approximately the same cost.

Freezer

Everyone has one, but few people give it the attention it deserves. Water freezes at 32°F., but a healthy freezer should hover closer to 0 to 5°F. This is critical for proper ice cream storage, because frozen desserts won't properly set up at warmer temperatures, and freeze into solid bricks if we're looking at sub-zero readings. If a thermometer isn't already built into your particular appliance, it's worthwhile to invest in a simple dial-type model for approximately $2 at most hardware stores. You can get fancier versions that have digital readouts and alarms to let you know about serious temperature variations, but such bells and whistles are completely unnecessary.

Keep an eye out for excessive frost and ice coating the sides of your freezer, because that's a sign of an insufficient door seal. The air from outside is finding a way in due to a faulty closure, and sticking to the insides, turning into that coating of ice crystals. For the proper storage of anything, beyond just frozen desserts, this issue should be looked at by a professional and repaired immediately. A poor seal also means that the temperature is likely not at the level it should be, which is downright unsafe for long-term food storage.

Ice Cream Machines

The single most critical item required for making your frosty treats, aside from the freezer itself, is the ice cream machine. Once a prohibitively expensive luxury item, both unwieldy to use and incapable of churning out any decent amount of ice cream, it's a whole new world of frozen dessert technology out there now. Making ice cream at home has never been easier or more accessible, with countless options to delight your inner gadget geek. Originally limited to different sizes of hand-cranked wooden buckets, you can now find machines that will mix the base, chill themselves, churn the ice cream, do your taxes, and all under thirty minutes. Okay, perhaps that's a slight exaggeration (it may take closer to forty-five minutes), but frozen dessert technology has come a long way. Prices rise precipitously with each additional feature, so be prepared to pay for the luxury of a self-contained unit that can freeze simply with the flip of a switch.

For starters, let's get one thing straight: I do not recommend hand-cranked machines. They may have an irresistible nostalgic quality, and the illusion of creating a more DIY experience, but trust me here, the novelty will wear off after the first batch, if not during the first batch. These archaic machines take much longer to freeze a quart of liquid base, can be terribly messy if they require salted ice as the chilling medium, and are downright exhausting. Plan to skip your workout if you're churning ice cream by hand; the amount of labor that goes into such a process is no joke. If this hasn't yet dissuaded you, bear in mind that at the point when it becomes thicker and even harder to crank, you must actually increase your vigor, to ensure that the finished ice cream has the smallest ice crystals possible, and thus the smoothest, richest mouthfeel.

One of the most basic, affordable, and thus popular models is the simple freezer bowl design, which, just as the name suggests, has a separate insulated bowl that must sit in the freezer for a minimum of twenty-four hours before each batch. It's essentially a giant ice pack shaped like a bowl, which rotates around a stationary but removable paddle. The downside is that you must plan your ice cream forays well in advance; a partially frozen bowl hastily pulled from the deep freeze will yield only slush. The big upside, however, is that $40 or $50 can get you one of these babies, brand spanking new. I would argue that these modest appliances are ideal for just about everyone, from newbie ice cream creators to those with intermediate experience. This is what I employed for many years, until the base fell on the ground one time too many and cracked beyond repair. Treat your machine nicely, and it should last your whole lifetime.

If you have a stand mixer, there is likely an ice cream attachment created for your particular brand that can be purchased separately. These are also of the freezer-bowl variety, but have the added benefit of making use of your existing appliance, saving space and hassle. Don't get me wrong, I'm a big fan of multitaskers, but there's also something to be said for specialized equipment that does one thing, and one thing very well. These types are fine options, but are actually a bit more expensive than the stand-alone sort, ringing up at about $70 to $100. Additionally, when trialing the attachment designed for my KitchenAid® stand mixer, I found that the resulting ice cream was slightly icier than average.

Panicked when I had to replace my trusty freezer bowl machine, I turned to the generosity of my grandmother. It occurred to me that my grandpa had made sorbet every Thanksgiving, but since his passing, that contraption hadn't seen the light of day. Luck was on my side, because my grandma was thrilled that I would take that bulky thing off her hands, since it had simply been collecting dust for nearly a decade, and also because it turned out to be a self-freezing unit. I shouldn't have expected anything less from my grandpa, a self-confessed gadget lover. Fond of having the top-of-the-line tools before anyone else on the block, though the machine was perhaps twenty years old, it was still a state-of-the-art ice cream churn. This variety of machine has in-set bowls that typically can't be removed, which makes for trickier clean up, but freeze from room-temperature to a state of readiness in about five minutes. You can generally churn consecutive batches to your heart's content, with a ten- to fifteen-minute pause in between. A good substitute for this outdated brand now would be the Cuisinart® ICE-50BC Supreme Ice Cream Maker, which has largely the same design and functionality. For hardcore frozen dessert divas, stand-alone countertop appliances are your best option, but they will set you back quite a few pretty pennies. Most start at about $250, and can escalate all the way to $1,000 and beyond, depending on the brand and capacity. For some, the investment is absolutely worth the expense, but most can get by just fine without such a fancy tool.

Pizzelle Maker/Waffle Cone Maker

Imagine a very flat, crispy waffle in cookie format, and you'd get the gist of the Italian snack known as pizzelles. Lovely floral patterns and various woven designs are seared right in using this machine, looking much like a panini press, which uses two hot iron plates to bake a thin round of batter into crispy submission. Still hot out from the iron, they're malleable enough to shape into cones, cups, cigars, cannoli, and even taco shells. These machines typically make two at a time, and while they're a little bit smaller than traditional ice cream cones, I think they're the perfect size for more reasonable portions. Taking a step up and getting an official ice cream cone maker will give you the same experience with a larger, single round plate, and typically comes with a handy metal or wooden cone form to ease the rolling process. I always lose the accessories that go with these things, so I've found paper cups, like the sort you'd find at an office water cooler, to be a great substitute in a pinch. Of course they're not as sturdy so you need to support them more during the rolling process, and they'll only last through one baking session, but they come in packs of about a million, so I think you can spare some every time you want to fire out a fresh batch of cones.

When shopping for a new model, you want to look for one with nonstick plates, a locking mechanism to hold it closed during the cooking process, and ideally some sort of indicator, be it lights or a timer, to show when the iron is hot and ready. You shouldn't pay more than $40 even for a top-of-the-line machine.

Popsicle Molds

For a low-tech and low-cost solution to possible ice cream–maker dilemmas, any sorbet or ice cream base can be transformed into popsicles with the right vessel. Hundreds of various shapes exist, so the main things to be on the lookout for are reusable sticks and the assurance of BPA-free plastic. The sticks may or may not have a drip-catcher at the base (a wider lid to help cut down on the mess) and preference for or against these is a personal choice. More important is that the "handle," so to speak, is included and can be used time and again, so you don't have to constantly keep buying more disposable pieces made of plastic or wood. Don't bother spending a dime more than $15–$20 for a standard nonstick plastic mold, because the additional investment doesn't add up to increased quality or longevity.

Still not sold on purchasing any additional equipment? That's okay, you still have plenty of options if you are a crafty DIY-er. Simple pop molds can be fashioned out of waxed paper cups and short wooden dowels in a pinch. Place six to eight 4-ounce cups on a small baking sheet so that you can transport them all together, and fill 'em up! Insert the sticks after about forty-five to sixty minutes into the freezing process to keep them standing up straight in the center.

Scoops

Even something as basic as an ice cream scoop deserves careful consideration. Sure, you can live a full and happy life with just a sturdy spoon, but the proper scoop can easily create more shapely rounds, cut through harder packed pints like butter, and spare your wrists when dishing out the goods for many hungry mouths at once. There are spades and paddles, which look like flat shovels, solid one-piece dishers, and spring-loaded trigger models. Those with squeeze handles are the most versatile, doubling as cookie scoops for baking, but also the most likely to break or mar the surface of the ice cream due to poorly aligned sweeping metal arms inside

the scoops. A sturdy, aluminum disher with an oval bowl will form the nicest, smoothest spheres, cutting into a fresh pint with ease, and last a lifetime. Standard sizes are about 3 to 4 ounces, but it's nice to have a smaller 1- to 2-ounce scoop for daintier parfaits and sundaes, too. Oh, and leave the trowels for gardening, please.

Silicone Baking Mats

If you're an eco-conscious baker who can't stand to waste sheet after sheet of parchment paper on each separate batch of cookies, I implore you to invest in two or three silicone baking mats right away. The reusable mats fit most standard sheet pans and allow anything baked on top to slide right off. No extra fats are needed to prevent your treats from sticking, so you can bake up healthier desserts while saving the planet from excess waste. Pretty incredible for inexpensive pieces of oven-safe plastic, huh? They last a lifetime, as long as you don't use a knife directly on them.

Springform Pans

When making ice cream cakes, having the right pans will make all the difference in the world. Frozen rounds of quickly melting custard won't easily turn out of a standard cake pan, no matter how many times you spray it with oil, and no matter what, you'll end up marring the surface trying to scrape it out of the bottom. What's worse, though, is if you do use a metal springform pan, but discover that it isn't perfectly sealed, only after your whole quart of fresh ice cream has dribbled out the bottom to coat the entire length of your freezer shelf. Trust me, once you experience it, you will pay any sum of money to never take the ice scraper out in July again. Silicone springform pans have been nothing short of life-changing in my ice cream cake construction. They have glass bottoms that allow you to see the brownness of traditionally baked crust, with soft, flexible sides that snap together snuggly and peel away without protest once the contents are fully set. I bought a set of two on Amazon, thinking it was a bit wasteful since I only needed one, only to have that "extra" become an equally indispensable part of my arsenal. Invest the $20 in a duo and it will pay for itself after a single use, at least in the stress and agony you've spared.

Stand Mixer

While hand mixers get the job done, a good stand mixer will save your arm a tremendous amount of grief, especially if you're a prolific baker. Though not necessary for most ice cream recipes, it will significantly ease the work that goes into any baked mix-ins or accompaniments. A high-quality stand mixer can be expensive, but it is usually worth its weight in gold. Powerful and independent, it is easy to multitask while this machine works its magic. If your kitchen space or budget doesn't allow for this luxury, then a hand mixer, or even the vigorous use of a whisk, will work whenever a stand mixer is noted.

Essential Techniques

Mastering a few simple procedures frequently called for in both baking and cooking will make any culinary task much less daunting. Skills are gained only through experience, so get into the kitchen and start practicing! Even the most timid novices should be able to get these basics down pat in no time.

Assembling Ice Cream Sandwiches

There are two methods for making picture-perfect ice cream sandwiches, depending on what sort of cookies you choose to use to enclose your slabs of ice cream.

When working with thin bars or uncut sheets of cookies, thoroughly chill before turning the whole batch out in one piece. Grab a pan a little bit larger than half the size of the single flat cookie (so for a recipe baked in a 9 x 13 baking dish, a 9 x 9 square pan is a good bet) and line it with aluminum foil. Cut the rectangle of cookie into two equal, mostly square halves, and fit one, upside-down, into the square pan, lined up flat against three of the sides (you will likely have an extra inch or so on one edge). Soften about 2 to 3 cups of any flavor of ice cream, and spread it in an even layer over the base cookie, pressing it all the way out to the edges. Top with the final half of the cookie sheet, and press down firmly so that it will adhere to and smooth out the ice cream center. Use your spatula to level off the exposed ice cream on the side, and quickly move the pan into the freezer. Allow it to set up for at least six hours or overnight before removing and using a sharp knife to cut the individual sandwiches into medium-sized squares or rectangles. Serve immediately, or quickly wrap each sandwich with plastic wrap and return to the freezer until you're ready for a treat.

For separate, round cookies, make sure the cookies have been well-chilled before you begin assembly. Place half of the cookies upside-down on a rimmed baking sheet or jelly roll pan, and make sure you clear space in the freezer to fit the whole thing later on. Take out your ice cream of choice, and scoop equal balls of ice cream onto each cookie. The amount will depend on the size of your cookie, but be fairly generous without going overboard. You should have a nice mound in the center of each while still maintaining a good margin of visible cookie all the way around. Take the remaining cookies and press each one firmly onto the top of each ice cream scoop, pressing down with your whole palm to prevent the cookie from breaking, until the ice cream reaches the outer edges. Repeat for each sandwich; then immediately move the whole baking sheet into the freezer for at least three hours before serving, or wrap individually in plastic wrap for later.

Churning According to the Manufacturer's Instructions

You'll see this phrase in various permutations all throughout this book. What does it really mean? All ice cream makers are different and have specific procedures that best suit their individual capabilities. Always read the manual for your particular machine (Yes, really! That bundle of papers is included for more than just padding!) and learn from your own experiences as you go along, too. If you have a freezer-bowl model, plan on having it frozen for at least twenty-four hours in advance, but from my own trials, I found thirty-six hours to be a safer bet. The amount of time your ice cream should churn is also highly variable, ranging from anywhere between twenty-five to ninety minutes. Just don't be afraid to crank up the machine and get churning to find out what works!

Freezing Ice Creams and Sorbets Without an Ice Cream Machine

Don't let the cost of a fancy ice cream maker stand in your way. Strictly speaking, all you really need to make your own frozen treats is a reliable freezer and a vessel to contain your base of choice. The caveat is that the results simply won't be quite as smooth or creamy, and will take a bit more work on your part, but the flavors will be just as delicious.

Pour your chilled base into a large metal baking pan, about 13 x 9 inches, and set it on a flat, stable surface in your freezer. Now is not the time to try some fancy Tetris-style stacking on top of frozen bagged veggies, trust me! Give it at least forty-five to sixty minutes in the deep freeze before opening the door again to check on it. Once the mixture begins to solidify around the edges, give the whole thing a vigorous whisk to break up any frozen chunks. Move the pan back into the freezer, and take another peek thirty to forty-five minutes later. Whisk again, and repeat until the whole pan of ice cream is frozen to at least a soft-serve consistency. This can take anywhere from two to four hours, depending on the amount of ice cream and the temperature of your freezer.

From that point, proceed as directed by the specific recipe regarding mix-ins, if applicable, and don't forget to transfer it into an airtight container when it's all done.

Grinding Whole Spices

Ready-to-use, ground spices have their place and work quite well in most cases, but if you just try grinding them from whole seeds to taste the difference, it may be hard to go back.

Using the same technique as you would to toast nuts over the stove top, toast your whole spices first. This will bring out the aromatic and flavorful oils, allowing them to have a stronger and fuller taste. Just keep a very close eye on them, as they tend to toast very quickly; about five to eight minutes should do it. They may not appear any different in color, but don't worry, you will definitely smell the difference. Let the spices cool completely before grinding down to a fine powder in a spice or coffee grinder. To achieve the finest consistency, you may want to first try freezing the spices. Measure out for your recipes only after completely ground, as whole and powdered spices measure out to very different amounts.

Properly Chilling Bases

The faster an ice cream freezes, the smaller the ice crystals, and the smoother the texture. That's why it's critical to start by chilling your base thoroughly before it ever hits the machine. Allow the cooked custard to first cool to room temperature, whisking occasionally to prevent a skin from forming on the surface, before moving it into the fridge. Allow a full two to three hours for the base to completely chill before switching on your ice cream maker and proceeding. You can speed up this process a little bit by first transferring the warm mixture into a cool metal bowl, which will conduct the heat outwards in less time than it would take to first cool down the hot metal pot it was cooked in.

Serving and Tasting Frozen Desserts

I trust that there's no need to instruct anyone on how to actually consume their finished treats, but for the optimal eating experience, there really is a way to maximize your enjoyment. First, make sure you let the ice cream sit out on the counter at room temperature for about ten to fifteen minutes, to become a softer consistency and also to bring out the full flavor profile. Our taste buds are dulled by foods that fall below a certain temperature, so frozen desserts straight out of the freezer will be perceived as less flavorful. For that same reason, serve your scoops with plastic, wooden, or biodegradable utensils—anything that isn't metal. The reason for this is that metal conducts heat, or in this case, cold, a bit too well, and thus freezes your palate before you ever get to taste the ice cream.

Storing Frozen Desserts

Air is the biggest enemy of ice cream, so the key to proper ice cream storage is investing in sturdy, airtight containers. BPA-free plastic is your best bet, since they have more flexibility, and can more easily withstand the rigors of freezing and thawing. Glass containers may be pretty and show off your hard work nicely, but they become exceedingly apt to break once frozen, and it really bites when you get shards of glass in your ice cream. If there's a lot of empty head room in your container after filling it with fresh ice cream, place a piece of parchment or waxed paper directly on the surface before closing up the container, to help stave off freezer burn.

Don't forget, the freezer doesn't cryogenically preserve foods, and even the most carefully packed edibles don't last forever. Be sure to label all containers with titles and dates either on stickers or pieces of masking tape, and keep frozen treats for no more than a maximum of four months (although that's never been much of a concern in my household).

Straining Custards

Lumps happen, and that's a fact of life. They *don't* have to ruin your ice cream, though! For the smoothest ice creams possible, it's a good idea to strain every single ice cream base before adding any mix-ins, to remove possible starchy clumps. Though technically an optional step, it's highly recommended. Use a fine-mesh sieve to filter out any offending particles, and try not to press the contents through with your spatula. Rather, tap on the side of the strainer firmly and rapidly to help gravity carry the custard through. Some bases are simply too thick to strain without a bit of additional pressure though, so don't be afraid to get a spatula in there if necessary. Discard any lumps you may catch.

Thickening a Custard

It's not at all hard to thicken an ice cream base (which is essentially a loose custard or pudding) but the key is that you must give it your undivided attention. Whisk vigorously before turning on the heat to break up any possible clumps hidden anywhere within the mixture, and then make sure that you never venture above medium heat. Medium-low is a better bet, as an extra measure of insurance.

Whisk occasionally at first, every few minutes, to ensure that nothing is sticking to or burning at the bottom of the pot. As bubbles begin to form around the edges, keep stirring constantly, with one hand hovering above the heat control. A rapid boil can quickly overflow the confines of any pot, so as soon as it's reached that stage, immediately kill the heat and move the pot off the burner. Keep whisking for a minute longer, to help facilitate the cooling process and ensure that no lumps form right at the end.

Toasting Nuts and Seeds

Many cooks recommend toasting nuts and seeds in the oven, but this isn't my method of choice. For one, why heat up the whole kitchen when you don't necessarily need the oven for the rest of your recipe? Secondly, I don't like the fact that I can't really watch over them or stir when necessary, which leads to horrifically blackened nuts far more often than I'd like to admit. Spare yourself the smoke and drama; try toasting over the stove instead.

Set a medium-sized skillet over moderate heat, and toss in your nuts or seeds. Toast only 1 to 2 cups at a time so that they can all have equal time getting direct heat, thus cooking more evenly. It may start slowly, but once you start smelling that nutty aroma, things move quickly, so don't walk away from this process. Stir every minute or two, until the nuts or seeds are golden brown and highly aromatic. This will take anywhere from seven to fifteen minutes, depending on your particular variety. Immediately pour the contents of your skillet out onto a plate, to prevent continued cooking and subsequent burning.

Using Whole Vanilla Beans

There may be some killer vanilla extracts on the market these days, but there's still no liquid elixir that can touch the potent, sweet essence of a whole vanilla bean. You want to seek out plump, supple beans that bend easily without snapping. They should have a strong scent that carries a natural sweetness with it. Using them in your recipes is simple: Slit one bean lengthwise with a sharp knife and scrape out the tiny seeds within. Add those seeds to your mixture, and be thorough to extract every bit of bean you can.

For additional flavor, toss the spent vanilla bean pods into the ice cream base as well, to infuse, and then remove before churning. Personally, I prefer to save the pods instead in a container of granulated sugar to create incredible vanilla sugar, which does wonders as the crust of crème *brûlée*.

Troubleshooting

Ice Cream or Sorbet Too Hard?

This is, hands down, the most common complaint I've heard (and also made myself). There are a number of culprits contributing to rock-solid, unscoopable ice cream. It's not necessarily the sign of a bad recipe or a cook's error. Simply let the ice cream thaw on the counter for ten to fifteen minutes before serving, and warm your ice cream scoop or paddle in hot water before scooping. It's helpful to let ice cream "warm" slightly regardless of the texture, as your taste buds are more capable of discerning delicate flavors when the food in question isn't eaten straight from the freezer.

Slush That Refuses to Fully Freeze?

The culprit here is an excessive measure of either sugar or alcohol, as both inhibit ice crystal formation. That's usually a good thing, but too much will prevent ice cream from solidifying at all. Your best bet is to bring the mixture back to room temperature, whisk in additional nondairy milk to dilute the base a bit, and re-churn.

Crunchy or Icy Texture?

If you're having trouble with icy results or simply want to guarantee the most luxuriously smooth texture possible, a pinch of homemade ice cream stabilizer can make a world of difference.

A generic term like "stabilizers" may sound like a euphemism for "barely food-grade chemicals of unknown origin," but fear not—there aren't any questionable additives to be found here! All of my recipes are formulated to make creamy, easily scooped frozen desserts, but to attain the level of smoothness and richness found within commercially packed pints, this little secret ingredient will do the trick. Just a tiny amount is needed, so even a small batch like the one detailed here will go a long way. Best of all, it can't go bad, so just keep the powder sealed in an airtight container and stashed in a cool place, and it can last for years.

The stabilizer makes ice cream "creamier" because it inhibits ice crystals, not because it's bringing any innate creaminess to the table. You can never turn a flat-out failed custard into incredible ice cream, but it sure does help improve a frozen dessert that just needs a tiny boost in the texture department.

Homemade Ice Cream Stabilizer

- 2 tablespoons guar gum
- 1½ tablespoons xanthan gum
- 1½ tablespoons fine soy lecithin powder (not granules)
- 1 teaspoon cornstarch

Stir everything together in an airtight container and store in a cool, dark place until needed. Using ¼ to ½ teaspoon of the powdered blend for every quart of ice cream base, incorporate the stabilizer by constantly agitating the liquid base while slowly sprinkling in the powder. It can clump very easily, so I would suggest churning it rapidly with an immersion blender or traditional blender while adding the powdered mix.

Note: This stabilizer will not work in sorbets.

Ice Cream That's Too Sweet?

For those with a more sensitive palate and a tendency toward less sweet desserts in general, you may wish to reduce the sugar slightly in some recipes. The amount of sugar is delicately balanced, though, so it's difficult to change the amount without throwing off the carefully calibrated ratio of remaining ingredients. Alcohol is also considered a type of sugar, so you can maintain a smooth texture if the amount of alcohol is increased while the granulated or liquid sweetener is decreased. Generally, try adding 2 to 3 tablespoons of vodka to remove up to ¼ cup of sugar, and don't be afraid to tweak accordingly. Bear in mind that these adjustments will inevitably alter the final flavor as well.

One of the best things about frozen desserts is that, in general, they're very forgiving; Most can be melted, tweaked, and churned all over again. Don't give up on a disappointing first spin!

SOLO SCOOPS

When you just want to dig into the freezer and pull out a pint worthy of spooning all by itself, there's a flavor here to suit every occasion, tame every craving, be it a classic vanilla or complex caramelized crunchy affair. Many of these are called for in the chapters that follow to form the base of other desserts, but consider them more like suggestions, rather than mandates. After all, this is your personal indulgence; adjust ingredients to taste, and don't be afraid to put your own twist on these creamy (or fruity, funky, salty, or savory) creations!

Any type of granola that strikes your fancy will work just fine, but it's best to avoid blends that include dried fruits. It varies depending on the variety, but they frequently freeze too hard to bite through comfortably.

Acai Bowl Sorbet

MAKES ABOUT 1½ QUARTS

Brazilians really know how to live. Taking life as it comes without rush or stress, and starting their mornings with what amounts to a thick, fruit-topped smoothie in a bowl, a bracing shot of espresso on the side. Little remembered is the fact that the original recipe was savory, in stark contrast to the syrup-lavished blue blends most popular today, garnished with fish, shrimp, or salted tapioca. For whatever reason, that version hasn't quite taken off in the same way—go figure.

Frozen acai packets are almost like sorbet starters in their natural state, so for anyone who wants to go au naturelle, you can keep it traditional and skip the churn altogether. Just blend up the fruits, adding juice sparingly, using enough to keep the blades spinning.

2 (3½ ounce) packs frozen unsweetened acai puree, thawed
1 medium-sized ripe banana
½ cup maple syrup
2 cups apple juice
1 tablespoon lemon juice
⅔ cup Super Seedy Granola Crunch (page 309), or store-bought granola

Bright pink pitaya is a very common substitute for the earthier blue acai blend, making for a brilliantly colored, albeit more mildly flavored, bowlful. Swap out the acai packets for frozen pitaya (also known as dragonfruit) to try it out.

Toss the acai puree, banana, and maple syrup in your blender. Thoroughly puree until completely smooth before slowly streaming in the apple juice and lemon juice. Blend to incorporate.

Transfer the sorbet base to your ice cream machine and churn according to the manufacturer's instructions. When it becomes the consistency of soft serve, scoop into an airtight container, layering in handfuls of granola with every spoonful. Store in your freezer for at least 3 hours, until firm enough to scoop, before serving.

Serve with fresh sliced berries, bananas, additional granola, and a drizzle of maple syrup for the full acai bowl experience!

Avocado Toast Ice Cream

Makes about 1 quart

Toast, the humblest of all morning meals, has taken the nation by storm. There is, admittedly, a lot to love about a crisp piece of bread smeared with a luscious, buttery, mashed avocado. The best renditions treat the toast more as a vehicle for conveying absurd mounds of the rich green mash, which is exactly what makes this frozen rendition so great. Reversing the ratios by suspending caramelized cubes of sourdough bread in a creamy avocado base, it's at once decadent and wholly satisfying. If you ask me, it's completely reasonable to serve a scoop or two for breakfast.

AVOCADO ICE CREAM

2 large, ripe avocados (about 1 pound)
1¼ cups plain nondairy milk
¾ cup full-fat coconut milk
⅔ cup granulated sugar
2 tablespoons lemon juice
¼ teaspoon salt
½ cup fresh spinach, firmly packed (optional, for color)

CARAMELIZED SOURDOUGH CROUTONS

2½ ounces (about 2 slices) sourdough bread, cut into 1-inch cubes
2 teaspoons olive oil
2 tablespoons granulated sugar

To make the ice cream, begin by pitting the avocados and scooping the flesh into your blender. Add all the remaining ingredients for the base, and thoroughly puree. Blend until no flecks of the spinach remain, if using, and the mixture is perfectly smooth. Chill in the fridge for at least 30 minutes before churning.

For the croutons, preheat your oven to 350°F. Toss the cubes of sourdough bread with the oil and sugar, stirring gently to evenly coat all the pieces. Spread them out on a baking sheet in one even layer and bake for about 15 minutes, until golden brown and lightly toasted all over. Let cool completely before proceeding.

Churn the base in your ice cream machine according to the manufacturer's instructions, adding the caramelized croutons in the final 5 minutes of processing. Scoop the soft ice cream into an airtight container and stash in your freezer for at least three hours before serving. This combination will be delicious immediately, but the croutons will continue to soften into more of a cake-like consistency over time. If you can let it sit and "ripen" for at least a day, your patience will be rewarded!

Bulletproof Coffee Ice Cream

MAKES ABOUT 1 QUART

Stronger than a little latte, more potent than mere caffeine, bulletproof coffee is a craze both loved and reviled with equal passion. A smooth, strong emulsion of brain-boosting fats from both coconut oil and butter, it's a rich brew that can serve as a full breakfast in a cup. Translated into ice cream, that means a bold scoop that packs a punch of intense coffee flavor, bolstered by the richest, creamiest consistency to ever melt luxuriously over your tongue. If you wanted to skip the formalities and spoon into a bowlful first thing in the morning, I certainly wouldn't judge.

1 cup strong brewed coffee or espresso
2 cups plain nondairy milk
¾ cup coconut sugar or light brown sugar, firmly packed
2 tablespoons arrowroot powder
2 tablespoons instant espresso powder
3 tablespoons vegan butter
1 tablespoon coconut oil

Whisk everything together in a medium saucepan, beating thoroughly and scraping the corners of the pot to ensure that there are no lumps whatsoever before turning on the heat to medium. Cook, whisking every few minutes, until the mixture comes to a rapid boil, and immediately remove from the stove.

Chill for at least 3 hours, until completely cold, before churning according to your ice cream manufacturer's instructions. Transfer into an airtight container, and stash in the freezer for at least 3 hours before scooping and serving.

Cactus Cooler Sorbet

MAKES 1 SCANT QUART

Modeled after a margarita but with bold dessert flare, the only thing shocking about this neon pink scoop is that it's crafted from only fresh fruit, straight from the cacti themselves. Nopales are best known for their edible paddles, typically filleted and sautéed to stuff burritos, tacos, and more. The fruit, known as cactus pears or prickly pears, are sweeter culinary delights. Think watermelon, but with a hint of cotton candy with a bubblegum top note, and you might have some idea of this naturally nectarous flavor. Though true to the name, their spiked exteriors can inflict some serious pain when handled without protective gloves, the sharp spines have already been removed by the time they hit most Latin markets and specialty stores.

1 pound fresh prickly pears (1 cup seedless puree)
1¾ cups water
½ cup granulated sugar
¼ cup tequila
¼ cup orange liqueur
3 tablespoons lime juice
¼ teaspoon salt

Unsurprisingly, it's hard to keep small hands away from these eye-catching pink scoops. Make a more kid-friendly version by replacing the alcohol with orange juice concentrate.

Breaking down one fruit at a time, slice off and discard both ends. Make one vertical slice down the full length of the prickly pear, cutting it clear in half. Work your fingers in between the flesh and skin, pulling away the exterior. Discard the skin, which is inedible.

Toss the flesh into your blender or food processor and puree until completely smooth, about 3 to 5 minutes, depending on how powerful your machine is. Pass the puree through a fine mesh sieve, pressing out all the liquid and discarding the dry pulp leftover. You should have about 1 cup of seedless puree. Save any leftovers for smoothies, overnight oats, or other desserts! It freezes beautifully in ice cube trays for easy portioning.

Transfer the seedless puree to a medium saucepan, along with the water and sugar. Bring to a gentle simmer over medium heat, cooking just to dissolve the sugar. Remove from the heat and stir in the alcohol, lime juice, and salt. Let cool to room temperature before moving into your fridge to chill thoroughly, at least 2 to 3 hours. Churn in your ice cream maker according to the manufacturer's instructions. Store in an airtight container in your freezer for at least 3 hours to solidify before serving.

For the full barhopping experience, serve scoops in margarita glasses rimmed with coarse sea salt.

Caramelized Green Grape Sherbet

MAKES ABOUT 1 QUART

Have you noticed the distinct lack of grape ice cream options? Not even grape sherbet? I'm here to restore grape flavor to proper prominence, featuring little more than the fresh, juicy green gems, heightened by the subtly astringent, pleasantly bitter edge of burnt sugar. Light on the palate yet bursting with a depth of nuanced flavor, it pays to invest in the best varietals here. There's such a spectrum of green grapes on the market, you may be surprised to taste the difference between seemingly similar fruits. So-called "cotton candy" grapes are shockingly true to the name, for anyone with a serious sweet tooth, while Riesling grapes, traditionally grown for producing white wine, are crisp, dry, and just higher in acidity. If you can't decide, go ahead and try a blend!

1 pound (about 4 cups) seedless green grapes
¾ cup granulated sugar
2 tablespoons lime juice
2 cups plain nondairy milk

To caramelize the grapes, place them in a medium saucepan over moderate heat along with the sugar and lime juice. Use the side of your spatula to roughly mash them against the sides of the pan, breaking down the fruits and releasing their juices. Bring the mixture to a boil before reducing the heat to a low simmer. Stir periodically, simmering gently for 35 to 40 minutes until the liquid has reduced considerably and the color has deepened to a pale amber. It should be the consistency of runny jam.

Transfer to your blender and puree. Leave it slightly chunky if you'd like a bit of texture, or keep processing until completely smooth for a perfectly silky spoonful. Measure out ⅓ cup and set it aside for the swirl.

Blend the remainder of the cooked fruit with the non-dairy milk. Once homogenous, chill for at least 1 hour in the refrigerator before churning in your ice cream maker according to the manufacturer's instructions.

Spoon the soft ice cream into an airtight container, swirling the reserved caramelized grapes in right at the end. Let rest in the freezer for at least 3 hours before serving, until solid enough to scoop.

Carrot Granita

MAKES ABOUT 1 PINT

Naturally sweet, pure carrot juice is a real treat on a hot summer's day. That's where this impossibly, laughably simple granita comes in. Little more than pure pressed carrots and a pinch of fresh mint, even the sweetener could be considered optional, depending on the flavor and intensity of your juice.

While most people think of carrots as salad vegetables, good for little more than color and crunch, I would implore you to open your mind (and mouth) to greater carrot consideration. It's remarkable what a little bit of time in the freezer can do.

2 cups 100% carrot juice
¼ cup granulated sugar, or 3 tablespoons agave nectar
1 tablespoon fresh mint leaves, finely minced

Simply combine all the ingredients and stir until your sweetener of choice has fully dissolved. Pour the mixture into a 9 by 13-inch baking pan and place on stable, flat surface in the freezer. Allow it to rest for half an hour.

Use a dinner fork to scrape any ice crystals that have begun to form on the sides and bottom of the pan. Place the pan back in the freezer and repeat this procedure, scraping and mixing every 20 to 30 minutes for a total of 3 to 4 hours.

Once mixture is thoroughly frozen, you should end up with light, fluffy flakes that look like dry orange crystals. Scoop into glasses and enjoy right away.

Cheddar-Style Ice Cream

MAKES ABOUT 1 SCANT QUART

Cheese . . . in a dessert? Clearly, some terrible mistake has been made . . .

Pondering what deranged, misled cook thought it was a good idea to top a perfectly good apple pie with little shreds of florescent orange cheddar cheese, the combination struck me as downright repulsive. Perhaps sheltered from such cheesy practices, it wasn't until reading about this oddity online, only a few years ago, did I even know such a thing existed.

It sounds bizarre, but the results were truly less shocking that I had imagined. Despite employing a whole package of the orange stuff, the flavor is quite mild. What's most striking about this scoop is the lovely bouquet of floral vanilla aroma, followed by the slightest hint of umami and a curiously sharp twang that might be hard for an unsuspecting taster to place. Moreover, what really made this frozen concoction special was the texture. Thanks to the stretchy, gooey, meltable shred, a richer, smoother, or creamier custard could not be imagined. For that reason alone, I implore you to break down your ideas of "normal" and give the recipe a go! If you're still intimidated by the idea of a cheesy ice cream, perhaps give a mild mozzarella-style cheese a spin instead, and rest assured that it's hardly present when paired with a strong enough vanilla extract.

2 cups vanilla nondairy milk
1 tablespoon arrowroot powder
½ cup granulated sugar
10 ounces (about 2 cups) vegan cheddar-style cheese shreds
1 teaspoon vanilla extract
⅛ teaspoon salt
⅛ teaspoon ground pepper

First, allow all the ingredients to come up to room temperature if they were previously refrigerated. This is critical, because the cheese shreds change considerably in texture, becoming much softer and easier to melt when already warm.

Combine the nondairy milk, arrowroot, and sugar in a medium saucepan, and whisk vigorously to break up any lumps. Place on the stove over medium heat, and add the cheese shreds into the pan, whisking gently until the mixture is smooth. Continue to whisk every couple of minutes, until the mixture comes to a boil. Cook for about a minute longer, until fully thickened, and turn off the heat. Add in the vanilla, and season with salt and pepper. Stir to incorporate.

Let cool, and chill thoroughly for at least 3 hours before churning in your ice cream machine according to the manufacturer's directions. Transfer the soft ice cream to an airtight container and store it in the freezer for another 3 hours minimum, until frozen solid, before serving.

Chile Lima Sorbet

MAKES 1 QUART

Fire and ice can mix, in this incendiary blend of hot chilies and tart, mouth-puckering lime, embedded within frosty scoops that appear on the surface as cold as arctic glaciers. Indeed, you'll get a blast of refreshing, cool sorbet, followed by an unexpected blast of piquant spice. Should chiles de árbol be unavailable, substitute good old ground cayenne pepper instead.

1½ cups granulated sugar
2 cups water
1 cup lime juice, freshly squeezed (from about 8–10 medium limes)
1 tablespoon lime zest
¾–1 teaspoon finely ground chiles de árbol

Easier than making agua fresca, all you need to do is stir, heat, and chill. Mix together the sugar, water, lime juice, zest, and ground chiles in a medium saucepan. Whisk gently, cooking over medium heat, just until the sugar has dissolved. Cool to room temperature before further chilling in the fridge.

Churn in your ice cream maker according to the manufacturer's recommendations. Transfer scoops of the soft sorbet to an airtight container. Let rest in the freezer for at least 4 hours to further solidify before serving.

Cucumber Raita Frozen Yogurt

MAKES 1 SCANT QUART

Is it a dip? Is it a salad? Perhaps it's just a condiment that needs no further definition. Either way, cucumber raita is a staple of any Indian meal, providing the cooling foil to spicy curries of every color. I'm such a fan of the yogurt-based topper that I think it deserves to be the main feature, not just a side. Frozen yogurt has proven itself as a tart, tangy base for countless flavors, so why not open it up to more vegetative options? While this scoop definitely qualifies as dessert, it works surprisingly well as a palate cleanser between courses, or melting into a dinner plate of red lentil dahl, too.

1 cup finely grated seedless cucumber (about half of an English cucumber)
½ teaspoon salt
1½ cups plain nondairy milk
¾ cup granulated sugar
2 tablespoons arrowroot powder
1¼ cups plain vegan yogurt
3 tablespoons finely chopped fresh mint or cilantro
¼ teaspoon crushed red pepper flakes (optional)

Use a manual cheese grater rather than the shredder insert for a food processor. It needs to be much finer than what most machines can produce.

To begin, toss the grated cucumber with salt and place in a mesh strainer lined with paper towels. Let sit for 15 minutes to extract some of the water. Press and squeeze firmly to drain away as much as possible. You should end up with about ⅓ to ½ cup cucumber after squeezing out the excess liquid.

In a saucepan set over medium heat, whisk together the nondairy milk, sugar, and arrowroot. Make sure the mixture is completely smooth before turning on the heat. Bring to a gentle boil, whisking frequently, to make sure none of the starch settles to the bottom and forms clumps or sticks to the pan. When bubbles burst rapidly on the surface and the liquid has thickened significantly, turn off the heat and let cool for at least 20 minutes. Whisk in the yogurt, chopped herbs of choice, and red pepper flakes, if using.

Place in your fridge to cool completely before churning in your ice cream maker according to the manufacturer's instructions. Add the shredded, drained cucumber in the final 5 minutes of churning, separating the strands to the best of your ability, rather than just dumping them all in at once. Transfer the soft, freshly churned frozen yogurt to an airtight container and place it in the freezer for at least 3 to 4 hours, until set and scoopable, before serving.

Dutch Licorice Ice Cream

MAKES ABOUT 1 QUART

As if black licorice wasn't polarizing enough, the Dutch are just twisted enough to take that divisive taste even further. Few other cultures embrace the shocking metallic twang of acid in addition to a strong dose of salt. Licorice has many beneficial health properties, which inspired the original inclusion of more medicinal ingredients. The addition of ammonium chloride yields an unforgettable candy known as salmiak, not to be consumed without fair warning. For thrill seekers and adventurous eaters, the blast of bold bitterness will resonate, like a sour gummy on acid—literally. If that doesn't quite ring your bell, there's no need to Dutch. Drop the acid and make licorice ice cream infused with only the standard dose of controversy.

- **1 cup granulated sugar**
- **2 tablespoons black cocoa powder**
- **2 tablespoons cornstarch**
- **1 tablespoon arrowroot powder**
- **1¼ teaspoons salt**
- **3 cups plain nondairy milk**
- **1 tablespoon anise extract**
- **1 teaspoon vanilla extract**
- **⅛ teaspoon almond extract**
- **1 teaspoon baking soda or cream of tartar (optional)**
- **⅔ cup chopped black licorice candy**

Cream of tartar, or tartaric acid, is a much tamer (and safer) than ammonium chloride, making it an easier, more accessible way to add sour power to your blend. It's commonly mixed with sodium bicarbonate, which is sold as baking powder, so you can use this everyday baking staple instead, without any adverse effects.

In a medium saucepan, combine the sugar, black cocoa, cornstarch, arrowroot, and salt. Before turning on the heat, whisk thoroughly to distribute all of the dry goods, breaking up all lumps, big and small. Slowly add the nondairy milk, whisking to incorporate. Turn the heat on to medium and whisk occasionally, until the mixture comes to a boil. Let cook at a full boil for 2 additional minutes, then remove the pan from the burner. Add in the anise, vanilla, almond extract, and baking soda or cream of tartar if using, stirring to incorporate.

Let cool to room temperature and then chill thoroughly for at least 3 hours before churning in your ice cream machine according to the manufacturer's directions. In the last 5 minutes of churning, slowly sprinkle in the chopped licorice candy so that the moving paddle of the machine incorporates and distributes the pieces throughout the ice cream. Transfer the soft ice cream to an airtight container, and store it in the freezer for another 3 hours minimum, or until frozen solid, before serving.

Garlic Ice Cream

MAKES ABOUT 1 QUART

Perhaps the most infamous element of the Gilroy Garlic Festival in California, garlic ice cream has become the main event for many, with tiny cones offered across the fairgrounds. Rather than playing it up as a token offering merely for shock value, my goal was to truly celebrate the sweeter side of garlic.

Slowly roasted to golden caramelized perfection, the cloves lose their assertive, harsh bite, bringing their natural sugars to the fore. Every cook and eater the world over has experienced this glorious transformation and knows the magic well. The real secret ingredient in my blend, however, is black garlic. Aged for at least 30 days, the cloves turn into spreadable nuggets of pure garlic candy. The mysterious process transforms the ubiquitous seasoning into an entirely new ingredient, difficult to describe but impossible to forget. It's the key here to balancing out the more savory undertones of the garlic, while maintaining its integrity. The end results should still taste like garlic, after all—not like syrupy scampi sauce.

Crunchy garlic chips aren't necessary to enjoy the full effect of this ode to garlic, but they do undeniably elevate it to a higher level, fit for a fancy affair if you should be so bold. Though they make the scoops look tiny, go for the oversized cloves found in elephant garlic, which are easily 4 times the size of the average bulb and far milder in flavor. They'll add a satisfying crunch to contrast with this creamy, cool treat.

Granted, this unusual frozen dessert will not be for everyone. Proceed with an open mind and a genuine love of garlic, and you will be in for a treat.

GARLIC ICE CREAM

3 cups plain nondairy milk
1½ tablespoons arrowroot powder
⅔ cup granulated sugar
2 tablespoons light agave nectar
¼ teaspoon salt
¼ cup vegan Cream Cheese (p. 282, or store-bought)
1 tablespoon black garlic, mashed
2 teaspoons roasted garlic, mashed

GARLIC CHIPS (OPTIONAL)

2–3 cloves elephant garlic
Olive oil spray

To make the ice cream, simply toss all the ingredients into your trusty blender or food processor. Thoroughly puree on high speed for 2 to 3 minutes, until completely smooth. Pass the mixture through a fine strainer to ensure a flawlessly silky texture, if desired. Transfer to a medium saucepan and set over moderate heat. Cook, whisking occasionally, until the mixture just comes to a boil. Turn off the heat and let cool. Chill for at least 1 hour in the refrigerator before churning in your ice cream maker according to the manufacturer's instructions.

Spoon the soft ice cream into an airtight container and let set in the freezer for at least 3 hours before serving, until solid enough to scoop.

For the garlic chips, peel and slice the giant cloves of elephant garlic as thinly as possible. If you have a small

mandoline to ensure consistency, now is when you want to break it out. Lay out the slices in one even layer on a silicone baking mat (or parchment paper-lined sheet), making sure that none overlap.

Lightly spritz with olive oil to evenly coat the pieces. Preheat your oven to 375°F. and bake for 15 to 30 minutes (depending on the thickness of your slices), rotating the pan and flipping over the slices every 10 minutes or so to ensure even cooking, until golden brown and crispy. Let cool and store in an airtight container at room temperature for 2 to 3 days, maximum. Top scoops of ice cream with garlic chips as desired.

Golden Latte Ice Cream

MAKES 1 SCANT QUART

When you want to feel like a million bucks, give yourself a sweet midday boost worth its weight in gold. Canary yellow turmeric, known for its powerful anti-inflammatory properties, has made a big splash in a most unexpected place. Baristas who would otherwise look down their noses at trendy flavored syrups or the alternative milk du jour are gleefully steaming cups of this liquid sunshine without an ounce of snark. Whether or not the dose reaches legitimately therapeutic levels is anyone's guess, but you will certainly feel your spirit lifted with every golden lick.

2 cups plain nondairy milk
⅔ cup brewed espresso or strong coffee, cooled
1 tablespoon cornstarch
1 tablespoon arrowroot powder
⅔ cup maple syrup or amber agave nectar
1½ tablespoons ground turmeric
1 teaspoon ground ginger
¼ teaspoon ground cardamom
⅛ teaspoon salt
1 teaspoon vanilla extract

In a medium saucepan over moderate heat, vigorously whisk together the nondairy milk, espresso or coffee, cornstarch, arrowroot, maple syrup or agave, turmeric, ginger, cardamom, and salt. Stir very thoroughly to make sure all the dry ingredients are blended in smoothly, with no clumps remaining.

Cook, whisking occasionally, until the mixture just comes to a boil. Turn off the heat and let cool. Chill for at least 1 hour in the refrigerator before churning in your ice cream maker according to the manufacturer's instructions.

Spoon the soft ice cream into an airtight container and let set in the freezer for at least 3 hours before serving, until solid enough to scoop.

Kalamata Caramel Ice Cream

MAKES ABOUT 1 QUART

Hey, you got olives in my caramel! No, you got caramel on my olives! Buttery, briny Greek olives get all mixed up in a prism of crisp amber almond brittle, and no matter how you look at it, everybody wins. Salt acts as a flavor enhancer, accentuating and adding complexity to any culinary equation, and the oily cured fruit offers a highly sophisticated way to balance out a sweet scoop beyond the basic sodium hit. They stay chewy even when frozen for a surprisingly satisfying bite in every spoonful. You might want to make a double batch of the brittle, though. It's an irresistible confectionery tour de force all by itself.

KALAMATA ALMOND BRITTLE

½ cup pitted kalamata olives
¾ cup granulated sugar
2 tablespoons water
½ cup sliced almonds

CARAMEL ICE CREAM

3 cups plain nondairy milk
1 tablespoon cornstarch
1 tablespoon arrowroot powder
1½ tablespoons olive brine
¼ cup olive oil
½ cup granulated sugar
¼ cup light brown sugar, firmly packed

For the brittle, preheat your oven to 200°F and line a baking sheet with parchment paper or a silicone baking mat. Slice the olives into thin rings and place on the prepared baking sheet in one layer, and place in the oven to dry for 1 hour. The goal is to remove some of the moisture without completely dehydrating the olives.

When the olives are ready, place the sugar and water into a small saucepan and cook over medium heat. Swirl the pan gently to mix, rather than stirring with a spatula, to prevent crystals from forming. It should come to a vigorous boil, bubbling angrily, but don't let it scare you into turning down the heat! Timing varies depending on the size of your saucepan and how much surface area has direct contact with the heat, so trust your eye, and your nose, on this one. Once the mixture is a deep amber brown in color and you can smell notes of roasted coffee or lightly burnt toffee, stir in the almonds and olives. Pour everything onto a fresh sheet of parchment paper or silicone baking mat, spreading it out thinly.

Allow the brittle to fully cool and harden, about 20 to 30 minutes, and then roughly chop.

For the ice cream, we're taking a shortcut by using brown sugar instead of going through the whole caramelization process again. Simply whisk together all the ingredients for the base in a medium saucepan over moderate heat.

Cook, stirring frequently, until the mixture comes to a boil. Continue for 1 additional minute before turning off the heat.

Let cool to room temperature and then chill thoroughly for at least 3 hours before churning in your ice cream machine according to the manufacturer's directions. In the last 5 minutes of churning, slowly sprinkle in the chopped brittle so that the churning process incorporates and distributes the pieces throughout the ice cream. Transfer the soft ice cream to an airtight container and store it in the freezer for another 3 hours minimum, or until frozen solid, before serving.

Mango A-Go-Go

MAKES ABOUT 1 QUART

This tangy tropical blend will make you want to jump up and dance! Smooth, soulful mango lays down a creamy baseline while zesty bites of lime belt out the high notes. Goji berries complete the bold trio, harmonizing beautifully while adding their own unique sweet-tart flavor to the melody. You won't be able to get this catchy combo out of your head after the first spin around the freezer.

2 cups chopped, ripe mango (about 1 pound)
¼ cup goji berries
1 tablespoon lime juice
½ teaspoon lime zest
2 cups plain nondairy milk
¾ cup granulated sugar
1½ tablespoons cornstarch
1½ teaspoons arrowroot powder
¼ teaspoon salt

Place all the ingredients in the container of your blender, and puree until the fruits are broken down to a smooth consistency. It's perfectly fine to leave a few flecks of goji berries remaining, as long as they aren't large chunks. Bigger pieces will freeze too hard to really be enjoyable.

Transfer the mixture to a medium saucepan and set over moderate heat. Whisk periodically, taking care to scrape the sides and bottom of the pan, until it comes up to a lazy boil. Cook for an additional minute before turning off the heat. Let cool to room temperature and then chill thoroughly for at least 3 hours before churning in your ice cream maker according to the manufacturer's instructions. Once churned, transfer the fresh, soft ice cream into an airtight container and stash it your freezer for at least 3 hours before serving.

Melted Truffle Dark Chocolate Ice Cream

MAKES 1 GENEROUS QUART

Rather than "death by chocolate," this sole scoop is proof, once and for all, that chocolate is a positively life-giving elixir. No truer, deeper expression of the dark arts can be found at any temperature. In fact, if you wanted to stop after cooking the custard and drink it hot, I certainly wouldn't judge.

3⅓ cups chocolate nondairy milk
4½ ounces (about ¾ cup) unsweetened dark chocolate, roughly chopped
¾ cup granulated sugar
6 tablespoons Dutch-process cocoa powder
2 tablespoons black cocoa powder
2 tablespoons cornstarch
½ teaspoon instant coffee powder or granules
½ teaspoon salt
1 teaspoon vanilla extract

Fresh out of black cocoa? Go ahead and substitute more Dutch-processed instead. The color won't be as dark, but the flavor will be every bit as rich.

In a medium saucepan, warm the chocolate nondairy milk over moderate heat and add in the chopped chocolate. Whisk occasionally to make sure that the chocolate pieces don't just settle to the bottom and burn, until completely melted and smooth. Meanwhile, combine the sugar, both types of cocoa, cornstarch, instant coffee, and salt in a separate dish, stirring well to evenly distribute.

Once the chocolate mixture on the stove is smooth and creamy, slowly sift in the dry ingredients, whisking vigorously to break up any clumps that may form. Continue to cook gently, stirring every few minutes, until the mixture comes to a boil and has thickened to a pudding-like consistency. Remove from the heat before introducing the vanilla.

Let cool to room temperature before moving the base into your fridge to chill, for at least 1 hour. Once it's nice and cold, process in your ice cream maker according to the manufacturer's instructions. Transfer the soft ice cream into an airtight container and let rest in the freezer for at least 3 hours before serving, until solid enough to scoop.

Mulled Wine Sorbet

MAKES 1 QUART

Drawn to the kitchen by the heady aroma of citrus and spice, the soothing scent of mulled wine evokes memories of the holidays, as warm and cozy as a thick knit sweater. Though typically enjoyed steaming hot to fortify against a cold winter's night, it's also quite delightful served over ice, which is where this much cooler rendition got its inspiration. Pull on your mittens and scarves to embrace this spirited yuletide treat!

2¼ cups cabernet sauvignon, or any fruity red wine
½ cup apple juice
⅓ cup light brown sugar, firmly packed
1 large navel orange (zest + ½ cup juice)
1 medium lemon (zest + ¼ cup juice)
1 cinnamon stick
4 whole cloves
1 star anise

Combine the wine, apple juice, and brown sugar in a medium saucepan over moderate heat. Use a paring knife to carefully trim the zest from both the orange and lemon, removing as much of the bitter white pith as possible. Juice the fruits, yielding approximately ½ cup from the orange and ¼ from the lemon, respectively. If you fall short, make up the difference with additional apple juice. Add the zest and juice to the pan, along with the whole spices.

Bring the mixture to a boil and immediately reduce the heat to low, keeping it at a gentle simmer for 15 to 20 minutes, until irresistibly aromatic. Cool to room temperature before transferring to your fridge. Chill thoroughly, for at least an hour, before processing in your ice cream maker according to the manufacturer's instructions.

Scoop into an airtight container and store in the freezer for another 3 hours at least, or until frozen solid, before serving.

Want a non-alcoholic tipple that will still tantalize? Replace the red wine and plain apple juice with apple cider.

No-Churn Vanilla Bean Ice Cream

MAKES 1 SCANT QUART

Plenty of low-tech methods exist for churning out frozen treats without fancy machinery (see page 20 for some tips and tricks), but let's be honest: few people, myself included, care enough to fuss with scraping around ice crystals or shaking a plastic bag of ice cubes all day, all for a few small bites of sweet satisfaction.

Your icy irritation ends here. All you need is a freezer, four ingredients, and an appetite. I would wager that you've already got two out of three already covered. The magic lies in the natural richness of concentrated coconut cream, providing a light, scoopable structure without any further agitation, or irritation.

2 (14-ounce) cans full-fat coconut milk, chilled
1 cup confectioners' sugar
1 tablespoon vodka
2 teaspoons vanilla bean paste or extract

Carefully open the chilled cans of coconut milk without shaking them, scooping off the top layer of thick coconut cream that will have risen to the top. Save the watery liquid left behind for another recipe that calls for plain nondairy milk.

Place the coconut cream in the bowl of your stand mixer and install the whisk attachment. Whip on high speed for about 3 minutes before slowly beginning to sprinkle in the sugar, just a few tablespoons at a time. Continue beating the mixture for up to 10 minutes, until light and fluffy. Finally, fold in the vodka and vanilla. Use as few strokes as possible to incorporate this final addition to keep the airy structure intact.

Spread the ice cream base into an airtight container and carefully move it into your freezer. Allow it to sit, undisturbed, for at least 6 hours before serving.

Ode to Soy Ice Cream

MAKES 1 QUART

In this sweet tribute to the endlessly versatile legume, I'm celebrating soy in all possible forms. Green edamame, tofu, and soy milk form the base, highlighting the nutty, beany flavor, while rather than balancing out the sugar with the bland sodium hit of salt, soy sauce provides a unique savory foil.

It's not such a stretch to suggest candied beans, strange as it may seem on a Western table. Amanatto, literally "sweet beans," have been part of the Japanese culinary repertoire for centuries. To enjoy them as a snack by themselves, toss the cooled, whole edamame in a second round of granulated sugar allow them to dry in a low oven, about 200°F., for about 1 hour. You might just want to make a double batch to throw into your next bag of trail mix, too.

CANDIED EDAMAME

1½ cups granulated sugar
1 cup water
½ teaspoon salt
2 cups shelled edamame

SOYBEAN ICE CREAM

1 cup shelled edamame
1 (12-ounce) package extra-firm silken tofu
2 cups unsweetened soy milk
¾ cup granulated sugar
2 tablespoons arrowroot powder
1 teaspoon soy sauce

Not *soy* crazy about this beige bean? Take another page from the creative Japanese school of thought and transform this blend into the best red bean ice cream you've ever tasted. Replace the edamame in both instances with cooked adzuki beans. If soy allergies are the issue, swap out tofu for 1½ cups of coconut or almond-based vegan yogurt, use ½ teaspoon of salt instead of soy sauce, and of course, feel free to use any nondairy milk you favor.

For the candied edamame, combine the sugar, water, and salt in medium saucepan over medium heat. Bring to simmer, stirring periodically. Once the sugar has dissolved, add the beans and continue to simmer for about 30 minutes, stirring every few minutes. Turn off the heat but leave the beans in the hot syrup until the entire mixture is completely cool. Drain the beans and spread them out on a baking sheet. Let air-dry for about an hour.

For the ice cream, place all ingredients in your blender and puree on high speed, pausing to scrape down the sides of the container as needed, until perfectly silky smooth. Pour the puree into a medium saucepan and set over medium heat on the stove. Whisk frequently until it comes to a full boil, taking care to scrape the bottom and sides of the pan so nothing sticks and burns. Cook for an additional 2 minutes before turning off the heat. Cool to room temperature and thoroughly chill in the fridge before churning according to your ice cream maker's instructions.

In the final 5 minutes of churning, slowly add in the candied edamame, allowing the machine time enough to mix the beans in. Spoon the soft ice cream into an airtight container and stash in the freezer until firm enough to scoop and serve; at least 3 hours.

POG Sherbet

MAKES 1 SCANT QUART

Did you play with pogs as a kid, or am I just dating myself here? Colorful, glossy disks that acted as tiny trading cards amongst those in the know, I'll be the first to admit that I have no idea how the game was played. Like a moth drawn to the light, I was lured in by those iridescent images, wanting nothing more than to collect and keep these flimsy cardboard caps for no discernable reason. Little did I know that the name came from one specific variety of fruit punch from Hawaii, whose moniker is an acronym for its contents: **P***assionfruit,* **O***range juice, and* **G***uava. The game itself peaked in the early nineties, then quickly faded back into obscurity, before anyone could figure out what to do with all that excess paraphernalia. While my own interest in pogs has waned, to say the least, my thirst for POG (the juice) has skyrocketed. Refreshing, breezy, and bright, it's an ideal base for a simple sherbet, enriched with a touch of coconut, but not so much as to smother the fruity flavors.*

1 pound fresh guava (1 large Asian)
½ pound fresh passionfruit, or ½ cup passionfruit puree
12 ounces frozen pulp-free orange juice concentrate, thawed
½ cup full-fat coconut milk

Asian guavas are my favorite variety for this preparation, since they're available all year round and have a mild sweetness with tart undertones, much like a Granny Smith apple. The entire fruit is edible, including the flesh, seeds, and skin. Simply chop the fruit into small pieces and place it in your blender along with the passionfruit pulp or puree, orange juice concentrate, and coconut milk. Blend on high speed until thoroughly pureed and completely smooth. Pass the mixture through a fine mesh sieve if you'd like to ensure the silkiest texture possible, or simply churn as is. Process in your ice cream maker according to the manufacturer's instructions, and transfer to an airtight container. Place in your freezer and let cure until firm enough to scoop; at least 3 hours.

Raspberry White Chocolate Frozen Yogurt

MAKES ABOUT 1½ QUARTS

Undulating ripples of raspberry jam flow freely through each creamy, silky spoonful of white chocolate ice cream, infused with the gentle essence of berries. On par with super-premium scoops, it may be hard to go back to store-bought pints after churning up a fresh batch.

½ cup raw cashews, soaked for at least 6 hours
1 (14-ounce) can (1½ cups) full-fat coconut milk
1 cup granulated sugar
¾ cup vegan raspberry yogurt
1 tablespoon vanilla extract
½ teaspoon salt
¼ cup cocoa butter, melted
½ cup seedless raspberry jam

Drain the water from the cashews and place in your blender along with the coconut milk, sugar, yogurt, vanilla, and salt. Blend on high-speed, pausing to scrape down the sides as needed, until completely pureed and creamy. With the motor still running, slowly drizzle in the melted cocoa butter to form a smooth emulsion.

Chill thoroughly for at least 2 hours before churning in your ice cream maker according to the manufacturer's instructions. As you transfer the soft ice cream into an airtight container, layer in dollops of the raspberry jam. Use a wide spatula to fold everything together, leaving thick ripples of jam throughout.

Place the container in your freezer for at least 4 hours before scooping and serving.

Rhubarb Sherbet

MAKES 1 SCANT QUART

Strawberries are wonderful, make no mistake, but why must they always be inseparably intertwined with rhubarb whenever the stalky vegetable makes an appearance? More than merely blushing red celery, rhubarb has a unique flavor that falls somewhere between tart green apples and sour lemons, ideal for balancing with a touch of sweetness. Rhubarb is an invigorating change of pace to finally feature as the headlining ingredient, with just a touch of ambrosial rosewater and vanilla to back it up. For a spicier punch, consider adding a pinch of fresh or ground ginger into the mix.

1 cup granulated sugar
2 tablespoons water
2 tablespoons lemon juice
¾ pound fresh rhubarb, cut into 1-inch pieces
1 teaspoon lemon zest
1 teaspoon vanilla paste or extract
½ teaspoon rosewater
1 cup unsweetened nondairy milk

Combine the sugar, water, and lemon juice in a medium saucepan over medium-low heat. Stir gently until sugar dissolves. Add the rhubarb, increase the heat, and bring to boil. Simmer until rhubarb is tender; about 10 minutes. Transfer the mixture to your blender or food processor and puree until smooth. Incorporate the lemon zest, vanilla, rosewater, and nondairy milk last.

Refrigerate the base until thoroughly chilled, or 1 to 2 hours. Pour the sherbet base into your ice cream maker and process according to the manufacturer's instructions. Transfer to an airtight container and store in the freezer until set, at least 3 hours.

Rose Gold Ice Cream

MAKES 1 SCANT QUART

Naysayers often get tangled up on their deep, earthy roots, describing beets in less favorable terms like "dirty" or "musty," but to them, I'd say you're talking about the wrong tuber. Golden beets especially are much more mild, higher in natural sugar and thus more palatable for even the pickiest eaters. If there's anything that might convince the critics, it's always going to be found in the final course. Yes, try eating beets for dessert! Blended with the floral bouquet of rosewater, the overall impact is reminiscent of the candied rose petals held in such high esteem in fine patisseries, bolstered by the soulful bass of golden beets. Don't drop these "phat" beets before you give them a try!

1½ cups plain nondairy milk
1 cup full-fat coconut milk
1 cup (about 6 ounces) peeled and finely chopped golden beets
½ cup granulated sugar
¼ cup maple syrup
2 tablespoons cornstarch
¼ teaspoon salt
2 teaspoons rosewater
1 teaspoon vanilla extract

In a medium saucepan over moderate heat, combine the nondairy milk, coconut milk, and chopped beets. Bring the mixture to a boil before reducing the heat to low, simmering gently for 15 minutes or until beets are fork-tender.

Carefully transfer the mixture to your blender or food processor and thoroughly puree. Blend to a perfectly silky-smooth consistency before adding in the sugar, maple syrup, cornstarch, and salt. Pour everything back into the saucepan and return the liquid to the stove. Bring to a boil once more, whisking frequently and vigorously, until significantly thickened. Turn off the heat and incorporate the rosewater and vanilla last.

Chill thoroughly in the fridge before churning in your ice cream maker according to the manufacturer's suggestions. Transfer the soft ice cream to an airtight container and stash in the freezer for at least 3 hours, until firm enough to scoop, before serving.

Sake Sherbet

MAKES 1 PINT

Sushi and sashimi, even when plant-based, are just small fish when sake sherbet is on the menu for dessert. In fact, so little sugar is used here that you could even serve these scoops between courses as a light, refreshing palate cleanser. A full-bodied, umami brew will enhance the flavors of anything it's paired with, making it a perfect to go with a cultured dairy-free cheese platter or ripe fresh fruits.

1 cup plain nondairy milk
1 cup dry sake
2 tablespoons confectioners' sugar
1 tablespoon lemon juice

No heat need apply, this cool contender just needs to chill out. Whisk everything together and churn in your ice cream maker according to the manufacturer's recommendations. Transfer the soft sherbet to an airtight container. Let rest in the freezer for at least 4 hours to further solidify before serving.

Sandia Agua Fresca Sorbet

Feeling fresh and fruity? Agua frescas are for you! Simply translating as "fresh waters," these cool libations can be made of pretty much any fruit or flower under the sun, but tend to favor the melon family for their easy accessibility, and of course, universally agreeable flavors. Juicy watermelons are the epitome of summer refreshment in my eyes, which makes them the only viable option for beating the heat. Chia seeds are a traditional addition, enhancing viscosity while lending their unique gel-like properties to the mix, but you can leave them out if you'd prefer to dive head-first into a pool of pure watermelon sweetness.

2¾ cups watermelon juice
¾ cup light agave nectar
½ cup coconut water
2 tablespoons lime juice
1 tablespoon chia seeds
⅛ teaspoon salt

No need to heat up the kitchen on a sweltering summer day; this recipe is simply blended and churned. Mix all the ingredients together and chill if not already properly cold. Process in your ice cream maker according to the manufacturer's instructions. Store the soft sorbet in an airtight container in the fridge until firm enough to scoop; at least 3 hours. Alternately, serve right away, straight out of the machine, for a supremely refreshing slushee.

Although I for one would buy it in gallons, pure watermelon juice is sadly unavailable for purchase. The fact that you can't even get the stuff online should speak volumes of its rarity. Luckily, it takes just minutes to make, and I can promise that it will taste 100 times fresher than anything out of a bottle. Just take either half of a good-sized personal (mini) seedless watermelon, or about ¼ of a standard watermelon, and cut the flesh into chunks. Pop the melon pieces into your blender, and let 'er rip on high, for 2 to 3 minutes or until completely pureed. If you have a high-speed blender, you can simply go straight to making sorbet, but if your machine is a bit less powerful, you'll be happier with the end results if you send the mix through a fine mesh strainer first. You will likely end up with a bit more juice than you need for this recipe, but that's the good news! It's delightful to drink all by itself.

To make baked banana boats as seen in the photo, just prior to serving, preheat your oven to 350°F. Place slightly underripe bananas on a baking sheet and roast for 15 to 20 minutes, until the skin is entirely jet-black. Remove from the oven and let rest for at least 15 minutes, or until cool enough to handle. Slice in half from tip to stem, but don't cut all the way through the peel on the opposite side. Gently pry the two halves apart, creating a neat little pocket to stuff with ice cream. Add as many scoops of ice cream as desired, and to really gild the lily, top with coconut whipped cream (page 17) and chopped nuts.

Slow-Roasted Banana Ice Cream

One can never have too many bananas, or so I tell myself as I pick up yet another bundle at the grocery store. Luckily, they only get better with age, and freeze like a dream. Banana bread is usually the go-to solution for using up massive amounts of the spotted brown fruits at a time, although most recipes still don't call for nearly enough to make the most of a truly intimidating stash. However, by roasting the bananas first, you not only concentrate the flavor and sweetness, but reduce their volume to pack even more banana goodness into every bite. Applying this wisdom to ice cream, you'll get the smoothest, creamiest blend yet, unapologetically banana-forward in the way that mere muffins can only dream of. Now you really can't have too many bananas, so stock up!

1¾ pounds (about 6 large or 8 medium) very ripe bananas
1 cup dark brown sugar, firmly packed
2 tablespoons vegan butter or olive oil
¼ teaspoon salt
2 cups plain nondairy milk
1½ tablespoons arrowroot powder
½ teaspoon ground cinnamon
1 teaspoon vanilla extract

So you say you still want to make that same old banana bread? Before you jump ship and pull out the loaf pan, try this cooler solution: Increase the cinnamon to 2 teaspoons and add ½ cup chopped walnuts, pecans, or chocolate chips. You'll get all the same satisfaction without beating any batter.

Preheat your oven to 325°F. Peel and place the bananas in a medium baking dish and toss with the sugar, butter or oil, and salt. Cover with foil and roast for 20 minutes. Pull the dish out and roughly mash the bananas until mostly smooth. Return to the oven, uncovered, and continue roasting for another 2 hours, stirring every 20 to 30 minutes, until darkly caramelized. Measure out ½ cup and set aside. Cool completely before proceeding.

Meanwhile, prepare the base by combining the nondairy milk, arrowroot, and cinnamon in a medium saucepan over moderate heat. Bring to a boil, whisking frequently, until significantly thickened. Cook for another minute before turning off the heat. Stir in about ¾ of the roasted banana along with the vanilla and chill in the fridge for at least 2 hours.

Churn in your ice cream maker according to the manufacturer's directions. Scoop the soft ice cream into an airtight container, interspersing each addition with spoonfuls of the remaining roasted banana. Lightly swirl everything together before securing the lid, stashing it in your freezer, and letting it cure for at least 3 hours. When it's solid enough to scoop, it's ready to serve!

Smoked Almond Ice Cream

MAKES 1 SCANT QUART

In much the same way that vegetables can be transformed into something spectacularly savory like the undulating waves of crispy bacon hot off the griddle, the kiss of smoke will utterly spin your ice cream world around. Liquid smoke can provide an easy, immediate flavor injection, but coaxing the same flavors out of inherently smoky ingredients can result in deeper flavor. Salted, smoked almonds are the foundation and inspiration, rippling through with satisfying crunch, amplified by the sweet spice of Spanish smoked paprika. If that's not enough of the woodsy, aromatic essence for you, go ahead and add a little sprinkle of coconut bacon (page 169) on top, too.

¾ cup smooth roasted almond butter
⅔ cup granulated sugar
2½ cups plain nondairy milk
1 tablespoon cornstarch
½ teaspoon smoked paprika
¼ teaspoon salt
1 teaspoon vanilla extract
½ teaspoon almond extract
½ cup roughly chopped smoked almonds

In a medium saucepan, vigorously whisk together the almond butter, sugar, nondairy milk, cornstarch, smoked paprika, and salt. Make sure that there are no lumps remaining, and place on the stove over medium heat. Whisk frequently but gently, taking care to scrape the bottom and sides of the pan as you go around while the base comes up to temperature. Cook until bubbles begin to break on the surface and the liquid seems significantly thickened. Remove from the heat and whisk in the vanilla and almond extract. Let cool before moving the mixture into the fridge. Chill thoroughly, or for at least 3 hours, before churning in your ice cream maker according to the manufacturer's instructions.

While the base spins, chop up the smoked almonds. In the last 5 minutes of churning, add in the nuts, allowing them time enough to incorporate into the mixture.

Transfer the soft ice cream into an airtight container and let rest in the freezer for at least 3 hours before serving, until solid enough to scoop.

Strawberry Shortcake Ice Cream

MAKES 1 QUART

Redefining this summertime staple in icier terms isn't a terrible stretch, since it rarely takes the form of cake, despite the misleading moniker. Delighting eaters across the United Kingdom and for centuries, it's most often made from biscuits, rather than quick bread. In that same spirit, my fruity scoops utilize any assortment of pastry additions. Whether you prefer the delicate, tender crumb of homemade lady-fingers, or the instant gratification of crunchy cookie crumbs, there's no wrong answer here! Of course, it wouldn't hurt to serve the finished ice cream over extra biscuits and fresh berries for maximum effect.

2¾ cups plain nondairy milk
¾ cup granulated sugar
2 tablespoons arrowroot powder
1 teaspoon cornstarch
¼ teaspoon salt
1 tablespoon vegan butter
2½ teaspoons vanilla extract
1 cup chopped Ladyfingers (page 297), Ice Cream Biscuits (page 259), or vanilla wafer cookies
⅔ cup strawberry jam or preserves

If your jam is too thick to easily spread across the frozen landscape, add 1 to 2 teaspoons of water and microwave for just a few seconds to loosen it up.

In a medium saucepan over moderate heat, vigorously whisk together the nondairy milk, sugar, arrowroot, cornstarch, and salt, making sure that there are no lumps remaining. Slowly bring the mixture up to a full boil, stirring frequently, scraping the bottom and sides of the pan to prevent anything from sticking and burning. Once it's at a rapid boil, reduce the heat slightly and cook for just a minute longer. Turn off the heat, whisking in the butter until it has fully melted and incorporated, followed by the vanilla. Let cool completely before chilling in the fridge for about 2 hours.

Churn in your ice cream maker according to the manufacturer's instructions. Spoon the soft ice cream into an airtight container, alternating with handfuls of chopped ladyfingers, biscuits, or cookies, and spoonfuls of jam. Once all three components are layered in, use a wide spatula to gently swirl everything together. Tap the container on the counter a few times to remove any air bubbles and smooth out the surface. Stash in your freezer for at least 3 hours or more, until firmly set, before serving.

Strawberry-Kiwi Swirled Sherbet

MAKES 1 SCANT QUART

Strawberry-kiwi, a classic combination since the beginning of time . . . Or is it? Kiwis are from China and strawberries are from France, so what gives? It seems the origins of this pairing can be traced back to the early nineties, owing to the creative marketing forces between California kiwi growers and an upstart brand of fruit drinks and teas, of all things. Luckily, the unlikely marriage is far more than a mere spring fling. The sweetness of strawberry and the tartness of kiwi are compelling counterpoints, proving, perhaps, that opposites do attract.

1 cup plain nondairy milk
¾ cup granulated sugar
¼ cup agave nectar
1½ pounds (about 3½ cups) fresh kiwis, peeled and sliced
¼ cup lemon juice
⅔ cup whole fruit strawberry jam or preserves

Place the nondairy milk, sugar, agave, kiwis, and lemon juice into your blender. Puree on high speed until completely smooth and the sugar has dissolved. This may take up to 10 minutes depending on how powerful your machine is, so be patient! Let rest in the fridge until thoroughly chilled if no longer cold by then.

Churn in your ice cream maker according to the manufacturer's instructions. Scoop the ice cream into an airtight container, alternating with dollops of strawberry jam. Gently swirl everything together to marble the jam with the ice cream. Store it in the freezer for at least 3 hours before serving, or until firm enough to scoop.

Sugar Snap Pea Ice Cream

MAKES 1 SCANT QUART

I'll take a second serving of this spring sensation, peas and thank you! When a vegetable is sweet enough to have "sugar" right in its name, it's destined for dessert, as far as I'm concerned. Matcha aficionados especially will appreciate the subtly grassy, vegetative notes intermingling with floral vanilla accents. In fact, that wouldn't be an unwelcome addition, either! Whisk in 2 teaspoons of matcha powder to experiment with a bold new hue of green tea ice cream, or take it in a more refreshing direction by blending in 1 cup of fresh mint leaves. Incorporate ½ cup cacao nibs or finely chopped semi-sweet chocolate for the boldest mint chip to ever grace a cone.

2½ cups plain nondairy milk
¾ cup granulated sugar
2 tablespoons arrowroot powder
½ teaspoon salt
1 cup fresh snap peas
⅔ cup fresh or frozen green peas
2 tablespoons olive oil
½ teaspoon vanilla extract

In a medium saucepan, vigorously whisk together the nondairy milk, sugar, arrowroot, and salt. Once smooth, set over medium heat and bring to a boil, stirring frequently. Add the snap peas and green peas, allowing the mixture to come back to a rapid boil, and cook for an additional minute or two. The vegetables should be bright green and the liquid base significantly thickened.

Cool for about 5 minutes before transferring to a blender. Puree on high speed, pausing to scrape down the sides of the canister as needed to incorporate all the pea-ness. When the base is perfectly smooth, keep the motor running while slowly streaming in the oil, followed by the vanilla extract. This process will keep it emulsified, much like if you were making salad dressing.

Thoroughly chill before churning in your ice cream maker according to the manufacturer's instructions. Place the soft ice cream in an airtight container and stash in the freezer for at least 3 hours, or until firmly set, before serving.

Sweet Heat Chipotle Pecan Ice Cream

MAKES ABOUT 1 QUART

Some like it hot, and if that describes you, then you'll like this spicy, smoky, sultry blend quite a bit, I daresay. Yes, of course it's still a frozen dessert, but the scorching hot flavor defies its physical temperature. The lingering burn of chipotles meets the warmth of sweet cinnamon along with the bite of fresh ginger. Buttery pecans complete the picture with a nutty finish that will leave you craving more.

2½ cups plain nondairy milk
¾ cup light brown sugar, firmly packed
2 tablespoons arrowroot powder
1 teaspoon cornstarch
1 chipotle canned in adobo, finely minced
2 teaspoons adobo sauce
1 teaspoon finely grated fresh ginger
½ teaspoon ground cinnamon
½ teaspoon salt
1 tablespoon vegan butter or coconut oil
2 teaspoons vanilla extract
½ cup toasted pecans, roughly chopped

In a medium saucepan, combine the nondairy milk, sugar, arrowroot, cornstarch, chipotle, adobo, ginger, cinnamon, and salt. Mix thoroughly to break up any clumps of ingredients. Set over medium heat on the stove and whisk occasionally, until the mixture comes to a boil. Let cook at a full boil for 2 additional minutes, and then remove the pan from the burner. Add in the butter or coconut oil and vanilla extract, stirring to incorporate and allowing the residual heat to melt the fat. Let cool to room temperature, and then chill thoroughly for at least 3 hours before churning.

Churn the base in your ice cream machine according to the manufacturer's directions. In the last 5 minutes of churning, slowly sprinkle the chopped pecans right into the machine, so that the paddle incorporates and distributes the pieces throughout the ice cream. Transfer dollops of the soft ice cream to an airtight container and store it in the freezer for another 3 hours minimum, or until frozen solid, before serving.

In case you *don't* like it hot, you can just as happily enjoy a mellow, creamy butter pecan ice cream instead by removing the pepper and spices. Add ¼ cup of pecan butter to the base after cooking but before churning, for an extra dose of nutty goodness.

Tamarind Ice Cream

MAKES 1 QUART

All at once tart, tangy, sweet, and sour, tamarind packs a powerful flavor punch unlike anything else. It doesn't get much love in the states, but in Asia and Africa, it's the not-so-secret ingredient giving everything from curries to candies an extra zing. The pods can be a bit tricky to track down, and a sticky mess to work with, so just start with the concentrate, which may also be labeled simply as tamarind paste. If you can't find it in the produce department or ethnic market, hit the Internet to get your fix. It's shelf stable until opened, and when refrigerated, all but indestructible.

¾ cup tamarind concentrate
1 tablespoon lemon juice
¾ cup full-fat coconut milk
2 cups plain nondairy milk
1 cup granulated sugar
2 tablespoons arrowroot powder
1 teaspoon vanilla extract

Combine the tamarind with the lemon juice before placing both in a medium saucepan along with the coconut milk, nondairy milk, sugar, and arrowroot. Whisk together over medium heat.

Bring the mixture to a steady boil. When the mixture has just started to boil, immediately remove from the heat and stir in the vanilla. Cool completely before placing in your fridge to chill before churning, for at least 3 hours.

Churn according to your ice cream maker's instructions. Store the soft ice cream in an airtight container and let set in the freezer until firm before scooping and serving, at least 3 to 4 hours.

Tiger Tail Frozen Yogurt

MAKES 1 SCANT QUART

Though unmistakable at a glance, streaked with jet-black ribbons of licorice, anyone outside of Canada is unlikely to identify this tiger based on its stripes. Found only in creameries up north, the orange base hasn't yet spread beyond the Canadian border, but once you try this recipe, you'll understand the appeal.

ORANGE FROZEN YOGURT

1½ cups vanilla vegan yogurt
1 (12-ounce) container frozen 100% orange juice concentrate, thawed
⅓ cup plain nondairy milk
½ teaspoon vanilla extract
Zest of 1 orange

BLACK LICORICE RIPPLE

2½ ounces (½ cup) black licorice candy
6 tablespoons water
¼ cup plain nondairy milk
1 tablespoon black cocoa powder
1½ teaspoons coconut oil

For the frozen yogurt, simply whisk all the ingredients together and chill if not already cold. Churn in your ice cream maker according to the manufacturer's recommendations.

For the licorice ripple, place the licorice candy, water, and nondairy milk in a small saucepan over medium-low heat. Cook gently, stirring often, until the candy melts into a smooth sauce. Vigorously whisk in the cocoa powder, turn off the heat, and allow the coconut oil to melt in. Set aside and let cool.

When the ice cream is done churning, scoop about ⅓ into an airtight container, drizzling ⅓ of the black licorice sauce on top. Repeat until both components are used up. Swirl together gently and stash in the freezer to set, at least 3 hours, before serving.

Toasted Vanilla Bean Sorbet

MAKES 1 SCANT QUART

It's a pale drink of cool water that's not flashy or complicated. It doesn't boast bold, intense flavors to grip you by the throat. It's so subtle that it might be described as ethereal; melting away in a quiet burst of refreshment as soon as it hits your palate, a haunting sweetness and understated sophistication. Meant as a palate cleanser rather than a full final course, the key is to emphasize only the highest quality ingredients and give them the utmost respect to coax out their full potential.

1 whole vanilla bean, cut into 1-inch pieces
3 cups coconut water
1¼ cups granulated sugar
1 teaspoon arrowroot powder

Set a small skillet over medium heat. Add the vanilla bean and toast, shaking the skillet to keep it moving the whole time, for about 5 minutes. It should start to dry out a bit and become irresistibly aromatic. Transfer to your blender or food processor, but let it cool for a minute or two before proceeding.

Add the coconut water, sugar, and arrowroot into the blender, and puree on high speed. Be patient and give it a good long time to completely break down the whole vanilla bean, rendering it into fine specks throughout the mixture. This may take as long as 10 minutes depending on your machine. Continue processing until the sugar has dissolved.

Chill in your fridge for about an hour before churning in your ice cream maker according to the manufacturer's instructions. Transfer to an airtight container and let set in the freezer for at least 4 hours, until firm enough to scoop, before serving.

Tostone Ice Cream

MAKES ABOUT 1 QUART

For anyone who's relished a midnight snack of crispy French fries dipped in a frosty milkshake, you're doing yourself a downright disservice if you don't give tostone ice cream a try. Twice fried plantains, starchy like a good old golden potato but with a subtle hint of tropical sweetness, find a cooler home this time around. Rather than dipping into garlicky guacamole, they plunge into a pool of dulcet custard, spike with a touch of citrus. It's a combination that tastes like a guilty pleasure but is nothing to be ashamed of. No one can deny the compelling allure of a perfect plantain, salted, sugared, and served up cold.

- 1 tablespoon coconut oil
- 1 pound plantains, diced
- ½ teaspoon salt
- 1 tablespoon orange juice
- 1 (14-ounce) can full-fat coconut milk
- 1 cup plain nondairy milk
- ⅔ cup granulated sugar
- 2 tablespoons arrowroot powder
- 3 ounces (about 1 cup) crushed plantain chips

In a medium saucepan over moderate heat, melt the coconut oil and add the diced plantains and salt. Sauté, stirring frequently, until the fruit has softened and is lightly golden around the edges, about 5 to 6 minutes. Add the orange juice to help loosen any pieces that might be sticking to the pan, scraping the bottom thoroughly.

In a separate bowl, whisk together the coconut milk, nondairy milk, sugar, and arrowroot, making sure there are no lumps of starch remaining before adding the mixture into the saucepan. Stir to incorporate. Bring to a full, rolling boil, stirring often, and turn off the heat. Carefully transfer the hot base to your blender or food processor and thoroughly puree. Alternately, you could use an immersion blender so you don't risk splashing hot liquid all over the place. Blend until completely smooth.

Chill in the fridge for at least 3 hours before proceeding. Due to the starches in the plantain, the mixture will continue to thicken as it cools, and may need to be reblended once again before churning.

Churn the base in your ice cream machine according to the manufacturer's directions. In the last 5 minutes of churning, slowly sprinkle the crushed plantain chips right into the machine, so that the moving paddle incorporates and distributes the pieces throughout the ice cream. Transfer the soft ice cream to an airtight container and store it in the freezer for another 3 hours minimum, or until frozen solid, before serving.

Triple Vanilla Frozen Custard

MAKES 1 QUART

Trends come and go, but vanilla ice cream is forever. Beating out all other flavors for as long as pollsters can discern, even classic chocolate offerings, vanilla ice cream is the #1 flavor in parlors across the globe. It's the one staple that transcends all cultural boundaries, ages, and seasons. It's also one of the most difficult flavors to perfectly capture, since such a pure, simple concept is challenging to execute with exactly the right nostalgic notes. Such a delicate, ephemeral essence provides nothing to hide behind, no exciting mix-ins to cover up off-notes or break up a slightly icy texture. It must evoke taste memories of all things custard, cream, birthday cake, frosting, and sugar cookies, and yet possess a distinctive flavor all its own.

Capturing the single perfect vanilla bean scoop is a lifelong quest, a holy grail which I can't claim to have achieved yet. That said, this triple threat custard that employs vanilla-flavored milk, whole beans, and extract, is the closest I've come. Owing its super-premium mouthfeel to an almost eggy base, this is clearly not your plain-Jane vanilla; in fact, it could redefine the category of "vanilla" as we know it.

3 cups vanilla nondairy milk
2 tablespoons arrowroot powder
2 teaspoons cornstarch
¾ cup light agave nectar
1 whole vanilla bean, split, and seeds scraped
¼ teaspoon salt
¼ teaspoon black salt (kala namak)
⅛ teaspoon ground turmeric (optional, for color)
2 tablespoons vegan butter
1 teaspoon vanilla extract

In a medium saucepan, vigorously whisk together the nondairy milk, arrowroot, and cornstarch so that there are no lumps of starch remaining. Set the pan over moderate heat and add in the agave, vanilla bean seeds, both salts, and turmeric, if using. Whisk occasionally, until it just comes to a boil, and the liquid has thickened significantly. Turn off the heat and immediately add in the butter and vanilla, whisking vigorously until the butter has melted and is fully incorporated. Let cool completely.

Chill for at least 3 hours, and then churn in your ice cream maker according to the manufacturer's instructions. Enjoy right away for a soft serve experience, or store in an airtight container in your freezer for at least 3 hours, or until firm enough to scoop, before serving.

If you don't have black salt (kala namak) and don't want to invest in a stash, you can simply use an additional ¼ teaspoon regular table salt instead. Black salt simply contributes a subtly eggy flavor more akin to traditional, rich custard.

Wholly Mole Ice Cream

MAKES ABOUT 1 QUART

Done right, making mole from scratch is an all-day affair. A murky, mysterious brew that could contain a hundred different spices, seasonings, and secret ingredients, each batch is as unique as the chef that makes it. Naturally, I can't claim to have expertise, let alone patience, when crafting my own sweet facsimile. Rather, my frozen blend takes inspiration from that diverse palate of ingredients but doesn't take hours to prepare. It's not quite instant gratification, but for mole, and for ice cream, it's pretty darn close.

MOLE ICE CREAM

2¾ cups plain nondairy milk
¾ cup coconut sugar or dark brown sugar, firmly packed
¼ cup Dutch-processed cocoa powder
2 tablespoons arrowroot powder
1½ teaspoons ground cinnamon
¼ cup raisins
¼ cup smooth roasted almond butter
1–2 tablespoons chili powder

DARK CHOCOLATE STRACCIATELLA

3 ounces (about ½ cup) unsweetened dark chocolate, chopped

Prepared chili blends are often stuffed with salt and questionable additives. Even if you find a high-quality option, who knows how long it's been sitting on the shelf? Make your own mix for the best results:

2 tablespoons smoked paprika
1½ teaspoons ground cumin
1 teaspoon garlic powder
1 teaspoon onion powder
1 teaspoon dried oregano
½ teaspoon sweet paprika
½ teaspoon cayenne pepper

Place everything in a small glass jar and shake it up! MAKES ABOUT ¼ CUP

For the ice cream, add all ingredients to your blender or food processor. Add chili powder to taste, depending on how spicy you'd like it. Bear in mind that the intensity will lessen once frozen. Blend on high speed for a solid 5 minutes, at least, pausing to scrape down the sides of the container as needed. You may still want to pass the mixture through a strainer to ensure a smooth texture once churned.

Transfer the liquid to a medium saucepan over medium-low heat. Stir constantly, scraping the bottom and sides of the pan with your spatula, to ensure that nothing sticks and burns. Once bubbles break on the surface, cook for an additional minute or two before turning off the heat.

Chill for at least 3 hours. Once fully chilled, churn in your ice cream maker according to the manufacturer's instructions.

For the stracciatella, when the ice cream is about 5 minutes away from finishing in the machine, melt the chopped chocolate, microwaving at intervals of 30 seconds and stirring until completely smooth. Slowly drizzle in a thin stream directly into the ice cream machine. It will freeze instantly on the surface of the ice cream, and the turning paddle will break it up into delicate, thin shards.

Transfer the ice cream into an airtight container, and store in the freezer. Let solidify in the freezer for at least 3 hours before serving.

SANDWICHES, STICKS, AND MISCELLANEOUS NOVELTIES

It's been irrefutably proven that food is just more fun when you can eat it with your hands, and that includes ice cream. The best methods employ edible vessels, such as the classic cone or soft cookies, but there's something special about the average wooden stick presentation, too. Novelties are what put ice cream trucks on the map, despite their movable quality, serving up smiles for miles with just a freezer chest in back. Way back before I could even run after a mobile ice cream dealer, sirens blazing through the quiet cul-de-sac, my mom would make the most basic of frozen treats out of leftover lemonade. Pour it into straight, cylindrical molds, stick a paddle in it, and call it a "party pop," they were the greatest reward us kids could ask for on hot summer afternoons. Sure, it was rustic, hard as a solid block of ice, and unrefined, but that didn't matter one lick to us kids. Evolving tastes and increasing knowledge of elevated ice cream experiences has guided a renaissance in distinctively gourmet novelties, far more ambitious than the likes of Mister Softee® would ever deliver. The following recipes can be quite a handful, but don't forget to make space for the old-school goodies, like I do for a round of party pops every now and then, in your freezer and in your heart.

Avo-Choco-Tacos

Makes 6 tacos

A taco without an avocado is like a camera without a lens; unfocused and unsatisfying. While I'm well aware that the original Choco Taco is composed of fudge-swirled vanilla ice cream stuffed in a folded waffle cone dipped in chocolate and peanuts, I still think that same sentiment applies. Avocados add unparalleled richness to dark, luscious, full-bodied chocolate ice cream. Not everyone is lucky enough to have their own waffle cone maker at home, which is why it's a good thing that the standard issue flour tortilla stands up to the task in this sweet preparation as well. Forming a crisp, neutral shell for all the glorious toppings your heart desires, choose your own adventure when it comes to the final flourish of toppings.

CRUNCHY TACO SHELLS

6 (5-inch) flour tortillas
Cooking spray/aerosol oil

AVOCADO CHOCOLATE ICE CREAM

2 ripe avocados, pitted and diced
1 can full-fat coconut milk
⅔ cup maple syrup
½ cup Dutch-processed cocoa powder
2 teaspoons vanilla extract

TO ASSEMBLE

1 batch Dark Chocolate Shell (page 285)
¼ cup sliced almonds, chopped peanuts, shredded coconut, cacao nibs, and/or sprinkles

Feeling more adventurous? Try spicing things up with a **Mexican Chocolate** variation. Add 1½ teaspoons ground cinnamon, 1 teaspoon instant coffee powder or granules, and ¼ to ¾ teaspoon chipotle powder (depending on how spicy you like it) right into the ice cream base. *Olé!*

For the taco shells, preheat your oven to 350°F. When hot, carefully drape the tortillas over the spaces on the oven rack. If they don't bend easily, microwave them for 15 to 30 seconds, until slightly softened and more pliable. Spray liberally with nonstick cooking spray on all sides. Bake until they're golden-brown; around 13 to 18 minutes. Remove and let cool completely.

For the ice cream, combine all ingredients in your blender and thoroughly puree on high speed, until completely smooth. Chill if not already cold, before processing in your ice cream maker according to the manufacturer's instructions.

Pack the soft ice cream into your taco shells, filling each one to the very edge. Quickly place each filled tortilla into your freezer on a foil-lined sheet pan, repeating until all the ice cream is used up. If you have extra tortillas, then break out the salsa! Let the tacos set in the freezer for at least 4 hours before proceeding.

When you're ready to serve, prepare the chocolate shell in a shallow dish. Have any toppings you want to use at the ready.

One by one, dip the entire exposed edge into the liquid chocolate. Sprinkle or dip your crunchy toppings all over. Place the taco on its side back on the foil-lined sheet in your freezer; the chocolate shell should set instantly. Repeat with the remaining tacos. Serve right away, or move them into an airtight container to store in your freezer for up to 2 months. Keep them separated by layers of foil or parchment paper for best results.

Banana Froyo Popsicles

MAKES 4–5 POPSICLES

Evocative of childhood memories of crunchy banana candies, I was inspired by crispy wafers flavored with America's favorite fruit. Real magic happens when they're stored in the icebox. Chilled, they suddenly taste like a fruit smoothie in stick form. That serendipitous discovery stemmed from an urge to clear overflowing counters. Instead, into the freezer the package of cookies went, and out came a brand new treat. No-churn banana ice cream, enlightened with a dollop of tangy dairy-free yogurt, perches temptingly on edible crème wafer sticks, every bite as satisfying and wholly refreshing as the last.

BANANA FROYO POPSICLES

2 (5.3–6 ounce) containers vanilla vegan yogurt
2 ripe, medium-sized bananas
2 tablespoons maple syrup
4–5 banana-flavored creme wafers (optional)

BANANA DIP AND GARNISH (OPTIONAL)

6 tablespoons coconut oil, melted
¼ cup 100% food-grade cocoa butter, melted
1 cup confectioners' sugar
1 teaspoon banana extract
¼ teaspoon ground turmeric
1–2 tablespoons Sprinkles (page 280, or store-bought)

To make the popsicles, simply combine the yogurt, bananas, and maple syrup in your blender and thoroughly puree until smooth. Divide the mixture evenly between popsicle molds and insert one wafer cookie into each. This will act as the stick, so make sure you press it deeply into the center, to prevent fallout later. Alternately, use standard wooden popsicle sticks if you can't get your hands on the right cookies.

Place the molds on a flat surface in your freezer and let chill until set, at least 8 hours and ideally overnight.

To make the banana dip, whisk together the coconut oil, cocoa butter, confectioners' sugar, banana extract, and turmeric in a small dish.

When ready to dip, release the popsicles from the molds by running them briefly under hot water. Dip halfway (or fully, if desired) and lay on a piece of parchment paper or nonstick silicone baking sheet. Top with sprinkles if desired. Return to the freezer until ready to serve.

Cannoli Cones

Makes 8–10 cones

Growing up, cannoli were always a great treat when in the vicinity of an Italian bakery, since no one in my household would fire up a vat of hot oil to fry and fabricate the shells from scratch. Without that edible container, there was no pastry at all—or so I thought.

After tireless taste tests, I can report that standard waffle ice cream cones have proven themselves as highly satisfying substitutes, every bit as crisp and crunchy, and far less greasy, to boot. In place of the typically heavy mascarpone filling, a combination of cream cheese and airy whipped coconut cream commingle to create an effortless mousse. Light as a cloud while still possessing that same characteristic tang of traditional cultured dairy, the mousse comes together in a matter of minutes. That's fast enough to strike down any craving in its tracks.

"MASCARPONE" MOUSSE FILLING

½ cup coconut cream
½ cup confectioners' sugar
4 ounces (½ cup) vegan Cream Cheese (p. 282)
, softened
½ teaspoon white miso paste
½ teaspoon nutritional yeast
½ teaspoon vanilla bean paste or extract

TO ASSEMBLE

3 ounces (½ cup) dark chocolate, finely chopped
8–10 Waffle Cones (page 313, or store-bought)
⅓ cup toasted pistachios, roughly chopped (optional)

To make the filling, place the coconut cream in the bowl of your stand mixer and install the whisk attachment. Whip on high speed for about 3 minutes before slowly beginning to sprinkle in the sugar, just a little bit at a time. Continue beating the mixture for up to 10 minutes, until light and fluffy.

In a separate bowl, mix together the cream cheese, miso, nutritional yeast, and vanilla, stirring until fully combined and completely smooth. Add in a few dollops of the whipped coconut cream at a time, using a wide spatula to gently fold it into the mixture. Be careful not to beat all the structure out of it to keep the filling light and airy. Keep refrigerated in an airtight container until ready to assemble.

To assemble, place the chocolate in a microwave-safe container and heat for 30 to 60 seconds, stirring thoroughly until the chocolate has completely melted. Dip the tops of the waffle cones into the liquid chocolate, allowing the excess to drip off, and carefully stand them in tall, narrow glasses to dry upright.

Pipe, spoon, or scoop the chilled mousse into your cones and top each with a sprinkle of toasted pistachios. Place in the freezer, still carefully balanced in glasses, and freeze until set, for at least 4 hours before serving.

Carrot Cake Pupsicles

MAKES APPROXIMATELY 8 SMALL TREATS OR 4 LARGE (DEPENDING ON SIZE OF MOLD)

Do you know a four-legged friend who would enjoy a little frozen treat, too? Of course you do! All dogs deserve to be spoiled at least occasionally, and although my own pup is hardly a picky eater, I can assure you that he fully endorses this veggie-loving blend. It's a good thing that the "sticks" are fully edible, made of baby carrots rather than wood, since he would have still wolfed them down in one bite, regardless.

A discerning palate may not find this take on carrot cake particularly sweet, but it's perfectly human-safe and would be delightful for all creatures, big and small, with an addition of 2 to 3 tablespoons of maple syrup, if desired.

1 cup (6 ounces) baby carrots, or sliced and peeled carrots
1 medium banana
1 tablespoon ground flaxseeds
¼ teaspoon ground cinnamon
¼ teaspoon ground ginger
¼ cup plain nondairy milk
4–8 baby carrots or carrot sticks

Place the carrots in a microwave-safe dish with a small splash of water and heat for 4 to 6 minutes, until very tender. Let cool for a few minutes before transferring the cooked vegetables to your blender along with the banana, flaxseeds, cinnamon, ginger, and nondairy milk. Blend, pausing as needed to scrape down the sides of the canister, until completely smooth.

Pour the mixture into popsicle molds. Place on a flat surface in your freezer, and let set for 30 minutes.

Meanwhile, shave the remaining carrots down to the size of popsicle sticks to accommodate your given vessels. Insert them into the centers of the partially frozen pops, and let fully solidify (at least 3 to 4 hours) before serving.

Cookie Dough Pudding Pops

Makes 6–8 popsicles, depending on the size of your molds

My love for cookie dough was fostered at a very young age, from some of my very earliest memories of baking with my mom. A lick from the beater or bowl, still coated in unbaked dough, evokes a certain nostalgia. When the steamy summer heat arrives, wouldn't you prefer to skip the oven to dive in with a spoon instead?

If you can delay gratification just a little bit longer though, I have an even cooler way to recall those childhood memories. Cookie dough pudding pops, with all the familiar flavors in a creamy, frozen package, may become the new nostalgic sweet treat.

Toasting the flour brings out the subtle nutty, roasted flavors imparted by baking, without the same intense heat. The base is otherwise prepared the same as any other cooked custard, so if you can stir a pot, you can whip up this buttery brown sugar pudding in no time. In fact, you may be tempted to eat the plain pudding prior to its trip to the freezer, and I wouldn't blame you. Just try to leave a little bit for the popsicles themselves; you'll be grateful to have them on hand (and in hand) the next time a craving strikes.

¼ cup all-purpose flour
1½ cups plain nondairy milk, divided
¼ cup light brown sugar, firmly packed
1 tablespoon vegan butter, melted
¼ teaspoon salt
1 teaspoon vanilla extract
¼ cup chocolate chips

Begin by lightly toasting the flour in a dry skillet. Place the skillet over medium heat and continuously, gently, stir the flour, until faintly golden brown all over. Slowly whisk in ½ cup of the nondairy milk to form a thick paste, beating out any lumps before proceeding. Continue to add in the remaining nondairy milk and whisk vigorously to smooth out the mixture. Incorporate the sugar, vegan butter, and salt, stirring well. Cook, stirring periodically, until bubbles break regularly on the surface and the liquid has thickened significantly.

Turn off the heat, cool to room temperature, and then let rest in the fridge until thoroughly chilled. Stir in the vanilla and chocolate chips before transferring the mixture to popsicle molds. Place in the freezer and let rest until frozen; at least 3 hours.

Frozen Strawberry-Balsamic Soufflé

Makes 3 servings

Lightened with cool, fluffy whipped coconut cream, this charming frozen soufflé is effortless to make. Unlike the traditional baked rendition, there's no fear of deflation before the lofty treats reach the table. Strawberries lend a pretty pink hue, but the first bite proves that this treat is far from child's play. Tangy balsamic vinegar smacks with acidity and brightness, jarring at first but an unexpectedly satisfying contrast to the fruity jam. The combined flavors linger, hauntingly, temptingly, long after dessert spoons have been licked clean.

Prepare to fall in love. After experiencing it once for yourself, it's hard to imagine being satisfied with anything else.

½ cup seedless strawberry jam or jelly
¼ cup vegan strawberry yogurt
¼ cup confectioners' sugar
2 teaspoons balsamic glaze or reduction
¼ teaspoon salt
1 (14-ounce) can full-fat coconut milk, chilled
Coconut whipped cream (optional)
Fresh strawberries, sliced (optional)

Set out 3 (4-ounce) ramekins on a small tray to more easily maneuver them in and out of the freezer. Cut 3 strips of aluminum foil or parchment paper to fit comfortably inside each ramekin, extending above the rim by about 2 inches. Tape the strips to ensure that they stay in place. Lightly grease and set aside.

In a large bowl, stir together the jam, yogurt, balsamic glaze, and salt until smooth. Set aside.

Carefully open the chilled can of coconut milk, being sure not to shake it, and scoop off the top layer of thick coconut cream. Save the watery liquid left behind for another recipe (it's great in smoothies, curries, or soups!). Place the coconut cream in the bowl of your stand mixer and install the whisk attachment. Whip on high speed for about 3 minutes before slowly beginning to sprinkle in the sugar, just a little bit at a time. Continue beating the mixture for up to 10 minutes, until light and fluffy. Add about half of the strawberry jam mixture, stirring lightly to incorporate. Fold in the remaining half more gently, keeping it as light and fluffy as possible.

Spoon the mixture into your prepared ramekins, dividing it equally and smoothing out the tops. Place the ramekins into the freezer on a level surface, and allow them to rest, undisturbed, for at least 3 hours or until set.

Remove from freezer 10 minutes before serving. Remove parchment collars and garnish with additional whipped coconut cream and sliced strawberries, if desired.

Ice Cream Doughnuts

Makes 6 ice cream doughnuts

Every day, there's a new absurd, excessive food trend blowing up on the Internet. Though many are over-hyped edibles we love to hate, it's impossible to deny the appeal of a select few crazy concepts. Thanks to the advent of flexible silicon molds, no food is safe from doughnut-ification. It didn't take long for visually stunning sushi doughnuts to emerge as a clear winner, captivating hungry followers across all social media platforms, but the hits keep on coming.

Trust me, ice cream doughnuts are more than just another excuse to capitalize on the irresistibly attractive ring shape. Haters will be the only ones with no chill, because these frozen treats are as much fun to admire as they are to eat! Pretty in pink, the glaze is actually a beet-tinted approach to magic shell, flavored with vanilla and finished with those classic rainbow sprinkles. It just wouldn't be a doughnut without them.

. . . Or would it? Almost as soon as the initial batch was devoured, I realized the opportunity that had been missed. Cinnamon sugar doughnuts, singing of warmth and comfort, are equally worthy candidates of imitation. Contrasting against the cold, creamy base, the spiced coating seals in a frozen surprise for the unsuspecting eater. Far more refreshing than the usual oily cake, it may even have an edge on the traditional treat, especially as temperatures outside skyrocket.

ICE CREAM DOUGHNUTS

1 pint Triple Vanilla Frozen Custard (page 103), or any smooth scoop

DOUGHNUT GLAZE MAGIC SHELL AND GARNISH

½ cup 100% food-grade cocoa butter, melted
1 tablespoon refined coconut oil, melted
¼ cup confectioners' sugar
2 tablespoons arrowroot powder
½ teaspoon beet powder (optional, for color)
½ teaspoon vanilla extract
⅛ teaspoon salt
1–2 tablespoons Confetti Quin Sprinkles (page 280, or store-bought)

CINNAMON CRUMB COATING

4 ice cream waffle cones
½ teaspoon ground cinnamon
1 cup full-fat coconut milk

For the doughnuts, have silicon doughnut molds at the ready and soften your pint of ice cream. Once thawed to the point of being spreadable but before it completely melts, smooth the ice cream evenly into your mold, taking care to fill any voids. Lightly tap the mold on the counter to remove any air bubbles before quickly sliding it into the freezer. Let chill until frozen solid, at least 4 to 6 hours but ideally overnight.

For the magic shell, mix the melted cocoa butter and coconut oil before whisking in the confectioners' sugar, arrowroot, and beet powder. Whisk vigorously until completely smooth and the beet powder has fully dissolved. Stir in the vanilla and salt. Retrieve your ice cream doughnuts from the freezer and pop them out of the mold. Either dip each one or drizzle with the magic shell before quickly topping with sprinkles; the glaze sets up almost immediately, so you need to be fast! Serve right away or return them to the freezer until ready to enjoy.

For the cinnamon crumb coating, place the ice cream cones and cinnamon in your blender or food processor and pulse until very finely ground. Transfer to a shallow dish. Place the coconut milk in a separate dish and dip each frozen doughnut into the coconut milk to ensure that the topping will adhere. Press the crumbs firmly into the doughnut until completely coated. Eat immediately or return the doughnuts to the freezer until ready to serve.

Inverse Affogato

Makes about 1–1½ pints ice cream; 4–6 servings affogato

Classically prepared with vanilla ice cream, a traditional affogato takes frosty scoops and drowns them in steaming hot espresso, mingling for those few fleeting seconds to create a sensation that vacillates between hot and cold, cold and hot, and finally hot once more. It's the kind of dessert that you can't get prepackaged; it must be enjoyed immediately, but above all else, thoroughly. Perhaps I love it so much because it really forces you to be in the moment, rather than mindlessly munching on stray cake crumbs or a few leftover cookies. It's more of an experience than a dish, when you get right down to it.

Of course, I'm hardly the sort to do anything traditional when it comes to food, so my flavors vary as wildly as the weather. The only constant has been that strong, dark shot of espresso poured on top . . . Until I discovered there was such a thing as chocolate tea. Instead of pouring espresso on top, why not freeze it as the ice cream instead? Steeped for twice as long and at double-strength, the chocolatey brew marries harmoniously with the creamy coffee ice cream, giving life to a new mocha flavor, as delicate as it is complex.

If the world is not black and white, why should all affogato remain merely vanilla and espresso?

ESPRESSO ICE CREAM

1 (14-ounce) can full-fat coconut milk
¼ cup granulated sugar
2 teaspoons instant espresso powder, or 1 tablespoon instant coffee powder
1 tablespoon arrowroot powder
¼ cup kahlua or coffee liqueur

CACAO NIB TEA

2 tablespoons cacao nibs, coarsely ground
2 cups water
2 teaspoons granulated sugar

To make the ice cream, simply toss all the ingredients except for the liqueur into a medium saucepan and whisk thoroughly. Make sure you break up any clumps before turning on the heat to medium. Whisk periodically until the mixture comes to a boil. Cook at a full boil for 2 additional minutes, and then remove the pan from the burner. Add in the liqueur last, stirring to incorporate. Let cool to room temperature and then chill thoroughly for at least 3 hours before churning in your ice cream maker according to the manufacturer's instructions. Once churned, transfer the fresh, soft ice cream into an airtight container and stash it your freezer for at least 3 hours before serving.

For the cacao nib tea, place the ground nibs in a tea bag or strainer and place in a medium saucepan along with the water. Cover, bring to a boil, and immediately turn off the heat. Let steep for 8 to 10 minutes to extract as much flavor as possible. Remove and discard the spent nibs. Stir in the sugar until fully dissolved.

To serve your affogato, simply scoop the ice cream into a heat-safe dish and pour as much of the hot cacao tea on top as desired. Eat immediately!

Most packaged marzipan found in the baking aisle these days should be vegan-friendly, but double-check labels to make sure there are no egg whites involved, as is traditional. To make your own marzipan from scratch, blend 2½ cups blanched almond meal with ½ cup light agave nectar and ½ teaspoon almond extract in a food processor to make a thick, doughy paste. Be careful not to over-process, which will make the mixture oily and separated. It should just hold together in a ball when finished.

Magnanimous Marzipan Bars

Makes 6–10 popsicles, depending on the size of your molds

Billed as the "ultimate ice cream indulgence," Magnum Bars were long highly esteemed within the frozen novelty hierarchy. One of the first commercial frozen treats to prioritize quality over quantity, the title was apt for some time. Vanilla bean ice cream, with actual, visible speaks of its namesake, rested softly within a crisp shell of chocolate that contained actual cocoa butter, not just waxy hydrogenated oils. Though they've kept up admirably with new plant-based almond milk options, I still think we can do them one better. Let's bring it back home with bolder, better flavors.

Almonds feature more prominently in my interpretation, rather than playing second string as a neutral background. Marzipan, the stuff of fine pastries the world over, lends a buttery, nutty, cake-like quality here. Crisp toasted almonds embedded into the thick chocolate coating ensure a satisfying crunch with every bite. Though it rests on a classic wooden pop, it's a far more refined treat than you can really shake a stick at.

5½ ounces (½ package) vegan marzipan
1 (14-ounce) can full-fat coconut milk
½ teaspoon vanilla extract
¼ teaspoon almond extract
⅛ teaspoon salt
1 batch Dark Chocolate Shell (page 285)
⅔ cup slivered almonds, toasted and finely chopped

Slice the marzipan into small pieces, about 1 tablespoon each, and place them in a small saucepan with the coconut milk. Heat gently over medium low just until the liquid comes to the brink of a boil. Turn off the heat immediately and transfer the contents to your blender, along with the vanilla and almond extracts, and salt. Blend until completely smooth.

Cool to room temperature before dividing the mixture between popsicle molds, and stash on a flat surface in your freezer. After about an hour, insert the sticks. Let set until completely firm; at least 4 hours, and ideally overnight.

To finish the bars, mix chopped almonds into liquified chocolate shell and pour into a tall drinking glass to help coat the bars. One by one, dip the entire length of each bar into the chocolate, allowing the excess to drip back into the glass, and place on a foil- or parchment-lined baking sheet. For the last ones, you may need to spoon the remaining topping over them to ensure full coverage. After repeating with all the pops, quickly move them back into the freezer.

Once set, serve right away, or move them into an airtight container to store in your freezer for up to 2 months. Keep them separated by layers of foil or parchment paper for best results.

Orange Dreamsicle Ice Cream Bars

Makes 6–8 servings

Go ahead, take it easy. Escape the heat, simplify your menu, but perish the thought of skipping dessert. These no-cook, no-churn treats were made for just such an occasion, rewarding a minimal amount of effort with sweet gratification well beyond some bland, freezer-burnt packaged confections. Instead, imagine the cool, creamy relief of an orange dreamsicle, without the cloying sugary wallop of early childhood memories. This rendition is brighter, bolder, and more brilliantly citrusy thanks to a hefty measure of zest added into the mix.

1 cup raw cashews, soaked for at least 6 hours, and drained
1 cup orange juice
½ cup full-fat coconut milk, divided
¼ cup light agave nectar or maple syrup, divided
1 tablespoon orange zest
1 teaspoon vanilla extract
¼ teaspoon salt

Place the soaked cashews, orange juice, half of the coconut milk, and half of the agave or maple syrup in your blender. Puree on high speed, pausing to scrape down the sides of the container if necessary, until completely silky-smooth. If you still see a few errant pieces remaining after 5 to 6 minutes of continuous blending, pass the mixture through a fine mesh strainer and discard any solids. Stir in the orange zest.

Separately, whisk together the remaining coconut milk and agave along with the vanilla and salt.

Pour the orange cashew mixture into popsicle molds, filling them about ⅔ of the way to the top. Add the vanilla coconut mixture to fill the rest of the space. Lightly swirl the two together with a popsicle skewer before inserting sticks and placing in the freezer. Let set for at least 6 hours, ideally overnight, before unmolding and enjoying.

Payday Ice Cream Bars

Makes 10–12 bars

Maximize your gustatory payoff with minimal output. Inspired by the chewy, crunchy combination of salted peanuts rolled in caramel, this chillier rendition tastes like a million bucks, looks like a nut-studded bar of gold, yet demands zero confectionary expertise. Now you can indulge your sweet tooth without cashing in your whole paycheck.

2 cups dry roasted, lightly salted peanuts, divided
1 cup granulated sugar
2 cups plain nondairy milk, divided
⅛ teaspoon salt
¼ cup creamy peanut butter
2 tablespoons tapioca starch
1 tablespoon vegan butter or coconut oil

Line an 8 x 8-inch square baking dish with aluminum foil and lightly grease. Spread out half of the peanuts evenly on the bottom and set aside.

Place the sugar and ¼ cup of the nondairy milk in a small saucepan and set over medium heat. Stir once to combine, and then keep your spatula out of it to prevent the mixture from crystalizing during this part of the process. Rather, gently swirl the pan to mix the contents.

Cook gently to caramelize the sugar, swirling frequently, until sugar turns mahogany brown in color. Pour in an additional ¾ cup of the milk, swirling to incorporate, followed by the salt and peanut butter. Whisk vigorously until smooth.

Separately, whisk together the remaining cup of milk with the tapioca starch, beating out any and all clumps. Pour this loose slurry into the pot and whisk constantly until the entire mixture has significantly thickened. Immediately remove from the heat, add the butter or oil, and whisk until it has fully melted in.

Cool to room temperature and gently dollop spoonfuls of the filling over the layer of peanuts in your prepared pan. Sprinkle the remaining peanuts on top and gently pat in to adhere. Place on a flat surface in your freezer until fully set; at least 4 hours, and ideally overnight.

Pull out the full sheet of bars, using the foil as a sling, and cut into single-serving sized rectangles. Serve right away, or wrap individually in fresh squares of foil and stash back in the freezer for future snack attacks.

Pistachio Ice Cream Truffles

MAKES A SCANT QUART OF ICE CREAM; 2–3 DOZEN TRUFFLES

These glorious green gems couldn't be simpler to prepare, and are the prefect offering for a party of any size. Best of all, they can be made well in advance, so all you have to do on the day of celebration is to bust them out and look like a total ice cream-churning, scoop-slinging pro. The creamy emerald interiors are sophisticated enough to suit the most discerning palates, while the shatteringly crisp chocolate coating adds sweetness and whimsy that is sure to appeal to a younger generation of food critics in training.

2 cups plain nondairy milk
1 cup shelled, toasted pistachios
⅓ cup fresh baby spinach, packed (optional, for color)
⅓ cup light agave nectar
2 tablespoons arrowroot powder
½ teaspoon salt
½ teaspoon vanilla extract
⅛ teaspoon orange zest
1 batch Dark Chocolate Shell (page 285)

To prepare the ice cream base, simply combine nondairy milk, pistachios, spinach (if using), agave, arrowroot, and salt into your blender or food processor. Blend on high for 5 to 6 minutes, pausing to scrape down the sides of the canister if necessary, until the mixture is thoroughly pureed, without a single fragment of pistachio to be found.

Pour the smooth mixture into a medium saucepan and set on the stove over moderate heat. Whisking frequently, scraping the sides and bottom of the pan to prevent anything from sticking and scorching, bring the liquid up to a gentle boil. Once bubbles begin to burst on the surface with increasing regularity, turn off the heat. Stir in the vanilla and zest last. Let the base cool to room temperature before moving it into the fridge to chill thoroughly; about 3 hours.

Churn the cooled base in your ice cream maker according to the manufacturer's instructions. Transfer the soft ice cream into an airtight container and let it "cure" in the freezer for at least 3 more hours before scooping out your truffles.

Use a small ice cream scoop to make neat little rounds of ice cream, placing them on a silicone baking mat- or parchment paper-lined baking sheet that can fit easily into the freezer. Scoop all your truffle balls and quickly move the whole baking sheet back into the freezer. You want the interiors to be solidly frozen before attempting to dip them, lest they melt once they hit the hot chocolate coating. Allow at least 3 more hours (yes, again!) or let them chill overnight before proceeding.

Finally, heat chocolate shell in a microwave-safe container for about 30 to 60 seconds. Stir thoroughly until fully liquefied. Use a fork to quickly submerge the frozen ice cream balls into the liquid chocolate and pull them out again, working as fast as you can. Place them back on their silicone mats and immediately return to the freezer upon finishing. They can be eaten immediately, or stored in an airtight container for up to 2 months.

Pom Ice Cream Pops

YIELD VARIES DEPENDING ON THE SIZE OF YOUR MOLDS

Can you guess what is shaped like a heart, and may also be good for your heart? Since research seems to indicate that pomegranates can fight heart disease, these frozen lollipops fit the bill quite nicely!

Though Valentine's Day may not be a holiday everyone enjoys, it does lend itself to a variety of fun treats that I'd otherwise have no excuse to create, and any reason to get into the kitchen is good enough for me. A healthier alternative to the generally cream- and butter-soaked bon bons one might give, such a carefully constructed morsel would make a much more thoughtful gift to someone you care for. Plus, who can resist food on a stick? Eat your heart out or just give it away; there are plenty of options for such symbolic sweets, whether romantic or macabre!

Meat of 1 young Thai coconut (about ½ cup), or ½ cup coconut cream
1½ cups 100% pomegranate juice
1 cup light agave nectar or maple syrup
1 (14-ounce) can sliced beets, drained
1 tablespoon lemon zest
1 teaspoon vanilla extract
Pinch of salt
Dark Chocolate Shell (page 285)

Pour any excess ice cream base into an airtight container, and store in the freezer as well. You can scoop this just like any normal ice cream after about 24 hours, no churning necessary! Bear in mind that it does become more solid the longer you leave it, however.

To make the ice cream centers, simply toss all the ingredients (except the magic shell) into your food processor or blender. Thoroughly puree, pausing to scrape down the sides of the bowl periodically, until the mixture is completely smooth. Once perfectly blended and creamy, carefully pour the mixture into the indentations of a small, heart-shaped silicon mold. Place on a level surface in your freezer, and let rest for at least 6 hours or overnight, until frozen solid.

Prepare your magic shell and lay out a silicone baking mat-lined baking sheet. Removing one heart from the mold at a time, carefully but firmly insert a lollipop stick into the bottom of the shape, pushing it straight in without twisting or jiggling it, as this will elongate the opening and make it more likely to fall off later. Dip the whole heart into the chocolate shell quickly, immersing the pop a little way up the stick as well to help "glue" it in place. Let the excess chocolate drip off and place on the baking mat. Repeat with the remaining hearts, pausing between every few to return all the ice cream hearts to the freezer for 15 minutes, to make sure they don't get too soft and become difficult to work with.

Stash the whole baking sheet in the freezer until you're ready to serve the pops. Eat immediately after removing from the freezer; these hearts melt fast!

Strawberry Shortcake Pops

Makes 4–6 popsicles

For fussy, hungry kids, plain yogurt can be a hard sell at snack time. Mix in some fresh fruit preserves and freeze it on a stick, though, and they'll clamor for seconds! These refreshing treats are modeled after the classic strawberry shortcake pops that feature sugary cake crumbs on the outside, but substituting crisp rice cereal provides a much more satisfying textural contrast, not to mention many fewer calories.

½ cup all-fruit strawberry jam or preserves
1 teaspoon lemon juice
⅔ cup vegan vanilla yogurt
½ cup plain nondairy milk
1 cup crispy rice cereal

Use equal parts chocolate and vanilla rice cereal for a sweet flavor sensation, as pictured here.

Whisk together the preserves, lemon juice, and yogurt until smooth, aside from any chunks of whole fruit, of course. Slowly drizzle in the nondairy milk until fully incorporated. Pour the mixture into popsicle molds, filling them up almost to the top. Allow for a little bit of space as the liquid will expand slightly as it freezes.

Carefully stash the molds on a flat surface in your freezer, and allow the pops to set for at least an hour before inserting the sticks. This will help ensure that the sticks remain straight and upright, as the mixture will have started to freeze and thicken to support them. Allow the pops to set overnight before proceeding.

To release the popsicles from their molds, quickly run the exterior under hot water, being careful not to splash any inside the molds. Lightly press the rice cereal on the outsides of the newly freed pops, place them on a plate, and return them to the freezer until ready to serve. If longer term storage is preferred, wrap each one individually in plastic before stashing them back in the freezer.

Superfood Fudgesicles

Makes 4–8 popsicles

Indulge your inner child and your inner health nut at the same time! Antioxidant powerhouses join forces but come out tasting like a treat.

½ cup full-fat coconut milk
3 ounces (about ½ cup) dark chocolate, finely chopped
2 (3½ ounce) packs frozen unsweetened acai puree, thawed
⅓ cup maple syrup
⅛ teaspoon salt

Heat the coconut milk for 60 to 90 seconds, until just on the brink of boiling, and pour it over the chocolate. Let sit for a few minutes to allow the chocolate to melt, and then stir well, until completely smooth. Pour in the acai puree, maple syrup, and salt, and mix thoroughly to combine. Let cool to room temperature and pour into popsicle molds. Place in the freezer and allow at least 4 hours before serving, or until the popsicles are completely solid.

Tex-Mex Ice Cream Sandwiches

MAKES 12–16 ICE CREAM SANDWICHES

Featuring an adventurous combination of cornmeal, coconut milk, and jalapeño, this recipe is a big winner by my estimation. At the center of it all, rich, creamy chocolate ice cream is accented with a bright pop of fresh peppery spice, combining the contrasting sensations of hot and cold all in one taste. Each slab of the frozen dessert is wedged between two thick, chewy cornmeal blondies sprinkled with big chocolate chunks. While each component is drop-dead delicious separately, they create one truly memorable treat when eaten together in one bite.

JALAPEÑO CHOCOLATE ICE CREAM

1¼ cups plain nondairy milk
1 (14-ounce) can coconut milk
1 large (approximately 2 ounces) fresh jalapeño pepper, finely chopped
½ cup granulated sugar
¼ cup natural cocoa powder
2 tablespoons cornstarch
1 tablespoon arrowroot powder
¼ teaspoon salt
¼ teaspoon cayenne pepper
¼ cup light agave nectar
3 ounces (about ½ cup) bittersweet chocolate, finely chopped
1 tablespoon tequila (optional)
½ teaspoon vanilla extract

CORNMEAL CHOCOLATE CHUNK BLONDIES

1½ cups yellow cornmeal
1½ cups all-purpose flour
⅓ cup garbanzo bean flour
1¾ cups granulated sugar
½ teaspoon smoked paprika
½ teaspoon salt
¼ teaspoon turmeric (optional, for color)
¼ teaspoon baking powder
1 cup semi-sweet chocolate chunks or chips
¾ cup frozen corn kernels, thawed
¾ cup olive oil
¼ cup maple syrup
2 teaspoons vanilla extract
1 teaspoon apple cider vinegar

For the ice cream, start by combining the nondairy milk, coconut milk, and jalapeño in a medium saucepan. Toss in the seeds and all, set it over moderate heat, and bring to a boil. Once bubbling vigorously, immediately turn off the heat, cover with the lid, and let infuse for about 2 hours. Strain, pressing all the liquid out of the spent pepper, and discard the solids.

In a clean saucepan, whisk together the sugar, cocoa powder, cornstarch, arrowroot, salt, and cayenne. Add in about ¼ cup of the jalapeño milk and stir into a thick paste, beating out any lumps of starch. When smooth, incorporate the rest of the liquid, along with the agave, and whisk thoroughly to blend. Set over medium heat, whisking occasionally as it comes up to a simmer. When bubbles begin forming around the edges of the liquid, add in the chocolate, letting the mixture sit without agitation for 2 minutes, to allow the chocolate to begin melting.

Switch over to a wide spatula, and stir gently, scraping the bottom and sides of the pan, to make sure that nothing sticks, and that the chocolate fully melts. Once the mixture comes up to a full

(Continued on next page)

boil, cook for just a minute or two longer, and as long as there are no more whole chocolate chunks remaining, turn off the heat. Stir in the tequila (if using) and vanilla extract and let cool completely before chilling thoroughly in the refrigerator; about 3 hours.

Churn in your ice cream maker according to the manufacturer's instructions. Once frozen but still soft, transfer the ice cream into an airtight container and let set up more solidly in the freezer before assembling the sandwiches.

To prepare the blondies, preheat your oven to 350°F. and lightly grease a 9 x 13-inch baking dish. In a large bowl, sift together the cornmeal, all-purpose flour, and garbanzo flour, and whisk in the sugar, paprika, salt, turmeric, and baking powder. Toss the chocolate chunks around in the dry goods to distribute them throughout and coat them with flour. This will help to prevent them from sinking to the bottom of the bars while baking. Set aside.

Place the corn, oil, maple syrup, vanilla, and vinegar into your blender or food processor, and thoroughly puree. Pause to scrape down the sides of the bowl as needed, until the mixture is completely smooth. Pour these wet goods into the bowl of dry, and with a wide spatula, gently stir the two together.

Transfer to your prepared pan, spreading the batter out evenly into the corners and smoothing down the top with your spatula. Bake for 25 to 30 minutes, until the top of the blondies appears set and is golden brown. Let cool before slicing.

When you're ready to assemble to bars, line an 8 x 8-inch square baking pan with aluminum foil. Slice the full rectangle of baked blondies in half so that you're left with two equal squares. Place one square into the prepared pan, lining it up flush with at least two of the pan's sides. If there's extra space between the other sides, construct a barrier with more foil and stand it up right next to the edge of the blondies. This will help prevent the ice cream from melting out initially.

Soften the ice cream slightly if needed and mound it on top of the blondie square as evenly as possible. Working quickly, place the second half of the blondies on top, pressing down lightly to smooth the ice cream and adhere the sheet of cookies. Move the whole thing back into the freezer on a flat surface. Let freeze until very solid before slicing. The longer the better; at least overnight.

Finally, turn the entire affair out onto a large cutting board, and with a very sharp knife, slice into 12 to 16 sandwiches. Wrap individually in plastic wrap, or transfer into a container with an airtight lid. Store the sandwiches in the freezer until you're ready to enjoy.

An alternate method for assembly: Slice the blondies into bars beforehand and store at room temperature in an airtight container. Simply top individual bars with a scoops of ice cream when desired, and press the second blondies on top.

This-Is-It

MAKES ABOUT 1 PINT ICE CREAM, 10–12 COOKIES, AND 5–6 SANDWICHES

Like any great origin story, the tale of the iconic It's-It ice cream sandwich begins with an unassuming start. When a man named George Whitney took a scoop of vanilla ice cream and sandwiched it between two oatmeal cookies in 1928, it didn't make headlines, to say the least. Of course, when he then boldly dipped the whole thing in chocolate, there was no looking back. An instant dessert dynamo, they were sold exclusively at San Francisco's Playland-at-the-Beach for more than four decades, adding to their elusive appeal.

The original It's-Its are now more widely available in high-end grocery stores across the nation but remain curiously deaf to the booming dairy-free demand. Of course, I think we can do Mr. Whitney one better by taking control into our own hands anyway, quickly whipping up a tangy, rich, and far more nuanced bourbon vanilla bean base. Lightly toasted, salted oats meet dark mahogany caramel, elevating the whole experience far beyond the realm of child's play.

NO-CHURN BOURBON VANILLA ICE CREAM

- **4 ounces (½ cup) vegan Cream Cheese (page 282, or store-bought)**
- **2 tablespoons bourbon**
- **1½ teaspoons vanilla bean paste or extract**
- **1 (14-ounce) can full-fat coconut milk, chilled**
- **⅔ cup confectioners' sugar**

SALTED CARAMEL OATMEAL COOKIES

- **1 cup quick-cooking rolled oats**
- **1 cup all-purpose flour**
- **1 teaspoon baking soda**
- **½ teaspoon salt**
- **¼ teaspoon ground cinnamon**
- **⅓ cup light brown sugar, firmly packed**
- **⅓ cup amber agave nectar**
- **¼ cup vegan butter, melted**
- **1 teaspoon vanilla extract**

TO FINISH (OPTIONAL)

- **Dark Chocolate Shell (page 285)**

For the ice cream, in a large bowl, beat together the cream cheese, bourbon, and vanilla until completely smooth. Set aside.

Carefully open the chilled can of coconut milk, being sure not to shake it, and scoop off the top layer of thick coconut cream. Place the coconut cream in the bowl of your stand mixer and install the whisk attachment. Whip on high speed for about 3 minutes before slowly beginning to sprinkle in the sugar, just a little bit at a time. Continue beating the mixture for up to 10 minutes, until light and fluffy.

Add about half of the cream cheese mixture, stirring lightly to incorporate. Fold in the remaining half more gently, keeping it as light and fluffy as possible. Leave a few streaks in the mixture if need be; it's better to under-mix than over-mix.

Pour the ice cream base into a loaf pan or airtight container and carefully move it into your freezer. Allow it to sit, undisturbed, for at least 6 hours before scooping.

For the cookies, preheat your oven to 350°F., and line a baking sheet with a silicone baking mat or parchment

(Continued)

paper. Set aside. Combine the oats, flour, baking soda, salt, and cinnamon. Stir to distribute all of the dry goods evenly and set aside.

In a separate bowl, thoroughly mix the brown sugar, agave, melted butter, and vanilla until smooth. Pour these wet ingredients into the bowl of dry, and mix until you achieve a thick batter, with no dry patches of flour remaining. Be sure to scrape down the sides of the bowl every now and then as you stir to make sure you don't miss any big lumps.

Scoop out about 3 tablespoons of dough for each cookie, roll into balls, and press them gently into flat rounds onto your prepared baking sheets. Aim for about ¼-inch in thickness. Bake for just 9 to 12 minutes, erring on the side of less time to ensure soft, chewy cookies. Slide the silicone baking mats or parchment papers off the hot sheets immediately after pulling the cookies from the oven, and let cool completely before sandwiching with ice cream, storing in an airtight container, or serving up with a tall glass of nondairy milk.

To assemble, sandwich scoops of ice cream between two cookies, pressing down gently until it spreads out to the edges. Immediately return to the freezer while reheating the chocolate shell. Once liquefied, dip the sandwiches halfway into the chocolate. Enjoy immediately or set on a piece of parchment paper, and return to the freezer until ready to serve.

Tirami-Sake Pops

When Italy meets Japan, the results are poetry on the plate. Taking classic tiramisu and infusing it with the traditional rice wine known as sake, a bold new world of flavor unfurls itself in this frozen reinvention. Forget about baking ladyfingers or any fussy cake. Since it will simply soften in the sweet, slightly tangy base, crushed vanilla cookies work perfectly well for this application, soaking up all the sake with ease.

- **1 (8-ounce) container (1 cup) vegan Cream Cheese (page 282, or store-bought)**
- **¼ cup granulated sugar**
- **¼ cup plain nondairy milk**
- **¼ cup coffee-flavored sake, divided**
- **1 teaspoon vanilla extract**
- **¼ teaspoon salt**
- **6 vanilla sandwich cookies, roughly crushed**
- **1 teaspoon instant coffee granules**
- **1 teaspoon Dutch-processed cocoa powder**

To make the creamy base, simply blend the cream cheese, sugar, nondairy milk, 2 tablespoons of the sake, vanilla, and salt together until smooth.

Separately, mix the crushed cookies, the remaining sake, instant coffee, and cocoa powder in a small bowl, stirring thoroughly until the coffee granules have dissolved.

Layer the base and the cookie mush into popsicle molds of your choice. Insert sticks and stash on a level surface in your freezer. Let rest for at least 4 hours, or until solid.

Granted, coffee-infused sake is a bit of a rarity in mainstream markets, but don't despair! You can simply blend ¼ cup of dry sake with ½ teaspoon instant coffee powder to make up the difference.

Vanilla Bean Bee's Knees Ice Cream Sandwiches

YIELD VARIES DEPENDING ON COOKIE CUTTERS

Break out the nice porcelain; it's teatime! Modeling my cookies after graham crackers while inserting fragrant black tea into the mix, these are much more than just ice cream conveyance devices. Crisp, buttery, aromatic, they are actually good enough to eat alone, unlike the standard issue biscuit. And then, there's the ice cream. The delicate nuances of floral vanilla bean and honey flavor are so clean and pure, they simply come alive. Everything works in perfect harmony.

VANILLA BEAN BEE'S KNEES ICE CREAM

3 cups full-fat coconut milk
2 tablespoons arrowroot powder
½ cup Honey Syrup (page 293), or honey-flavored agave nectar
1 whole vanilla bean, split, and seeds scraped

BLACK TEA GRAHAM CRACKERS

1¼ cups white whole wheat flour
½ cup graham flour
1¼ cups confectioners' sugar
¼ teaspoon salt
6 teaspoons black tea (about 6 bags)
1 teaspoon baking powder
½ cup vegan butter
2 tablespoons Honey Syrup (page 293), or honey-flavored agave nectar
2 tablespoons plain nondairy milk
1 teaspoon vanilla extract

Start by preparing the ice cream. In a medium saucepan, vigorously whisk together the coconut milk and arrowroot so that there are no lumps of starch remaining. Set the pan over moderate heat, and add in the syrup and vanilla bean seeds. Whisk occasionally, until it just comes to a boil, and the liquid has thickened significantly. Turn off the heat, and let cool. Chill for at least 3 hours, and then churn in your ice cream maker according to the manufacturer's instructions. Move the freshly churned and still soft ice cream into a 9 x 9-inch square baking pan, smooth it down into as even a layer as possible, and stash in the freezer until frozen solid; at least 6 hours.

For the crackers, preheat your oven to 325°F., and line two baking sheets with parchment paper or silicone baking mats. Place both flours, sugar, salt, tea leaves, and baking powder in your food processor, and pulse briefly to combine. Cut the vegan butter into chunks, and add it as well, pulsing to incorporate, as if you were making a pie crust. Once you achieve small, pea-sized pebbles and a coarse texture in general, add in the syrup, nondairy milk, and vanilla, and pulse just until the dough comes together into one cohesive mass. Divide it into two equal pieces.

Take one piece and lay it out on one of your silicone baking mats. Place another silicone baking mat or piece of parchment paper on top, to prevent the dough from sticking to your rolling pin, and roll it out to about ⅛- to 1⁄16-inch in thickness. If it's really sticky and difficult to work with, just stick it in the fridge for 15 to 20 minutes.

Remove the top silicone baking mat or parchment, and bake for about 15 minutes, until the edges are lightly browned. Quickly cut out whatever shapes you desire while still hot, and then let the cookies cool before removing the excess. Repeat with the remaining half of dough.

To assemble your sandwiches, use the same cookie cutter, or the same shape in one size smaller, and cut out slabs of ice cream. Sandwich them between two cookies, and eat immediately, or return them to the freezer for later consumption. Personally, I actually like them better after they've been sitting for a couple days and the cookies have had a chance to soften.

Wild Blueberry Cheesecake Ice Cream Sandwiches

MAKES 9–12 ICE CREAM SANDWICHES

Regular blueberries, picked at the height of summer, are pretty special as they are. Wild blueberries, however, are on an entirely different level. Tiny, concentrated flavor bombs that explode with rich, jammy flavor, deeper than any fruit snack could ever dream of tasting—their only downfall is the difficulty of pairing that intensity without smothering the accomplice.

Cheesecake is a luscious foundation that serves to best highlight these natural, edible gems. Bumping up the intensity with a bold pop of citrus, lemon zest turned the simple flavor pairing into a full-fledged taste sensation. Sandwiching that indigo swirled scoop between two thick squares of graham cracker cookie bars, each bite sparkles with sunshine and sweetness.

WILD BLUEBERRY SWIRL

5 ounces (about ¾ cups) frozen wild blueberries, thawed
2 tablespoons granulated sugar
1 teaspoon lemon zest
1 teaspoon cornstarch

GRAHAM CRACKER COOKIE BARS

¾ cup vegan butter
¼ cup dark brown sugar, firmly packed
3 cups finely ground graham cracker crumbs
2 tablespoons whole flaxseeds, ground
½ teaspoon salt
¼ teaspoon ground cinnamon
2 tablespoons vegan sour cream or plain yogurt

LEMON CHEESECAKE ICE CREAM

½ cup (4 ounces) vegan Cream Cheese (p. 282)
⅓ cup granulated sugar
¾ teaspoons vanilla extract
1 cup plain nondairy milk
1 teaspoon lemon zest
Pinch of salt

For the swirl, combine all ingredients in a medium saucepan, stirring well before turning on the heat to break up any possible lumps. Cook over medium heat, stirring periodically, until the mixture comes up to a full boil. Turn down the heat slightly so that it stays at a lively simmer, and cook for 1 minute longer, until thickened. Remove from the stove, cool to room temperature, and then place in the fridge to chill; about 2 to 3 hours.

For the cookies, preheat your oven to 350°F. and lightly grease a 9 x 13-inch rectangular baking pan. Place the butter and sugar in the bowl of your stand mixer and cream the two together using the paddle attachment. Once thoroughly beaten, pause the mixer and add in the remaining cookie ingredients. Starting at the lowest speed, gently incorporate, and continue stirring until the entire mixture is moist will and stick together when pressed.

Transfer to your prepared pan and spread it out evenly. Press it firmly into a smooth layer, using your hands or the bottom of a flat measuring cup.

Bake for 12 to 15 minutes, until golden brown. Let cool completely before turning the whole cookie sheet out of the pan and onto a cutting board. Use a very sharp knife to slice it cleanly down the middle, forming two

(Continued on next page)

equal pieces. Trim away the dark edges so that they each measure about 8 inches wide and 5 to 6 inches long.

Line an 8 x 8-inch baking pan with aluminum foil, and carefully place one of the squares inside, fitting it snugly against three of the four edges. Pull the foil up against the remaining side that comes up slightly short. Place the pan and the remaining square of graham cracker cookie in the fridge.

For the ice cream, simply pile all the ingredients into your blender and puree briefly, just until smooth, then churn according to the manufacturer's instructions. Pull out your square baking pan and spoon the soft ice cream on top of the graham cookie sheet. Smooth out to evenly cover the cookie. Spread the blueberry swirl mixture on top, and use a spatula to swirl both components together. Finally, place the remaining rectangle of graham cracker cookie on top, and press down gently. Immediately move the pan into your freezer and let rest until solidified; at least 8 hours. Slice the large ice cream sandwich into smaller rectangles and enjoy.

Yukimi Daifuku

MAKES ABOUT 12 SERVINGS

Otherwise known in America as "mochi ice cream," the name is literally translated as "snow-viewing" rice cakes, alluding to the frosty visions barely visible beneath a thin sheath of pounded sticky rice. Taking the state by storm, traditional Japanese flavors like red bean and matcha often take a backseat to more crowd-pleasing tastes, predictably favoring the basics like strawberry, chocolate, and beyond. Happily, there's room for everyone's favorite flavor in these little chewy bundles! Feel free to take a shortcut here and start with packaged ice cream if you'd like, but don't let conventional choices limit your creativity. While smooth scoops without inclusions are generally easiest to work with while you're still mastering the mochi-making technique, there are no hard rules when it comes to soft ice cream!

1 pint ice cream (any flavor, homemade or store-bought)
¾ cup shiratamako or mochiko
⅓ cup confectioners' sugar
¾ cup water
½ cup potato starch, tapioca starch, or cornstarch

Think outside the scoop! Infuse another layer of flavor into your ice cream creations by using fruit juice instead of water, like orange, pomegranate, or pineapple, just for starters, and pair the creamy center accordingly.

First, create the ice cream centers by using a small ice cream scoop to make neat little rounds of ice cream about the size of golf balls, placing them on a silicone baking mat- or parchment paper-lined baking sheet that can fit easily into the freezer. Portion the entire pint into balls and quickly move the whole baking sheet back into the freezer, for at least 3 to 4 hours or overnight. You want the interiors to be solidly frozen before attempting to wrap them.

When the ice cream cores are solidly frozen, it's time to make mochi. Though this would traditionally involve pounding cooked grains of sticky rice, taking a shortcut by using the microwave makes the process a whole lot easier. Place the shiratamako or mochiko in a medium microwave-safe bowl along with the sugar and water. Whisk vigorously until no lumps remain.

Loosely cover the bowl with plastic wrap and microwave for 1 minute. Use a slightly dampened nonstick spatula to stir before re-covering and microwaving for an additional minute. Stir again, cover once more, and microwave for a 30 final seconds. It should be doughy, slightly gelatinous, and almost translucent.

Line a baking sheet with parchment paper and dust generously with your starch of choice. Place the hot mochi on top, cover with additional starch, and let cool until you can comfortably handle it. Use a rolling pin to flatten the ball out to about

(Continued)

¼-inch in thickness. Add more starch as needed to prevent it from sticking. Chill the whole sheet for about 10 to 15 minutes, until firm and cool to the touch.

Use a 3½-inch cookie cutter to cut out rounds. Press the scraps back together and re-roll to cut additional circles, bearing in mind that they may be a bit tougher and therefore harder to work with later. Lightly brush away the excess starch.

To assemble, take one piece of mochi at a time and place a firmly frozen ball of ice cream on top. Pull the edges up and around the ice cream to fully enclose it in the mochi, pinching the top together with your fingers. Place the seam at the bottom and press gently to slightly flatten. Quickly return the finished yukimi daifuku to the freezer to prevent the core from melting. Repeat with the remaining ice cream and mochi.

For the best eating experience, let the mochi sit at room temperature for about 5 minutes, until the outer layer has returned to a soft and chewy texture.

Shiratamako or Mochiko are both sweet glutenous rice flours and can generally be used interchangeably, although the end results will vary slightly in texture. Shiratamako yields a more elastic dough that will take longer to harden, making it ideal for making yukimi daifuku. Mochiko tends to be more readily available in the import section of many mainstream grocery stores, which gives it an instant upper hand; just bear in mind that it can be a bit more difficult to work with. Contrary to the suspicious-sounding origins, neither contain any gluten, so celiac suffers can safely partake.

SUNDAES EVERYDAY

Like any good origin story, the original invention of what we know as an ice cream sundae is surrounded in controversy, intrigue, and scandal. Okay, it's maybe slightly less gripping than your average telenovela, but quite mysterious all the same. Prevailing lore has it that an inventive druggist first began slinging the lavishly garnished scoops back in the later 1800s, when soda fountains were essentially viewed as health clinics, combining medication with refreshments. Exactly who, and from what town, can lay claim to this concept remains unknown.

Luckily, the future of the ice cream sundae is far clearer than its murky past, and you don't even need to wait for the weekend to indulge. A sundae, by definition, is simply ice cream with a topping. Any topping, and any number of toppings are perfectly suitable, be it a combination of sweet or salty, syrupy or crunchy, fluffy or chewy, fruity or nutty. The very best sundaes balance out these contrasting sensations to create an experience that exceeds the sum of its parts. Sometimes that means going the extra mile to make toffee bits from scratch, and sometimes, it means taking it easy and buying hot fudge sauce at the grocery store, for that finishing touch. I've provided recipes for absolutely every component you could possibly cram into the glass, but by all means, swap and substitute as desired.

Apple Pie Sundae

MAKES ABOUT 1 QUART ICE CREAM, 6–8 CRUST CUPS, AND ABOUT 2 CUPS APPLES

First gradually, and then suddenly, the seasons shift once more. Progressively cooler breezes blow in every night until thick, knit blankets reemerge from storage, unfurling upon beds like the triumphant victory flags of fall. Golden leaves tumble from their branches, crunching and snapping underfoot, dusting every pathway like freshly fallen snow. Tastes adjust as well, directing cravings towards the comfort of warmer, richer foods. When it comes to dessert, no dish better represents this transitory period than the classic apple crisp. A foolproof formula for success, the combination of tender apples, bubbling away in their own cinnamon- and nutmeg-spiked juices holds universal appeal.

Bearing all the best characteristics of the classic pastry but in with a considerably cooler core, a rich scoop of apple butter-rippled ice cream perches atop warm, fork-tender apples, gently poached and delicately cradled by a single-serve flaky crust. Incorporating the faintly woodsy flavor of burnt sugar, these treats don't just welcome autumn's return, but celebrate it with gusto.

APPLE BUTTER SWIRL ICE CREAM

1 cup apple butter, divided
1 (14-ounce) can full-fat coconut milk
½ cup dark brown sugar, packed
¼ cup maple syrup
3 tablespoons bourbon or dark rum
¼ teaspoon salt

PIE CRUST CUPS

1¼ cups all-purpose flour
1 teaspoon granulated sugar
¼ teaspoon salt
6 tablespoons vegan butter, chilled, cut into small pieces
1½ teaspoons lemon juice
1–2 tablespoons ice-cold water
1 tablespoon aquafaba

SIMMERED APPLES

2 tablespoons vegan butter or coconut oil
2 large apples, peeled, cored, and diced
¼ cup dark brown sugar, firmly packed
1 teaspoon ground cinnamon
¼ teaspoon ground nutmeg
¼ teaspoon ground cloves

For the ice cream, simply combine ¾ cup of the apple butter in a large bowl with the remaining ingredients, whisking vigorously until smooth. Chill if not already cold, and process in your ice cream machine as per the manufacturer's instructions. Transfer into an airtight container, alternating scoops with spoonfuls of the reserved apple butter. Swirl the layers together lightly and freeze until solid, for at least 4 hours, before serving.

For the pie crust cups, place the flour, sugar, and salt in the bowl of your food processor and pulse to combine. Add the butter and pulse 6 or 8 times, until the mixture resembles coarsely ground almond meal. A few small chunks should remain, but nothing larger than the size of peas. Sprinkle lemon juice and first tablespoon of water down the chute while pulsing a few times to incorporate. If the dough holds together when squeezed, you're good to go. If it remains crumbly, keep adding water while pulsing, just a teaspoon at a time, until it holds together.

Press into a ball and flatten into a disk about ½-inch thick. Wrap tightly with plastic wrap and chill in the fridge for at least an hour, or up to a week. To save the unbaked dough even longer, store in your freezer for up to 6 months.

When you're ready to roll, preheat your oven to 425°F. and lightly dust a clean, flat surface with an even coating of flour. Lightly coat both sides of the dough with additional flour. Starting at the center of the disk, use your rolling pin to apply gentle pressure while moving outwards to the edges. Keep rolling until it reaches about ⅛-inch in thickness. Cut circles using a 4-inch round cookie cutter, rerolling the scraps and repeating until all the dough is used.

Alternately, make pie crust crisps to serve alongside the scoops by use small cookie cutters to stamp out shapes, or simply use a sharp knife to cut into basic rectangles or squares.

For the cups, gently ease the rounds into ungreased muffin cups, pressing into the corners and smoothing out the sides. For crisps, transfer the pieces to a baking sheet lined with parchment paper or a silicone baking mat. Lightly brush with aquafaba and bake for 14 to 18 minutes, until golden brown all over. Let cool completely.

To make the simmered apples, melt the butter or coconut oil in a medium skillet over medium heat. Toss the apples with the brown sugar and spices and add to the skillet. After about a minute, reduce the heat to medium-low and continue to cook, stirring frequently, until the apples are tender; about 10 minutes. Remove from the heat and let cool before serving warm, or storing an airtight jar in the fridge for up to 5 days. Makes about 2 cups.

To assemble, spoon simmered apples into crust cups and top with a heaping helping of apple butter ice cream. Serve immediately, while the apples are still warm, and the ice cream is still frozen!

Make this treat easy as pie by simply topping with crumbled graham crackers instead of making the crust.

Baklava Sundae

MAKES 12 SERVINGS

Towering stacks of gossamer-thin pastry, impossibly crisp and glistening with sticky syrup, gleam from within bakery cases across the globe. Though typically filled with crisp walnuts and warm spices, baklava is no stranger to alternative approaches. Considering that it's been at the mercy of creative bakers for centuries, this well-loved treat has managed to maintain its core identity far better than most, thanks in no small part to its sheer simplicity.

All you need is phyllo dough and a bit of patience to bring this Mediterranean staple to life in brilliant golden glory. Swapping in a frosty filling with an ice cream core, walnuts become the crowning glory for this frozen rendition, encased in amber toffee. Ambrosial notes of cinnamon and floral syrup, closely reminiscent of honey, are sure to satisfy traditionalist and more adventurous eaters alike.

WALNUT BRITTLE

1 cup granulated sugar
3 tablespoons Honey Syrup (page 293), or amber agave nectar
2 tablespoons water
2 tablespoons vegan butter
¾ cups toasted walnuts, roughly chopped
1 teaspoon ground cinnamon
⅛ teaspoon ground cardamom
¼ teaspoon baking soda
¼ teaspoon salt
1 teaspoon orange blossom water

PHYLLO CUPS

12 sheets (about 8 ounces) frozen phyllo dough, thawed
⅓ cup vegan butter, melted

TO ASSEMBLE

1 pint Smoked Almond Ice Cream (page 85) or Triple Vanilla Frozen Custard (page 103)
¼ cup Honey Syrup (page 293), or amber agave nectar

For the brittle, in a large saucepan, combine sugar, Honey Syrup or agave, and water. Cook over medium heat, stirring, until sugar dissolves. Bring to a boil before blending in the butter. Swirl the pan occasionally rather than stirring, to prevent the sugar from boiling over. Cook until the syrup hits 300 to 310°F. (the hard crack stage) according to a candy thermometer.

Meanwhile, lay a silicone baking mat out on a baking sheet nearby. Combine the walnuts, cinnamon, cardamom, baking soda, and salt in a medium bowl.

Once the hot sugar syrup hits the proper temperature, immediately turn off the heat and quickly stir in the dry ingredients. Add the orange blossom water last and mix thoroughly. Without pausing, scrape the hot candy out of the pan and onto your prepared baking sheet, pressing it out with a spatula to achieve a flat, thin shape.

Let cool completely before breaking into small pieces and either eating right away, or storing in an airtight container at room temperature. In a dry climate, the brittle should keep for 1 to 2 weeks.

For the phyllo cups, preheat your oven to 400°F. Keep your phyllo dough covered with a lightly moistened, but not damp, kitchen towel at all times to prevent them from drying out.

Start by placing one sheet on your work surface and lightly brush with melted vegan butter. Top with another

Fearful of working with finicky phyllo? Take it easy and grab a pack of ready-made phyllo cups straight out of the freezer aisle in your local grocery store. They tend it be fairly small, but they work nicely to cradle a mini ice cream scoop, making for daintier one- or two-bite treats.

sheet of phyllo, brush with more butter, and repeat this sequence until you've stacked up 12 sheets of flaky pastry.

With kitchen shears or very sharp, clean scissors, cut the stack into 12 (4-inch) squares. Form the cups by pressing these squares into muffin tins, with the corners extending above the edges. Bake for 5 to 8 minutes or until golden brown. Cool completely in the pan. While they can be kept in an airtight container for up to 3 days, they're best enjoyed the same day they're baked for the best crisp texture. To revive leftover cups, you can pop them back in the oven at 350°F. for 3 to 5 minutes.

To serve, fill each phyllo cup with ice cream and top with chopped walnut brittle and a drizzle of honey syrup or agave.

Blue Ribbon County Fair Sundae

MAKES 5–6 SERVINGS

Pay a visit to an American county fair and brace yourself for a bombardment of bright lights, brilliant face paint, and raucous laughter. Ferris wheels spin endlessly upwards into the summer sky while kids below try their luck at games of chance, always shooting for the biggest, fluffiest teddy bear on display. Throughout the grounds is the smell of the concession stands. Deep fried delights, popcorn cooked in enormous vats, and freshly spun cotton candy lend a sweet, salty, irresistible perfume to the air. Every bit as essential to the experience, extravagant carnival foods are the stuff that childhood dreams are made of.

Bring the festival back home with a taste worthy of a blue ribbon. Funnel cakes, simply webs of thick fried dough, may seem intimidating to make from scratch, but can be spun together in a snap from basic pantry staples. Served à la mode with bright pink cotton candy ice cream, crunchy kernels of sweet and salty kettle corn peek out from tufts of additional candy clouds. Step right up and take your chances; this dessert is a winner every time.

COTTON CANDY ICE CREAM

2 cups plain nondairy milk
4 teaspoons tapioca starch
4 ounces cotton candy
1 ounce (about 2 tablespoons) cocoa butter, melted
½ teaspoon vanilla extract

KETTLE CORN

2 tablespoons coconut oil
¼ cup popcorn kernels
3 tablespoons granulated sugar
½ teaspoon salt

FUNNEL CAKES

1 quart neutral vegetable or peanut oil, for frying
1 cup all-purpose flour
2 tablespoons granulated sugar
1 teaspoon baking powder
⅛ teaspoon salt
¼ cup aquafaba
½ cup water
¼ teaspoon vanilla extract

TO ASSEMBLE

Additional cotton candy (optional)
Coconut Whipped Cream (page 17, or store-bought)
Maraschino Cherries (page 301, or store-bought)
Sprinkles (page 280, or store-bought) (optional)

Beginning with the ice cream, vigorously whisk together the nondairy milk and tapioca starch in a medium saucepan. Make sure there are no lumps before turning on the heat to medium. Add the cotton candy, and stir until it has completely dissolved. Continue to cook, whisking periodically and scraping the bottom of the saucepan to make sure that nothing sticks, until it comes to a full boil. Add the cocoa butter and combine thoroughly. Turn off the heat and mix in the vanilla.

Cool and chill in the fridge for at least 3 hours. Churn in your ice cream maker according to the manufacturer's instructions. Transfer to an airtight container, and stash in your freezer for at least 3 hours before scooping.

Prepare the kettle corn by setting a large stock pot over medium heat. Add the oil and cover with a lid. Toss just a few kernels of popcorn in at first; once they pop, the oil is hot enough to accommodate the full batch.

Add in the remaining popcorn kernels along with the sugar and salt. Cover and begin shaking the pot aggressively every 10 seconds or so. Don't be afraid to get fierce! The popcorn needs to keep moving to keep unpopped kernels closer to the heat, while moving those that have already popped up to the top. Continue until you hear the popping noises slow, then pour into a large

bowl and let cool for a few minutes. Leftovers will keep in an airtight container for up to 3 days, but is best eaten fresh.

For the funnel cakes, set a tall saucepan or stock pot over medium heat and add oil to fill halfway. Allow the oil to reach 350°F while you prepare the batter.

In a large bowl, whisk together the flour, sugar, baking powder, and salt. Separately, combine the aquafaba, water, and vanilla. Add this liquid mixture into the bowl of dry ingredients, mixing until just combined. Transfer the batter to a plastic squeeze bottle, like you would use to dispense ketchup or mustard, and keep in the fridge until the oil is ready.

Once the oil hits the proper temperature, squeeze the bottle of batter into the pot, dispensing it in a circular, overlapping pattern to make a neat little web. Use about ¼ to ⅓ cup of the batter, cooking just one funnel cake at a time. Fry for 2 to 3 minutes until golden brown, then carefully flip with tongs or a flat spatula. Allow an additional 1 to 2 minutes or until cooked through.

Use a slotted spoon to retrieve the finished funnel cake, draining away excess oil before transferring to a baking sheet or plate lined with paper towels. Let cool for at least 10 minutes before enjoying. You should end up with 5 to 6 gorgeous, golden funnel cakes.

To complete this masterpiece, place a funnel cake on a plate and top with kettle corn, additional cotton candy (if desired), one or two big scoops of ice cream, whipped cream, and a cherry on top. Finish with a flurry of sprinkles if you'd like a bit of extra color and fun.

Boba Tea Sundae

MAKES 4–6 SERVINGS

Shooting through fat straws everywhere, the bubbles found in many refreshing summer drinks aren't merely effervescence, but tangible spheres that you can chew. Known interchangeably as bubble tea, pearl tea, and boba tea, this Taiwanese import has almost as many names as it does flavors. Though it was only invented as recently as the mid-eighties, the sudden availability makes it hard to imagine life without these sweet drinks now. Their unlikely textural combination makes for an irresistible treat.

Take it down a few degrees cooler by transforming the sweet brew into a sundae that straddles the line between drink and dessert. Wait long enough for it to melt, and you can sip it up, too!

MILK TEA ICE CREAM

1 (14-ounce) can full-fat coconut milk
2 cups plain nondairy milk
¼ cup loose black tea leaves (assam and darjeeling)
1 cup granulated sugar
2 tablespoons arrowroot powder
1 tablespoon cornstarch
⅛ teaspoon salt
1 teaspoon vanilla extract

BOBA

½ cup large tapioca pearls
6 cups cold water
3 tablespoons dark brown sugar, firmly packed
⅛ teaspoon salt

TO ASSEMBLE

Sweetened Condensed Cashew Milk (page 310)

Flavor variations are endless for this tall drink of icy sweetness. Just take a gander at the average boba shop menu, and you'll see what I mean. The most popular variations after classic black tea are matcha, strawberry, honeydew, coffee, and Thai tea. Feel free to substitute any of your favorite scoops, homemade or store-bought, to suit your cravings.

For the ice cream, in a medium saucepan, combine the coconut milk and nondairy milk, along with the tea leaves. Bring the mixture up to a full boil before turning off the heat. Cover and let the mixture steep and infuse for 20 to 30 minutes. Strain out and discard the spent tea before returning the liquid to the saucepan.

Separately, whisk together the sugar, arrowroot, cornstarch, and salt, mixing well. Slowly sift this mixture into the saucepan while whisking briskly. Give it another good whisk through before turning on the heat to medium, to ensure that there are no remaining clumps. Stir periodically, to make sure that the base doesn't scorch, and bring to a vigorous boil. Turn down the heat to medium-low and simmer for an additional 2 minutes, at which point the mixture should have thickened quite a bit. Turn off the heat and add the vanilla extract. Cool and chill in the fridge for at least 3 hours, until completely cold all the way through.

Churn in your ice cream maker according to the manufacturer's instructions. Transfer to an airtight container, and stash in your freezer for at least 3 hours before scooping and serving.

For the boba, place the tapioca and cold water in a medium saucepan and set over medium heat. Bring to a boil and then immediately reduce the heat to low, simmering very gently for 45 to 50 minutes. When they're done, the pearls should be mostly translucent with only a tiny speck of opaque white remaining in the centers. Drain in a fine mesh sieve and rinse thoroughly in cold water

"Real" boba from Taiwan is typically multicolored or plain black, slightly larger than plain white tapioca, and softer. They keep longer in the fridge—up to 4 days in an airtight container—and have a genuinely "bouncier" chew. In the event that you can secure a reputable supply of these toothsome morsels, feel free to substitute them here for a more authentic experience. They only need to be cooked for 15 minutes at a rolling boil, and then allowed to sit and steam for an additional 15. Add only 1 tablespoon of brown sugar for the same amount of tapioca if they come presweetened.

to stop the cooking process. Transfer the soft pearls to a small bowl, add brown sugar and salt, stirring gently to combine. Let the tapioca soak in the sugar for at least 15 minutes before using. Covered and stored in the fridge, prepared tapioca can be kept for up to 2 days. This will yield approximately 1½ to 2 cups ready-to-eat tapioca pearls.

To assemble, alternate scoops of ice cream with spoonfuls of chilled Boba in tall glasses, and top with Sweetened Condensed Cashew Milk. Spoon and slurp it up!

Breakfast in Bed Sundae

MAKES 2 SERVINGS

It's never too late, nor too early, to say I love you. And as such, there are plenty of treats suitable for sharing with your sweetheart first thing in the morning. For something truly special, my thoughts drift to a surprise breakfast in bed. Pancakes, fresh fruit smoothies, and even a bowl of cereal seem like extraordinary pleasures when served in the comfort of a cushioned throne, clad in pajamas, sunlight just beginning to filter between gently parted curtains.

With just a little bit of advanced planning, you can rise to the occasion with a wake-up call sure to exceed your beau's wildest dreams. Combine all the best reasons to rise and shine into one short stack. Fluffy pancakes made with cornflake cereal, still hot off the griddle, gently melt the no-churn, no-sugar-added smoothie ice cream mounded on top like a dollop of blueberry butter, but so much better.

CORNFLAKE PANCAKES

1½ cups (about 1½ ounces) cornflake cereal
¾ cup all-purpose flour
1 tablespoon granulated sugar
1½ teaspoons baking powder
⅛ teaspoon salt
1 cup plain nondairy milk
2 tablespoons olive oil
1½ teaspoons apple cider vinegar

BLUEBERRY BANANA SMOOTHIE ICE CREAM

2 ripe bananas, sliced and frozen
1 cup frozen blueberries

TO ASSEMBLE

¼ cup cornflake cereal
Fresh blueberries and sliced bananas
Maple syrup (optional)

If you're not such an early riser, the pancakes can be prepared in advance and kept in the fridge for up to 5 days, or frozen for up to 3 months.

For the pancakes, start by crushing the cereal by either pulsing it in your food processor or pounding it with a rolling pin. When properly broken down, it should measure about ½ cup in volume. Transfer to a large bowl and add in the flour, sugar, baking powder, and salt. Mix well to combine.

Separately, whisk together the nondairy milk, oil, and vinegar before adding the liquid mixture into the bowl of dry ingredients. Stir lightly, just to bring the batter together. Don't try to get it completely smooth, as it will be lumpy from the cereal, and you'll only risk overmixing.

Heat a nonstick skillet over medium heat and lightly grease. Ladle about ¼ cup of batter for each pancake onto the hot surface, cooking 2 to 3 at a time. Cook until bubbles begin to burst on the surface, and the bottom is golden brown, about 5 to 6 minutes. Flip and cook for another 4 to 5, until equally browned on the other side. You should end up with about 8 pancakes.

For the ice cream, place both ingredients into a food processor or blender and pulse until smooth. Scrape down the sides as necessary. Serve immediately for a soft-serve consistency, or place it in an airtight container and freeze for 1 to 3 hours to get a scoopable texture.

To assemble, simply stack up as many pancakes as you'd like on a plate and top with half the cornflakes, fresh fruit, and blueberry banana smoothie. Serve immediately.

Cookie Monster Sundae

MAKES 5–6 SERVINGS

For anyone who's gotten caught with their hand in the cookie jar, I know the struggle; deciding on a single flavor is almost too much to bear! For everyone else who wants it all, your dream dessert has arrived.

Approximately equal parts cookie to ice cream base, this is a solid scoop meant for dough lovers only. Typically relegated to a tiny portion of a largely unexceptional pint, I'm bringing cookies of all types and textures into the spotlight for this bakery bonanza that would make Cookie Monster himself blush. Simple sandwich cookies are mixed into the ice cream itself, with the resounding bite of mini chocolate chips for good measure. Things really start to get golden brown and delicious when it's scooped up alongside sizable chunks of unbaked chocolate chip cookie dough, eggless and perfectly safe to eat as-is. Speculoos joins the party as a creamy sauce, redolent of cinnamon sweetness, thick as hot fudge. Just to gild the lily, crushed graham crackers and more sandwich cookies add that final kiss of crunchy decadence.

COOKIES 'N CREME ICE CREAM

3 cups plain nondairy milk
3 tablespoons cornstarch
¾ cup granulated sugar
¼ teaspoon salt
1 tablespoon vanilla extract
1½ cups quartered Faux-reos (Cream Filled Chocolate Wafer Cookies) (about 14–15) (page 286, or store-bought)

SPECULOOS SAUCE

½ cup creamy speculoos spread
½ cup plain nondairy milk
2 tablespoons maple syrup

COOKIE DOUGH BITES

2 tablespoons vegan butter
¼ cup granulated sugar
¼ cup dark brown sugar, firmly packed
½ cup all-purpose flour
⅛ teaspoon salt
2 tablespoons mini semi-sweet chocolate chips, or finely chopped semi-sweet chocolate
¼ teaspoon vanilla extract
1–2 tablespoons plain nondairy milk

TO ASSEMBLE

1–2 roughly chopped or crushed graham crackers
2–4 Faux-reos (Cream Filled Chocolate Wafer Cookies) (page 286, or store-bought), cut into quarters

---

Starting with the ice cream, in a medium saucepan, combine the nondairy milk, cornstarch, sugar, and salt. Whisk vigorously before turning on the heat. Turn the burner up to medium heat and whisk occasionally, until the mixture comes up to a boil. Let cook at a full boil for 2 minutes, and then remove from the heat. Stir in the vanilla. Let cool to room temperature and then chill thoroughly for at least 3 hours.

Once properly chilled, churn in your ice cream machine according to the manufacturer's directions. Transfer spoonfuls of the soft ice cream into an airtight container, sprinkling quartered sandwich cookies over each addition. Fold the last addition in with a wide spatula, scooping all the way to the bottom and out, to fully mix and distribute. Freeze for at least 3 hours before serving. Makes about 1½ quarts of ice cream.

For the speculoos sauce, simply place all the ingredients in a microwave-safe dish and heat for 30 to 60 seconds, just to loosen up the spread. Stir vigorously to combine, until the mixture is completely smooth. Serve warm or at room temperature, and store in an airtight container in the fridge for up to 2 weeks.

For the cookie dough, melt the butter, and combine it with both sugars, flour, salt, and chocolate chips. Stir in the vanilla; then drizzle the nondairy milk in slowly, one tablespoon at a time, until the mixture comes together into a cohesive dough and no pockets of dry ingredients remain. Press the dough out into a square or rectangle about ½-inch thick and use a sharp knife to cut it into ½-inch cubes. Chill the dough a bit if it's too sticky to cut cleanly. Stash the cubes in an airtight container in the fridge until ready to serve (or simply snack on).

To present your masterpiece, start by placing two or three scoops of ice cream in your favorite dishes or parfait glasses. Top with a generous drizzle of speculoos sauce, a handful of cookie dough bites, and crushed graham crackers and sandwich cookies. Unleash your inner cookie monster!

Elvis Banana Split

MAKES 4 SERVINGS

Long live the king! Elvis was infamous for his legendary food cravings, especially the peanut butter, banana, and bacon sandwich. Clearly the man was a gastronome ahead of his time, combining sweet, salty, and savory well before anyone knew what umami or flavor pairing was. It sounds crazy on paper, but give it the benefit of the doubt and just try a bite; for reasons not fully known, it works.

COCONUT BACON

1 tablespoon soy sauce
½ tablespoon liquid smoke
½ tablespoon maple syrup
½ tablespoon olive oil
⅛ teaspoon ground black pepper
1 cup coconut flakes

PEANUT BUTTER SAUCE

½ cup creamy peanut butter
⅓ cup maple syrup
1–2 tablespoons nondairy milk
⅛ teaspoon salt

TO ASSEMBLE

4 ripe bananas, peeled and halved
Smoked Almond Ice Cream (page 85) or Triple Vanilla Frozen Custard (page 103)
Coconut Whipped Cream (page 17), (optional)

For the coconut bacon, preheat your oven to 300°F. and set aside a 9 x 13-inch baking pan. Stir together the soy sauce, liquid smoke, maple syrup, oil, and pepper in a large mixing bowl. Toss the coconut in and stir with a wide spatula, coating the flakes thoroughly with the liquids. Be gentle to prevent the coconut from breaking into small pieces.

Pour everything, including the excess marinade, into your waiting pan. Bake for about 28 to 32 minutes, stirring every 10 minutes or so to keep the entire batch cooking evenly, until golden brown all over and highly aromatic. The flakes can burn very easily and surprisingly quickly, so stand by and keep a close eye on it. Straight out of the oven, the "bacon" will still be slightly soft to the touch but will crisp up nicely once cool.

Let cool completely and store at room temperature in an airtight container. The "bacon" will keep for up to 2 weeks in a dark, cool place. Makes about 1 cup of bacon.

For the peanut butter sauce, in a small, microwave-safe bowl, combine peanut butter, maple syrup, and 1 tablespoon of nondairy milk. Microwave for 20 to 30 seconds, until the mixture just begins to bubble. Remove from microwave carefully, and stir until smooth. Stir in the salt and thin with additional nondairy milk if needed to reach your ideal viscosity.

To assemble, place two halves of banana cut sides down on a plate and top with generous scoops of your ice cream of choice. Lavish with peanut sauce and a healthy handful of coconut bacon. Pipe or dollop coconut whipped cream on top, if desired. Repeat for the remaining plates. Live like a king and eat well!

Eton Mess Sundae

MAKES 4–6 SERVINGS

One of England's more traditional desserts is truly a beautiful mess. Believed to originate from Eton College, legend has it that it was first served at a cricket match in 1893. Smashed meringues, macerated strawberries, and smears of soft-whipped cream are jumbled together in delicious disarray. It may not look like much on the plate, but this ugly duckling exceeds all expectations once you dig in. Doubling down on the strawberry component, rosy pink meringues grain flavor and their brilliant blushing hue from freeze-dried berries, which are far less exotic than they may sound. There's nothing wrong with bright white vanilla cookies should you choose to omit the added fruit, of course, but be sure you make up for it with twice as much sauce in your sundae. Of course, I would just ladle it on with a heavy hand no matter what.

STRAWBERRY MERINGUE COOKIES

½ cup granulated sugar
⅓ cup freeze-dried strawberries
¼ teaspoon cream of tartar
⅓ cup aquafaba
1 teaspoon vanilla extract

FRESH STRAWBERRY SAUCE

½ pound strawberries, fresh or frozen and thawed, roughly chopped
1 tablespoon maple syrup
2 teaspoons lemon juice
½ teaspoon lemon zest
¼ teaspoon vanilla extract

TO ASSEMBLE

Strawberry Shortcake Ice Cream (page 87) or Triple Vanilla Frozen Custard (page 103)
1 cup fresh strawberries, sliced or chopped
Coconut Whipped Cream (page 17)

To make the meringues, preheat your oven to 200°F. and line a baking sheet with parchment paper. Blitz the sugar together with the freeze-dried strawberries in a very clean, bone-dry spice or coffee grinder, pulsing until the mixture is finely powdered. Sift out any large pieces and re-process if needed. Stir the cream of tartar in to incorporate and set aside.

Place the aquafaba in the bowl of your stand mixer and begin beating on low speed. Once frothy, start beating on high, and slowly sift the sugar mixture in, just a few spoonfuls at a time. Continue to whip, pausing to scrape down the sides of the bowl with a spatula as needed, until the mixture can stand at stiff peaks. This can take between 8 and 10 minutes, so be patient! Gently fold in the vanilla.

Transfer the meringue to a pastry bag fitted with a large star tip, or spoon dollops for each cookie onto the prepared baking sheet. Bake for 1½ to 2 hours, rotating the pans halfway through. It can be difficult to gauge doneness since they shouldn't brown, but be dry and firm to the touch. Don't worry if they seem slightly soft, as they'll continue to crisp as they cool. Just bear in mind that larger cookies will take longer, and smaller will of course take less time. Worst comes to worst, you can always pop under-baked cookies back into the oven to bake again until they reach the correct texture.

Store finished meringues in an airtight container in a cool, dry place. They are best eaten that same day, but if your environment is very dry (not humid), they can last for up to a week.

For the strawberry sauce, in a blender or food processor, combine the strawberries, maple syrup, lemon juice, lemon zest, and vanilla. Blend until smooth, and pass through a fine mesh strainer if needed to remove any errant seeds. Strawberry sweetness will vary by the batch, so taste your sauce and add more maple syrup if desired. That's all there is to it! The sauce is ready to serve right away, or can be stored in an airtight jar in the fridge for up to 5 days. This will yield approximately 1¼ cups of sauce in all.

To assemble, scoop about ½ cup of your ice cream of choice into a glass or bowl, lavish generously with strawberry sauce, sprinkle with fresh strawberries, dollops of coconut whipped cream, and top with as many crumbled and/or whole meringues as desired. Don't waste time admiring your homely creation, stunning as it may be; enjoy before it becomes an even bigger mess as it melts!

Balsamic reduction is readily found alongside the other vinegar options in any well-stocked supermarket, but it's super simple to make at home, too. Simple place about 1½ cups balsamic vinegar in a medium saucepan and cook over medium-high heat. When it comes to a boil, reduce the heat to keep the mixture at a steady simmer for 40 to 45 minutes. Reduce to about ½ cup. Pour into a separate container and let cool; it will continue to thicken. Reheat prior to serving if necessary.

Fried Cherry Pie Sorbet

MAKES ABOUT 16 SERVINGS

Much ado is made about "fried" ice cream, but why not sorbet? Uniting a crispy, buttery crust with the cold comfort of a luscious frozen scoop, this fruit-forward approach allows intense cherry flavor to shine. Contrary to the name, fried ice cream is not plunged into a vat of hot bubbling fat, but coated with a crunchy layer of crushed cereal, sweetened breadcrumbs, or some other starchy substance. I prefer a homemade crumb coating, much like you would find perched atop coffee cake, but with a bit more heft to properly enrobe a full scoop. It's a heck of a lot easier than making pie dough or splattering the kitchen with scalding droplets of hot oil, that's for sure!

CHERRY SORBET

1 pound (about 3 cups) pitted sweet cherries, fresh or frozen and thawed
1 cup 100% apple juice
⅔ cup granulated sugar
1 teaspoon lemon juice
¼ teaspoon ground cinnamon

FAUX-FRIED PIE CRUST CRUMBS

½ cup granulated sugar
1½ cups all-purpose flour
⅓ cup vegan butter or coconut oil, melted
½ teaspoon salt

TO ASSEMBLE

Balsamic reduction or Hot Fudge Sauce (page 295, or store-bought)
Coconut Whipped Cream (page 17, or store-bought)
Maraschino Cherries (page 301, or store-bought)

For the cherry sorbet, simply place all the ingredients in a blender or food processor, and puree on high speed for up to 10 minutes depending on how powerful your machine in, until completely smooth. Pass the mixture through a fine mesh strainer if needed, and chill if no longer cold.

Process in your ice cream maker according to the manufacturer's instructions. Transfer to an airtight container and let cure in the freezer until firm enough to scoop; at least 4 hours, and ideally overnight.

Line a baking sheet with aluminum foil or parchment paper, and scoop out full rounds of the sorbet, placing them evenly spaced apart on the sheet. Quickly return to the freezer.

Prepare the crumb coating by preheating your oven to 300°F. In a large bowl, mix together all ingredients. The mixture should form coarse, chunky crumbs.

Transfer to a lightly greased baking dish and bake for 20 minutes. Let cool, then break apart the biggest clumps by hand, leaving it a bit chunkier, or toss it back into the food processor for a couple pulses to pulverize more finely. Transfer to a shallow dish.

Roll the frozen sorbet balls in the crumb mixture, gently pressing to adhere and fully coat each scoop. Return to the freezer until ready to serve.

For the final presentation, arrange each crumb-covered sorbet scoop on a plate, drizzled with balsamic reduction or chocolate sauce, a swirled of whipped coconut cream, and a cherry on top. Easy as pie!

Frosty Fruit Nachos

MAKES 2–3 SERVINGS

At the height of summer, all I want out of a frozen treat is some cool, refreshing goodness, and this is the power snack to beat all: Fresh fruit nachos! Raw, whole foods are all it takes to make a decadent dessert that won't leave you in a sugar coma. The most "complicated" part is making banana ice cream, so you'll never need to let sweet cravings get the best of you. Consider your summertime snack attacks officially solved.

3 ripe bananas, sliced and frozen
2 tablespoons maple syrup, divided
¼ medium seedless watermelon
1–2 tablespoons cacao nibs

For the ice cream, pop the bananas into your blender along with 1 tablespoon of maple syrup and puree until smooth and creamy. Pause to scrape down the sides of the container with your spatula if needed, to keep everything incorporated.

Meanwhile, cut the watermelon into thin triangles and arrange overlapping on a plate. Top with scoops of banana ice cream, cacao nibs, and a drizzle of the remaining maple syrup. Dig in right away before it all melts down!

Gingersnap, Crackle, and Pop Sundae

MAKES 4 SERVINGS

Some gingerbread creations are merely accented by warm spices, but this one has a real spark. Ginger blazes brightly through molasses-tinted scoops, set off by effervescent fireworks of fizzy ginger ale. Crispy cereal sprinkles create a cacophony of crackling, both audibly and gustatorily, creating a perfectly symphonic experience. This is a sundae that you can eat with a spoon and drink through a straw simultaneously, bringing together all the best parts of a hard-packed pint and soda float in one.

GINGERBREAD ICE CREAM

3 cups plain nondairy milk
¾ cup dark brown sugar, firmly packed
¼ cup molasses
2 tablespoons tapioca starch
1 tablespoon ground ginger
1½ teaspoons ground cinnamon
¾ teaspoon ground allspice
½ teaspoon ground cloves
¼ teaspoon ground nutmeg
¼ teaspoon salt
2 tablespoons vegan butter
1 tablespoon bourbon (optional)
⅓ cup crystallized ginger, finely chopped

GINGERSNAP COOKIES

½ cup vegan butter
⅔ cup granulated sugar
2 tablespoons molasses
1½ cups all-purpose flour
2 teaspoons ground ginger
1 teaspoon ground cinnamon
¼ teaspoon ground cloves
1 teaspoon baking soda
⅛ teaspoon salt

TO ASSEMBLE

½ cup crispy rice cereal
4 tablespoons molasses
2 cups ginger ale soda

For the ice cream, since it will take the longest to properly set: In a medium saucepan, whisk together the nondairy milk, sugar, molasses, starch, all the spices, and salt. Beat vigorously to combine, making sure there are no lumps before proceeding.

Cook over medium heat, whisking frequently, until the mixture comes to a full boil. Remove the pan from the heat and add in the vegan butter, stirring until it has completely melted and is smoothly incorporated into the mixture, followed by the bourbon if using. Cool to room temperature before chilling thoroughly in the fridge, at least 3 hours, before churning.

Pour the mixture into your ice cream maker and process according to your machine's directions. In the final 5 minutes of freezing, slowly add in the crystalized ginger, allowing the paddles to distribute it evenly throughout. Transfer the soft ice cream into an airtight container and stash in the freezer until firm enough to scoop, at least 3 to 4 hours, or overnight.

For the cookies, preheat your oven to 350°F. and line a baking sheet with parchment paper or a silicone baking mat. Install the paddle attachment on your stand mixer, and place the vegan butter in the bowl first, beating it briefly on low speed. This will soften it up a bit and make it easier to incorporate the dry goods. Add in the sugar and molasses, and cream thoroughly, pausing to scrape down the side of the bowl as necessary. The mixture should be grainy but otherwise homogenous, with no ribbons of unmixed molasses.

(Continued on next page)

In a separate bowl, lightly whisk together the flour, ginger, cinnamon, cloves, baking soda, and salt. Add this flour mix into your stand mixer and combine. Be patient; it may take a few minutes for the dough to come together.

Using 1 to 2 tablespoons' worth of dough at a time, roll into smooth balls in the palms of your hands. Space the cookies about 1 inch apart on your prepared baking sheet and press down lightly to flatten out the tops. You should end up with approximately 18 cookies, giving you plenty of extras to snack on!

Bake for 8 to 12 minutes and let cool on sheets. If you prefer chewier cookies, aim closer to the shorter time; bake longer if you'd like them to have more of a crunch.

To assemble the sundaes, scoop the ice cream into 4 glasses (and don't feel compelled to use it all up; it makes a generous amount). Smash 1–2 cookies per sundae and sprinkle the crumbles on top, along with the rice cereal and an extra drizzle of molasses. Finish each one with ½ cup of ginger ale right before serving. Garnish with an extra whole cookie, if desired.

Halo Halo

MAKES 4–6 SERVINGS

A riot of colors and textures in a glass, halo halo is Tagalog for "mixed," which is a very dull way to describe such a dazzling Filipino sensation. Extravagant by design, the only consistent component across all interpretations is crushed ice drizzled with evaporated or condensed milk. Too much is never enough when it comes to toppings, which could include anything from mashed ube, sweetened red, white, or black beans, coconut strips, tapioca pearls, gulaman (seaweed gelatin), pinipig (toasted pounded rice), nata de coco (fermented coconut water jelly), nuts, fresh fruit, candied fruit, flan, and of course, most importantly in my eyes, a scoop of ice cream. Some of the typical suspects are still a bit difficult to track down stateside, but the beauty of this exotic ensemble is that truly, anything goes. I've taken some shortcuts and shrewd swaps to approximate the genuine article. Use what you want, leave out what you don't, and feel free to wing it with your own unique adaptations.

UBE ICE CREAM

6 ounces peeled, cubed, or grated ube (sweet purple yam)
1 (14-ounce) can full-fat coconut milk
½ cup light agave nectar
¼ teaspoon salt
¼ teaspoon vanilla extract

SHORTCUT NATA DE COCO

1 cup coconut water
2 teaspoons coconut milk
1 teaspoon agar powder

TO ASSEMBLE

½ cup sweetened white beans
½ cup fresh coconut meat, diced, or unsweetened coconut flakes
¼ cup Maraschino Cherries (page 301, or store-bought), chopped
½ cup ripe jackfruit or pineapple, fresh or frozen and thawed, sliced
2 cups ice cubes
⅓ cup coconut cream
2 tablespoons light agave nectar
1 ripe banana, sliced
¼ cup crispy rice cereal

Prepare the ice cream by placing the ube and coconut milk in a small saucepan, cover, and bring to a gentle simmer. Cook for about 20 minutes, until fork-tender, and let cool. Transfer to your blender or food processor along with the agave, salt, and vanilla, and puree until completely silky-smooth.

Chill in the fridge for 2 to 3 hours before churning in your ice cream maker according to the manufacturer's instructions. Store in an airtight container in the freezer, and allow at least 3 hours for the ice cream to set and become a more scoopable consistency.

For the nata de coco, simply combine everything in a small saucepan over medium heat, whisk vigorously to combine, and bring to a boil. Cook for 2 minutes at a rolling boil before pouring the mixture into a lightly greased square container. The exact dimensions aren't critical, since you'll be dicing it fairly small later.

Let the coconut mixture cool to room temperature before transferring to the fridge. Chill until set, about 1 hour. Slice into small squares and store in an airtight container in the fridge until ready to use. It will keep for up to 1 week.

(Continued)

To assemble, break out 4 to 6 of your nicest parfait glasses or champagne flutes! Spoon about 2 tablespoons of the diced nata de coco into the bottom of each. On top of that, divide the sweetened beans, coconut, cherries, and jackfruit or pineapple equally between the glasses.

Make "shaved" ice by placing the ice cubes in your blender or food processor, and pulse until they're broken down to the consistency of coarse snow. Move quickly now, since it will melt away just as quickly, too. Distribute the ice between your glasses.

Mix together the coconut cream and agave before drizzling it over the layer of ice. Pull out your ube ice cream and add generous scoops on top. Finally, finish the parfaits with sliced bananas and a sprinkle of crispy rice cereal. Spoon, slurp, and enjoy! You've certainly earned a cool, refreshing snack break after all that.

Some of these ingredients bear further explanation.

Ube, which also known as purple yam, is a tuberous root vegetable. Hailing from southeast Asia, some say the delicate taste has notes of pistachio and white chocolate. It varies in color between a deep purple and even white. Taro and Okinawan sweet potatoes are very similar and can be substituted interchangeably, but flavors and hues will vary.

You can make your own **sweetened beans** by combining 1 can of navy or cannelini beans with ½ cup granulated sugar and ¼ cup water. Simmer gently until the sugar has dissolved. Let cool and store in the excess syrup, sealed in an airtight container in the fridge, for up to a week. Drain thoroughly before using.

When preparing the **nata de coco**, this could be a great opportunity to use the liquid left in the can of full-fat coconut milk after skimming off the cream! Just substitute it for the full measure of coconut water and milk combined.

Mangonada

SERVES 2

In a frosty amalgamation of many quintessential flavors and ingredients that define Mexican street snacks, the mangonada (sometimes referred to as a chamoyada) checks the boxes for sweet, salty, spicy, and tart all at once. Blitzing fresh mangos with ice, orange juice, chili powder, and chamoy, these slushees get their twang from a thick swirl of chamoy sauce. Traditionally made from fermented fruit, salt, sugar, and chiles, chamoy sauce can be found in the Latin section of most stores but is simple to whip up in your own kitchen. The same can be said for Tajin, and both should have permanent residence in your pantry in any case. A tiny bit of each can enliven everything from crisp apple slices to hot French fries.

SHORTCUT CHAMOY SAUCE

2 chipotles in adobo, or 2 teaspoons chipotle powder
1 cup apricot jam
¼ cup lime juice
½ teaspoon salt

TAJIN (CHILI-LIME SEASONING)

1 tablespoon chili powder, chipotle powder, or paprika
1 teaspoon lime zest
½ teaspoon ground cumin
¼ teaspoon ground cayenne pepper
¼ teaspoon ground coriander
¼ teaspoon salt

MANGO SOFT SERVE

2½ cups (about ¾ pound) frozen mango chunks
½ cup orange juice
2 tablespoons lime juice

TO ASSEMBLE

1 fresh mango, diced
1 lime, halved

Prepare the chamoy sauce by placing the chipotles in your blender or food processor and pulsing to break them down into more manageable chunks. Add in the jam, lime juice, and salt, pulsing to combine. Keep blending if you'd prefer a smoother texture, or keep it slightly chunky for more of a bite. Store in an airtight container in the fridge for up to 2 months.

To make the tajin, simply mix all the seasonings until thoroughly distributed throughout. Stored at room temperature in an airtight jar in a dark place, the blend will keep indefinitely.

For the soft serve, place the frozen mango chunks, orange juice, and lime juice into your blender and puree until smooth. Juice half of a lime into each glass then add 1 to 2 tablespoons of chamoy and 1 teaspoon of tajin to each. Swirl the mixture together and up the sides of each glass.

To assemble, add scoops of the frozen mango mixture into each glass and top with fresh diced mango, more chamoy, and a sprinkle of tajin seasoning. Serve immediate to keep it cool . . . Yet spicy, too!

> You can purchase commercial tajin seasoning, but by making it yourself, you can adjust it specifically to your tastes. Want a smokier chili lime seasoning? Use chipotle powder instead of chili powder. Want a milder spiciness? Use generic mild paprika instead of chili powder or cut down the amount of cayenne used.

Santa's Secret Stash

MAKES 4 SERVINGS

When he's on his epic Christmas Eve odyssey, Santa is powered by the laughter of children, reindeer magic, and the holiday spirit itself, but we all know he needs to stop and refuel on something more substantial every so often. If I were going to treat Mr. Claus, it would be with this magnificent collection of seasonal specialties. It all starts with a thick, chewy sugar cookie, because tradition does mandate the classic offering. Instead of a wan glass of milk, though, I'm topping it with a generous scoop of eggnog ice cream, melting into the warm skillet while rivulets of tart cranberry sauce burst through each nook and cranny. Lightly spiced nuts crunch through each layer, adding a refreshing textural contrast. Old Saint Nick never tasted a midnight snack quite like this.

EGGNOG ICE CREAM

1 cup raw macadamia nuts, soaked for at least 6 hours
2½ cups nondairy milk
½ cup light agave nectar
2 tablespoons arrowroot powder
½ teaspoon ground nutmeg
½ teaspoon black salt (kala namak)
¼ teaspoon ground cinnamon
¼ teaspoon ground turmeric, for color
¼ cup dark rum
1 teaspoon vanilla extract

QUICK FRESH CRANBERRY SAUCE

6 ounces (about 2 cups) fresh cranberries
½ cup orange juice
¼ cup granulated sugar
¼ teaspoon ground cinnamon

SPICED BOURBON PECANS

2 tablespoons aquafaba
1 tablespoon bourbon
¼ cup granulated sugar
¾ teaspoon ground cinnamon
¼ teaspoon ground ginger
½ teaspoon salt
2 cups pecan halves

DEEP DISH SUGAR COOKIES

¼ cup vegan butter
¼ cup dark brown sugar, firmly packed
2 tablespoons aquafaba
1 tablespoon ground flaxseeds
1 teaspoon vanilla extract
1 cup all-purpose flour
¼ teaspoon baking soda
¼ teaspoon salt
1 tablespoon turbinado sugar

For the ice cream, place everything for the ice cream base into your blender and let it rip on high. Puree, until completely smooth, pausing to scrape down the sides if needed. Give it at least 4 to 8 minutes to ensure there are no gritty particles of the nuts remaining. Don't rush the process to achieve a truly silky texture. Pass the base through a fine mesh strainer to remove any tricky pieces that may not have been blended. Chill the mixture thoroughly, for at least 3 hours in your fridge, before churning.

Churn according to your ice cream maker's instructions. Scoop the fresh ice cream into an airtight container and store in your freezer for at least 3 hours, until firm enough to scoop, before serving.

(Continued on next page)

To make the cranberry sauce, bring the cranberries, orange juice, sugar, and cinnamon to a simmer over medium heat, stirring frequently. Continue cooking, for about 10 minutes, until most of the cranberries have popped. Use the side of your spoon to lightly mash them if they need a bit of convincing to reach the right consistency. Let cool for at least 30 minutes before spooning out or storing for later. When stored in an airtight container in the fridge, the sauce can be prepared up to a week in advance.

For the candied pecans, preheat your oven to 275°F. In a medium bowl, lightly whisk the aquafaba by hand, until frothy. Add the bourbon, sugar, cinnamon, ginger, and salt, whisking thoroughly to incorporate. Introduce the pecans last, tossing to coat. Once all the spices are evenly distributed across the nuts, spread the mixture onto a baking sheet. Bake for about 45 to 50 minutes, stirring gently every 15 minutes, until evenly golden brown and dry to the touch. Let cool completely before storing in an airtight container. Candied pecans will keep at room temperature for at least 2 weeks.

For the sugar cookies, preheat your oven to 325°F. Lightly grease 4 (4-ounce) oven-safe custard cups, mini skillets, or ramekins. Using your stand mixer with the paddle attachment installed, beat together the vegan butter and brown sugar until smooth and homogeneous, pausing to scrape down the sides with your spatula as needed. Add aquafaba, flaxseeds, and vanilla, mixing until smoothly incorporated. Sift together the flour, baking soda, and salt before adding them to the wet ingredients. Stir well to bring the batter together.

Divide the cookie dough between your prepared dishes, pressing it out to fill each in an even layer. Sprinkle with turbinado sugar and bake for 15 to 18 minutes, or just beginning to turn golden brown around the edges and set in the center.

Remove from oven and let rest for at least 5 minutes before serving. They're great at any temperature, but best served warm! To complete the sundae, top the single-serve cookies with scoops of ice cream, cranberry sauce, and candied pecans, as desired. 'Tis always the season for ice cream!

Sesame Potting Soil Sundae

MAKES 3–4 SERVINGS

Roll up your sleeves and dig in! You don't need a green thumb to cultivate a crop of black sesame sweets to be the envy of any gardener. Blending a straightforward base of whole fruits allows the full range of nutty, toasted black sesame flavors to shine, crowned with a crunchy crumb topping. Delicate candied rose petals blossom on top, but for a more nostalgic sort of treat, there's no shame in tossing some homemade gummy worms on top. To make gummy worms, refer to the recipe on page 277, and simply use a worm-shaped mold instead. No matter how your garden grows, it's sure to blossom with brilliant flavors.

INSTANT BLACK SESAME ICE CREAM

¼ cup toasted black sesame seeds
⅛ teaspoon salt
1 ripe avocado, pitted, diced, and frozen
1 ripe banana, sliced and frozen
¼ cup maple syrup

SESAME SOIL

¼ cup toasted black sesame seeds, divided
¼ cup granulated sugar
½ cup all-purpose flour
2 tablespoons vegan butter or coconut oil, melted
¼ teaspoon salt

CANDIED ROSE PETALS

1 unsprayed rose
3 tablespoons aquafaba
½ cup granulated sugar

TO ASSEMBLE

3–4 tablespoons green colored sugar or sprinkles

Craving a more classic childhood dirt cup? Replace the black sesame seeds in the mousse with Dutch-process cocoa powder, and simply use ground sandwich cookies for the crumb topping.

For the ice cream, place the sesame seeds in your food processor first, grinding them down to a very fine powder. Once it's a flour-like consistency, add all the remaining ingredients and process, pausing to scrape down the sides of the bowl, until perfectly smooth and creamy. Transfer to a piping bag or simply scoop into individual dishes and stash in the freezer until ready to serve.

For the edible soil, preheat your oven to 300°F. Make sure your food processor is thoroughly cleaned and dried before grinding down 3 tablespoons of the sesame seeds. Add the sugar, flour, melted butter or coconut oil, and salt. Pulse to incorporate, mixing until just combined. Stir in the remaining sesame seeds by hand and spread the stiff batter onto a baking sheet lined with parchment paper or a silicone baking mat. Press it down in an even layer about ¼-inch thick.

Bake for 20 minutes, until dry to the touch. Let cool completely, then either break apart by hand, leaving it a bit more chunky, or toss it back into the food processor for a couple pulses to break apart (as pictured).

For the rose petals, gently separate the petals; discard the stem. Use a pastry brush or paintbrush (used only for food, please!) to carefully apply the aquafaba to each petal before tossing them with the sugar. Once fully coated, retrieve the petals by using tweezers, to prevent all the sugar from just falling back off. Lay them

(Continued)

out on a baking sheet in a single layer, allowing enough space for air to circulate. Let dry at room temperature for 2 to 6 hours, depending on how humid your climate is. Use within 2 to 3 days for best results.

To bring it all together, retrieve the ice cream from the freezer and top with sesame soil, candied rose petals, and green colored sugar. Way to grow!

Spaghetti Eis

MAKES 4 SERVINGS

Spaghetti eis, a.k.a. spaghetti ice cream, is exactly what it sounds like. Not a savory entrée served below the freezing point, but a fun trompe l'oeil made from strands of sweet frozen custard intertwined with pools of red berry "marinara" and a flurry of shredded coconut "cheese." Anyone can make this from pantry staples in a flash, or go all out with a fully homemade version, complete with chocolate truffle "meatballs" for a more substantial treat.

Invented in Germany, this is still mostly a Teutonic treat, not seen widely abroad. The original method calls for extruding vanilla ice cream through a spaetzle press, but if you don't have one, a potato ricer works just as effectively, squeezing out fine noodles with the greatest of ease.

CHOCOLATE MEATBALLS

½ cup (3 ounces) semi-sweet chocolate chips, melted
¼ cup almond meal
¼ cup confectioners' sugar
¼ cup chopped walnuts
¼ cup unsweetened, shredded coconut
⅛ teaspoon salt

STRAWBERRY RED SAUCE

½ cup strawberry jam or preserves
1 tablespoon orange juice

TO ASSEMBLE

1 batch Triple Vanilla Frozen Custard (page 103) or Garlic Ice Cream (page 54)
Shredded coconut, confectioners' sugar, or white sprinkles
Fresh mint leaves

For the chocolate meatballs, combine all the meatball ingredients. Stir thoroughly to create a very thick, coarse dough. Let stand for 10 to 15 minutes for the chocolate to further set and become easier to handle; you can speed this process up by sticking it in the fridge for about 5 minutes instead.

Use a small cookie scoop to scoop out about 1 tablespoon of the dough for each ball. Roll between the palms of your hands to smooth and round them out evenly. You should get between 9 to 10 finished "meatballs," which can be made up to 2 weeks in advance if stored in an airtight container in the fridge.

For the red sauce, simply combine the jam and juice in a small microwave-safe dish and heat for 30 to 60 seconds, to soften the jam. Stir thoroughly, until smooth.

When you have all the components completed and ready to go, place four plates and the potato ricer into the freezer. Keeping them chilled will prevent the ice cream from melting on contact.

To assemble, scoop about 1 cup of ice cream into the potato ricer at a time. Holding the ricer over the frozen sundae plate, squeeze the ice cream through the holes, swirl it onto the plate as artistically as possible, to imitate fresh spaghetti noodles. Quickly stash the plate back in in the freezer. Repeat for the other plates.

Pour the strawberry sauce over each ice cream "noodle" creation, top with chocolate meatballs and fresh mint leaves, and sprinkle with coconut. Serve immediately.

Yellow Butter Brickle Road Sundae

Put on your ruby slippers and follow me down the yellow brick road, to a taste sensation beyond your wildest imagination. Gleaming brighter than gold itself, this invaluable culinary currency shines with crunchy bites of buttery toffee and toasted almonds, paving the way back home with marshmallow sauce spackling and a dab of fudge for good measure. Just tap your heels together three times and say, "there's no place like the kitchen." We're off to see the Wizard, the wonderful Wizard of Ice!

BASIC BUTTER BRICKLE

1 cup vegan butter
1 cup granulated sugar
¼ teaspoon salt
½ teaspoon vanilla extract

BUTTER BRICKLE ROAD ICE CREAM

¼ cup vegan butter
⅔ cup dark brown sugar, firmly packed
2 cups plain nondairy milk
2 tablespoons arrowroot powder
½ teaspoon ground turmeric
¼ teaspoon salt
1 teaspoon vanilla extract

TO ASSEMBLE

Maple Marshmallow Sauce (page 299)
Hot Fudge Sauce (page 295)
Chopped almonds

For an utterly irresistible treat worthy of the fanciest candy platters, mix 1 cup of sliced almonds into the butter brickle at the same time you incorporate the vanilla. Let set, and top with 1½ cups melted semi-sweet chocolate chips on top. Spread evenly all over, and voilà; like modern magic, you've just created a mouthwatering sheet of English toffee. Break into larger chunks for solo snacking.

For the brickle, melt down the vegan butter in a medium saucepan over moderate heat. Add the sugar and salt once liquefied, stir to incorporate, and then keep your spatula out of it from that point forward. Cook until the sugar caramelizes to a deep amber color; about 10 to 15 minutes. Incorporate the vanilla and immediately pour onto a piece of parchment paper or silicone baking mat to cool. Let rest for 1 to 2 hours, until solidly set, before breaking or chopping into small pieces. Stored in an airtight container at room temperature, the butter brickle can keep for 5 to 7 days.

For the ice cream, place the vegan butter and brown sugar in a medium saucepan over moderate heat. Cook until the butter melts and the sugar dissolves smoothly, without any grainy texture.

Separately, whisk together the nondairy milk, arrowroot, turmeric, and salt, making sure the mixture is completely smooth and lump-free before gently pouring it into the saucepan. Whisk frequently, until it reaches a rolling boil and has thickened significantly. Turn off the heat and add the vanilla, whisking vigorously to incorporate. Let cool completely before stashing in your fridge to chill for at least 3 hours before churning.

Churn in your ice cream maker according to the manufacturer's instructions. In the final 5 minutes of churning, while the ice cream is still soft, slowly add 1 cup of the finely chopped butter brickle into the mix, allowing the paddle to distribute the pieces throughout. You should still have plenty of candy leftover for topping. Transfer the freshly churned ice cream to an airtight container and let rest in the freezer for at least 4 hours, or until set solid enough to scoop. The butter brickle will continue to soften and melt into the base the longer that it sits, which is just as delicious, too!

To assemble each sundae, place 2 to 3 generous scoops of ice cream into your desired dish and top with marshmallow sauce, fudge sauce, leftover butter brickle bits, and chopped almonds, to your heart's content. Keep on following the yellow brick road and dig in!

CELEBRATION CAKES

Growing up, birthdays were always grand events for me. Even better than a national holiday, all my favorite people came out to play, party, and feast. At least, that's how I imagined it, bursting with excitement at daybreak. Best of all, there would be two separate parties to look forward to; one with my family, and one with my friends. That also meant two cakes would grace the table in short time. The first was always a unique creation lovingly baked and sculpted by my mom, often in the shape of my obsession du jour. Old photos still exist of a flamingo cake, complete with neon pink peppermint frosting, and a dark chocolate penguin cake dressed up in his finest cocoa tuxedo. The second cake, though, was always the same, and entirely non-negotiable: A simple ice cream cake straight off the shelf from a local parlor, chocolate and vanilla, with chocolate crunchies in the center. As much as I loved the finery of my mother's handiwork, I relished the cold comfort of this reliable quick fix with nearly equal enthusiasm.

The ice cream cakes that follow are considerably elevated in tastes, from the complex to the nostalgic, but should ultimately elicit that very same feeling of child-like joy with the very first slice. Bear in mind that building frozen cakes is a delicate art, not to be attempted by the meek, the ambivalent, the impatient, or those of limited freezer space. When you want a next-level grand finale for a truly special occasion, these are the keys to the kingdom. Read through the entire recipe twice, toss out the forgotten, freezer-burnt loaves of bread to make room, and assemble the full fleet of ingredients before diving in. We have some merrymaking to create.

Feel free to dissect these recipes for the core components if the entire assembly is just too intimidating. Ice creams can be churned as solo scoops, sauces and sides taste just as sweet gracing other dishes, and there are plenty of gems to enjoy as entirely unique desserts, no ice cream need apply.

Pull out your party hat and strike up the band; the celebration is waiting to begin.

Brooklyn Blizzard Blackout Cake

MAKES 16–20 SERVINGS

Sink your fork into this one and close your eyes. This sensation, this euphoric, intoxicated, suddenly blissful feeling you're experiencing? This isn't death by chocolate, it's life by chocolate! The original Brooklyn Blackout Cake, iconic for its jet-black crumb coating and pudding-smothered layers, really does mean well, but doesn't quite reach the frosty peaks that my ice queen here does. Firm yet supple layers stacked up with a no-churn chocolate custard beckon, reviving jaded chocolate lovers with one bite. Kids and adults alike will clamor to help "clean up" the fallen crumbs left behind.

CHOCOLATE BLACKOUT CAKE

½ cup olive oil
2 cups granulated sugar
1 cup plain vegan yogurt
1½ cups brewed and cooled coffee
2 teaspoons vanilla extract
3 cups all-purpose flour
⅔ cup Dutch-processed cocoa powder
1 teaspoon baking powder
1 teaspoon baking soda
¾ teaspoon salt

NO-CHURN FROZEN CHOCOLATE CUSTARD

1½ cups granulated sugar
½ cup potato starch
¼ cup Dutch-processed cocoa powder
½ teaspoon salt
4 cups plain nondairy milk
½ cup (about 3 ounces) semi-sweet chocolate chips or finely chopped dark chocolate
¼ cup vegan butter
1 teaspoon vanilla extract
½ cup unsalted, raw cashew butter

GANACHE ICING

1 cup (about 6 ounces) semi-sweet chocolate chips or finely chopped dark chocolate
1 cup plain nondairy milk

For the cake, preheat your oven to 350°F. and lightly grease 2 (8-inch) round cake pans. Set aside. In a large bowl, whisk together the oil, sugar, yogurt, coffee, and vanilla extract.

Separately, sift the flour and cocoa into a second bowl. Whisk in the baking powder and soda, and salt. Add these dry ingredients into the bowl of wet and use a large spatula to fold the two together. Mix until just combined, being careful not to overmix. The resulting batter should be fairly thick, and it's fine to leave a few lumps remaining.

Divide the batter equally between the two cake pans, smooth out the tops, and bake for about 35 to 40 minutes, or until a toothpick inserted in the centers comes out clean. Remove from the oven to cool completely before proceeding.

Prepare the custard by combining the sugar, potato starch, cocoa, and salt in a large saucepan. Whisk thoroughly to distribute the dry ingredients and break up any clumps before slowly pouring in the nondairy milk, whisking vigorously the whole time. This will help incorporate the liquid more smoothly, so take your time.

Cook over medium-high heat, whisking frequently, until the mixture begins to thicken and is close to a boil. Adjust the heat as needed to get a full boil, but don't let it be so high that the bottom scorches. When you reach

(Continued on next page)

a full boil, immediately remove the saucepan from the stove. Add in the chocolate, vegan butter, and vanilla, stirring until everything melts from the residual heat. It may take a bit of time, so be patent. When the mixture is completely smooth and everything is incorporated, vigorously beat in the cashew butter until the custard is smooth once again.

Transfer to a large bowl and place a piece of plastic wrap directly on the surface to prevent a skin from forming. Cool to room temperature before refrigerating until completely cold, at least 3 hours.

To bring the cake together, have an 8-inch springform pan at the ready. Slice the two cake rounds in half horizontally, setting 1 layer aside, leaving you with three to work with. Place one down at the bottom of the springform pan and top with half of the custard. Top with a second round of cake, and then the remainder of the custard. Finish off with the last cake layer, pressing down gently but firmly to smooth and even out all the layers, pushing out air bubbles at the same time. Stash the whole pan in the freezer until solidly set; at least 8 hours and ideally overnight.

Prepare the icing by heating the chocolate and nondairy milk together in the microwave at intervals of 30 seconds, stirring thoroughly between each one, until smooth. Chill, stirring every 15 minutes, for about 45 minutes, until cool and thickened, but still pourable.

Unmold the cake, transferring it to a serving platter. Carefully pour the icing over the top, spreading it evenly down the sides. Crumble the remaining round of cake and press the crumbs all over the outside. Immediately return the cake to the freezer until ready to serve.

Chocolate-Covered Cherry Bombe

MAKES 10–12 SERVINGS

Detonate this explosive sweet and spicy dessert at your next party and you'll blow everyone away. Creamy cherry ice cream crackles with sparks of hot cinnamon candies buried like a minefield of flavor within, but the real surprise is a liquid core of gooey chocolate fudge. Set all of that atop of base of nutty brownie crumbles, enrobed in a crisp shell of chocolate, and you might start to get an idea of how to have a real blast.

WALNUT BROWNIE BASE

¼ cup vegan butter
½ cup granulated sugar
⅓ cup natural cocoa powder
¼ teaspoon vanilla extract
⅛ teaspoon salt
¼ cup aquafaba
¼ cup all-purpose flour
⅓ cup walnuts, toasted and chopped

HOT CHERRY ICE CREAM

1 pound (about 3 cups) pitted sweet cherries, fresh or frozen and thawed
¾ cup plain nondairy milk
1 (14-ounce) can full-fat coconut milk
⅔ cup granulated sugar
2 tablespoons tapioca starch
1 teaspoon lemon juice
⅛ teaspoon salt
⅛ teaspoon almond extract
½ cup red hot cinnamon imperial candies

TO ASSEMBLE

1 Cup Hot Fudge Sauce (page 295)
1 batch Dark Chocolate Shell (page 285)
Colored sugar or sprinkles (optional)

For the brownie base, preheat your oven to 325°F. and lightly grease an 8-inch round cake pan. Melt the vegan butter in a small heatproof bowl in the microwave or set over a pot of barely simmering water. In a separate bowl, mix the sugar, cocoa powder, vanilla, and salt, whisking thoroughly to break up any lumps. Pour the melted butter on top, followed by the aquafaba, and stir until smooth.

Toss the flour and walnuts together to coat before adding both in last. Mix well, until completely incorporated. Transfer the batter to your prepared baking pan and use a wide spatula to spread it evenly across the bottom. It may seem thin, but I promise, there's enough to cover! Bake for 15 to 18 minutes, until firm to the touch and a tester inserted into the center comes out with moist crumbs, not runny batter, clinging to it. Let cool completely.

For the ice cream, place the cherries, nondairy milk, coconut milk, sugar, tapioca starch, lemon juice, and salt in your blender or food processor. Puree on full power, until completely pureed and silky smooth. Transfer to a medium saucepan on the stove. Turn on the heat to medium and cook, whisking occasionally, until it reaches a rolling boil and is thickened significantly. Turn off the heat and add the almond extract, whisking vigorously to incorporate. Let cool completely before stashing in your fridge to chill for at least 3 hours before churning.

Prepare your bombe form by lining a 2-quart bowl with plastic wrap or aluminum foil. Have a smaller bowl at the

(Continued)

ready that roughly matches the same shape, about 1 cup in capacity. Warm the chocolate sauce just enough to make it pourable, but not hot.

Churn the ice cream in your ice cream maker according to the manufacturer's instructions. In the final 5 minutes of churning, while the ice cream is still soft, slowly add the cinnamon candies into the mix, allowing the paddle to distribute the pieces throughout. Spoon the ice cream into the large lined bowl, smearing it up the sides and packing it firmly. Use the smaller bowl to press an indentation into the center, leaving a hollow core. Quickly pour the liquid chocolate sauce inside. Waste no time in placing the entire bowl into the freezer on a flat surface. Let rest and set for at least 8 hours, and ideally overnight.

Crumble the brownie base into chunks and press them firmly onto the exposed surface, evenly covering the all the ice cream and fudge. Return the bomb to the freezer while you prepare for the final chocolate coating.

Set a wire rack over a jelly roll pan to catch any excess drips. Prepare the magic shell and have it ready before getting the bombe from the freezer. Unmold ice cream and place it on the rack, removing plastic or foil. Evenly pour chocolate shell all over, starting from the top and moving slowly down the sides to ensure complete coverage. Use a flat spatula to touch up any holes and if using, immediately top with decorative sprinkles without delay; the coating will begin to set almost instantly.

Transfer the cake to an appropriate serving platter and stash it back in the freezer until ready to serve. Bombes away!

Completely Coconuts Ice Cream Cake

MAKES 12–14 SERVINGS

To the bounty hunter who can never catch enough coconuts, this little number may just be your biggest score yet. They said it was impossible, that it was outrageous, maybe even absurd, but here we have the one, the only, the epic ice cream cake made almost solely of pure coconut goodness. A vision in white, all elegance and grace, you won't have to look hard to uncover tropical flavor so decadent, it should be downright criminal.

COCONUT CAKE LAYERS AND CREAM FILLING

6 ounces (about 10) graham crackers
3 cups unsweetened shredded coconut, divided
½ cup coconut oil, melted
4 (14-ounce) cans full-fat coconut milk, chilled
1½ cups granulated sugar
2 teaspoons vanilla extract

TO ASSEMBLE

1 batch Coconut Whipped Cream (page 17)
1 cup toasted coconut flakes or chips

For the coconut layers, lightly grease 2 (9-inch) round springform cake pans and set aside. Place the graham crackers and 2 cups of the coconut flakes in a food processor and pulse to fine crumbs. Drizzle in the melted coconut oil and whiz until well combined. Divide the crumb mixture between the two pans, pressing down firmly into even layers.

Carefully open the chilled cans of coconut milk, being sure not to shake them, and scoop off the top layer of thick coconut cream. Discard or save the watery liquid left behind for another recipe. Place the coconut cream in the bowl of your stand mixer and install the whisk attachment. Whip on high speed for about 3 minutes before slowly beginning to sprinkle in the sugar, just a little bit at a time. Continue beating the mixture for up to 10 minutes, until light and fluffy.

Gently fold in the remaining cup of shredded coconut along with the vanilla extract, stirring as little as possible to incorporate without beating the air out of the mixture. Divide equally between the two cake pans, tapping them gently on the counter to release large bubbles, and smoothing out the tops with your spatula. Place on a flat surface in your freezer and let rest for at least 6 hours, ideally overnight, until firmly set.

To assemble, remove cakes from pans and place the first round, cookie crust side down, on a cake stand or serving platter. Top with a thin layer of whipped coconut cream to act as edible spackling, and gently place the second frozen layer on top. Finish with a generous plume of whipped coconut cream a festive sprinkle of toasted coconut flakes. Store in the freezer or serve immediately.

Confetti Cake Batter Birthday Cake

MAKES 20–26 SERVINGS

Redundant enough for you? Hardly! Accurately over the top, the title calls out the distinct cake batter flavor infused into every layer of this celebratory spectacle, complete with rainbow sprinkles and whipped cream frosting, of course. It's just the right amount of "extra."

CAKE BATTER ICE CREAM

⅔ cup all-purpose flour, divided
3 cups nondairy milk
1 cup granulated sugar
2 teaspoons vanilla extract
⅛ teaspoon almond extract
⅛ teaspoon salt
2 tablespoons vegan butter
¼ cup Confetti Quin Sprinkles (page 280, or store-bought)

FROSTING SWIRL AND TOPPING

1 cup vegan butter
4 cups confectioners' sugar
1 teaspoon vanilla extract
2 teaspoons blue matcha or spirulina, for color (optional)
2–3 tablespoons nondairy milk

FUNFETTI CAKE

½ cup vegan butter
2½ cups granulated sugar
½ cup olive oil
½ cup unsweetened apple sauce
1 tablespoon vanilla extract
4 cups all-purpose flour
4 teaspoons baking powder
1 teaspoon baking soda
1 teaspoon salt
2 cups plain nondairy milk
2 teaspoon apple cider vinegar
½ cup Confetti Quin Sprinkles (page 280, or store-bought)

Beginning with the ice cream, you'll want to lightly toast the flour to get some of that raw wheat flavor out. This can be achieved by spreading ⅓ of a cup in an even layer over a microwave-safe plate. Heat for just 60 seconds, until it smells very lightly nutty. Place the toasted and raw flour in a medium saucepan along with the nondairy milk and sugar, whisking very vigorously to combine. Be sure to beat out any and all lumps before turning on the stove.

Cook over medium heat, whisking frequently and taking care to scrape along the bottom and sides to prevent burning, until the mixture comes to full boil. Continue to cook, whisking constantly, for about 1 minute longer. It should have significantly thickened to the consistency of loose pancake batter.

Turn off the heat and whisk in the vanilla extract, almond extract, salt, and vegan butter. Stir until the butter has melted and everything is smoothly combined. Place a piece of plastic wrap directly over the surface and place in the fridge to chill. Allow at least 3 hours before churning.

Prepare the frosting by beating together the vegan butter and confectioners' sugar in your stand mixer using the whisk attachment. Add the vanilla and coloring agent of choice (if using), and slowly drizzle in nondairy milk, until the frosting is smooth, light, and fluffy. Measure out 1 cup of the frosting for the swirl, reserve the rest for decoration.

For the cakes, preheat your oven to 350°F. and lightly grease and flour 3 (8-inch) round cake pans. Be sure to tap out any excess flour so that only a thin coating remains. Set aside. Place the vegan butter and sugar in

(Continued on next page)

the bowl of your stand mixer with the paddle attachment installed and beat until homogenous. Pause to scrape down the sides of the bowl with your spatula as needed, to keep everything incorporated. Add the oil while mixing on slow speed and beat to combine. Follow that with the applesauce and vanilla, blending thoroughly. Don't worry if it looks a bit chunky and curdled at this point; it only gets better from here!

In separate bowl, sift together the flour, baking powder, baking soda, and salt. In yet another bowl, mix the nondairy milk and vinegar. With the mixer on medium-low speed, gradually add the dry ingredients alternately with the milk, incorporating about ⅓ of each at a time. Stir until each addition is mostly incorporated before adding the next. Finally, add the sprinkles and fold them in by hand, using a large spatula. Stir just enough to evenly distribute them throughout the batter without overmixing.

Divide the batter between your prepared cake pans, smoothing out the tops. Bake for 35 to 40 minutes, or until a toothpick inserted in the centers comes out cleanly, or with few moist crumbs—not wet batter.

Remove cakes from oven and let to cool for 15 minutes in the pans. Run a thin butter knife between each cake and the inside of the pan to loosen, and invert each onto a cooling rack. Allow to cool completely, then chill in the fridge.

When you're ready to get this party started, churn the ice cream in your machine according to the manufacturer's instructions. In the final 5 minutes of churning, add in the sprinkles, allowing the paddle to incorporate the pieces throughout the mixture.

Ease one of the cake layers into the bottom of an 8-inch round springform pan. When the ice cream is ready but still soft out of the machine, spoon about half of it on top. Use a wide spatula to spread it out to the edges of the pan. Take ½ cup of the frosting reserved for the swirl and place dollops of it all over. Marble it throughout the layer of ice cream with a thin spatula or knife. Tap the whole pan gently on the counter to smooth it down and knock out any air bubbles at the same time.

Top this layer with another round of cake, pressing down firmly. Repeat the process with remaining ice cream and frosting. The final layer of cake will likely protrude well above the lip of the pan, as this is a very tall cake. We don't mess around when it comes to birthdays, okay?

Immediately place the whole assembly on a flat surface in your freezer. Let rest until solidified, at least 8 hours and ideally overnight.

For the finishing touches, release the sides of the springform pan and transfer the cake to a serving plate. Trim the sides with a very sharp serrated knife, evening out all the layers and revealing the beautiful edible confetti baked within. Spoon the remaining frosting in a piping bag and decorate as desired. Finish with a last handful of sprinkles on top, if you'd like, because there's no sense holding back now.

Slice and serve, but don't forget to blow out the candles first!

Ferocious Rocher Bombe

MAKES 12–16 SERVINGS

"Life is like a box of chocolates. You never know what you're gonna get." Forrest Gump gets a lot of credit for this nugget of wisdom, but I would beg to disagree. Like any serious chocolate lover, I routinely seek out the very best bites, deftly picking over the bubblegum pink marshmallow fillings and stale, stringy coconut cores, quickly figuring out precisely which morsels will dazzle my palate.

No need to play any guessing games with this supersized frozen confection. Roasted hazelnut ice cream lies at the heart of this ode to a certain European candy, supported by a creamy chocolate base and enveloped in a crisp dark chocolate coating, crisp wafers and nuts embedded for a resounding crunch. If you've never had a chocolate like this in your box before, are you really living your best life?

HAZELNUT PRALINE ICE CREAM

1½ cups raw hazelnuts
1 cup granulated sugar
¼ cup water
2 cups plain nondairy milk
2 tablespoons olive oil
1 teaspoon vanilla extract
¼ teaspoon salt

EASY CHOCOLATE ICE CREAM

1 (14-ounce) can full-fat coconut milk
½ cup Dutch-processed cocoa powder
⅓ cup maple syrup
1 teaspoon vanilla extract
¼ teaspoon salt

TO ASSEMBLE

1 batch Dark Chocolate Shell (page 285)
1 cup roughly crushed Waffle Cones (page 313, or store-bought)
¼ cup toasted, skinned hazelnuts

Snag a pint of your favorite chocolate ice cream to use for the base if you'd rather not deal with churning two ice cream bases at once. I promise, your secret is safe with me.

For the hazelnut ice cream, begin by preheating your oven to 300°F. Spread the hazelnuts out in an even layer on a baking sheet and toast for 10 minutes, until fragrant. Let cool for at least 15 minutes, or until you can comfortably handle them. Transfer to a clean dish towel and rub vigorously to remove the papery skins. Don't try to get every last bit of it off because you'll drive yourself crazy. Just get them as clean as possible for the smoothest texture.

Place the sugar and water in a medium saucepan over moderate heat. Stir to combine and bring to a boil. Afterwards, swirl the pan to mix the contents at this point in the process, rather than stirring, to prevent the sugar from crystalizing. Allow the sugar to cook until it caramelizes to a deep amber color; about 10 to 15 minutes. Quickly add in the hazelnuts, stir to coat with the hot sugar, and immediately transfer everything out to a silicone baking mat or piece of parchment paper. Let cool completely before breaking it into chunks.

Roughly chop about ⅓ of the caramelized hazelnuts and set aside. Toss the remainder into your blender, along with the nondairy milk, olive oil, vanilla, and salt. Pulse to break down the brittle to a coarse consistency, and then let the motor run until very smooth. It may take as long as 10 minutes, so be patient. Transfer the base to

(Continued)

a container to cool, and chill in the fridge for at least 3 hours before proceeding.

Churn in your ice cream maker according to the manufacturer's instructions. Meanwhile, line a 2-quart bowl with plastic wrap or aluminum foil. Add the remaining chopped hazelnut praline in the last 5 minutes of churning. Scoop the soft ice cream into the bowl, tapping it on the counter lightly to remove any air bubbles and smoothing out the top. Stash it in your freezer for at least 6 hours, until firmly set.

For the chocolate ice cream, simply whisk all the ingredients together until smooth. Chill if not already cold, and churn in your ice cream maker according the manufacturer's instructions. Yes, it's really that easy!

Spoon the soft ice cream into the large bowl, right on top of the solidified hazelnut praline ice cream, and smooth it out into an even layer. Tap the bowl lightly on the counter to knock out any air bubbles and return it to the freezer to set, at least 6 more hours.

For the final flourish, liquefy the chocolate shell and stir in the crushed cones and hazelnuts. Set a wire rack over a jelly roll pan to catch any excess drips. Remove the ice cream dome from the bowl and place it on the rack, removing plastic or foil. Evenly pour chocolate shell all over, starting from the top and moving slowly down the sides to ensure complete coverage. Use a flat spatula to touch up any holes but don't delay; the coating will begin to set almost instantly. Transfer the cake to an appropriate serving platter and stash it back in the freezer until ready to serve.

Simplify this stunning supersized frozen truffle by simply blending ½ cup hazelnut butter and ½ cup sugar into the hazelnut praline ice cream, skipping the whole toasting, skinning, and caramelization process. Mix in an additional ½ cup chopped hazelnuts right at the end.

Frosty Pumpkin Roulade

MAKES 10–12 SERVINGS

The cult of pumpkin spice is unstoppable, growing in tenor and ferocity with every passing season. Pumpkin spice lattes, pumpkin spice candles, pumpkin spice lip gloss—they're all real! If it can be infused with the flavor (or scent) that dominates all of fall, it absolutely will be. Pumpkin pie is at the very top of the Thanksgiving dessert hierarchy of course, as the purest, original manifestation of the flavor sensation.

Typically filled with airy mounds of vanilla-spiked whipped cream, this roulade gains even greater appeal with buttery pecan ice cream instead. Wrapping up two desserts into one, pumpkin spice fanatics will have a fresh focus for their seasonal obsession, and fair-weather fans will be mightily pleased, too.

Roll cakes can be intimidating at room temperature, let alone when handling a frozen filling, but never fear; it's a lot more difficult on paper than in real life. Accept the beauty of imperfection, prepare yourself for a reasonable mess, and discover the ease of adding one secret ingredient into the mix: Xanthan gum. Typically included in gluten-free baking, it adds an extra dose of flexibility for this conventional flour blend, making it less liable to crack or break while rolling.

PUMPKIN ROLL CAKE

¼ cup aquafaba
1 cup pumpkin puree
1 cup dark brown sugar, firmly packed
¾ cup plain nondairy milk
1 teaspoon ground cinnamon
½ teaspoon ground ginger
¼ teaspoon ground cloves
¼ cup olive oil
1 teaspoon vanilla extract
1 teaspoon apple cider vinegar
1 cup all-purpose flour, plus additional for dusting
2 tablespoons tapioca starch
1 teaspoon baking powder
½ teaspoon baking soda
½ teaspoon xanthan gum
¼ teaspoon salt

BUTTERY PECAN ICE CREAM

¾ cup toasted pecan halves, chopped and divided
1 tablespoon vegan butter
¼ cup maple syrup
⅓ cup dark brown sugar, firmly packed
½ teaspoon ground cinnamon
¼ teaspoon salt
2 tablespoons cornstarch
1½ cups plain nondairy milk

Beginning with the cake, preheat your oven to 375°F and line a 10 x 15-inch jelly roll pan with parchment paper, making sure the edges are completely covered. It's important to use a baking sheet that's close to these dimensions or the cake will be too thick or thin to roll properly.

Pour the aquafaba into the bowl of your stand mixer with the whisk attachment installed and gradually increase the speed up to its highest setting. Once you have a steady froth going, whip at full power for 5 to 7 minutes, until you achieve a sturdy meringue that stands up at firm peaks.

In a separate bowl, whisk together the pumpkin puree, brown sugar, nondairy milk, and all the spices. Once smooth, slowly pour in the oil, whisking to incorporate, followed by the vanilla and vinegar. Stir until homogenous and emulsified.

Sift together the flour, tapioca starch, baking powder, baking soda, xanthan gum, and salt, blending until the dry ingredients are thoroughly distributed throughout the mixture. Add this blend into the bowl of spiced pumpkin puree, stirring lightly until just combined. Add

(Continued on next page)

about half of the whipped aquafaba, using a wide spatula to gently fold it in. Try to keep it light and airy, mixing just enough to combine without beating out all the air bubbles. Repeat the procedure with the remaining fluff.

Spread the batter out evenly across your prepared jelly roll pan. It may seem like a very thin layer, but fear not! It shouldn't be very tall, as that would make it impossible to roll. Smooth out the top before sliding it into the oven. Bake for 15 to 18 minutes, or until golden brown all over. Let cool for 5 minutes in the pan.

Use the edges of the parchment paper as a sling to gently lift the cake out of the pan. Lightly dust the top with additional flour, and place a clean dish towel on top. Roll the cake lengthwise, from short end to short end, peeling away the parchment paper up and wrapping in the dish towel as you go. The cake will be the most fragile at this stage so try to keep it fairly loose and handle the cake as little as possible. Cool to room temperature before transferring to the fridge to chill. It needs to be at least cool before wrapping around the ice cream so that the filling doesn't instantly melt.

For the ice cream, set aside ¼ cup of the chopped pecans for later, then place the rest in a medium saucepan, along with the vegan butter. Cook over medium heat until aromatic.

Meanwhile, whisk together the remaining ingredients in a separate container. When the whole kitchen begins to smell nutty and toasty, pour in the liquid mixture and cook, stirring often, until the mixture comes up to a rapid boil. Turn down the heat slightly so that it doesn't bubble over, and continue to stir for another 2 minutes. Remove the pan from the heat.

Carefully pour the hot base into your blender and gradually crank the machine up to full power. Puree thoroughly, until the nuts are completely broken down and smooth. If you don't have a high-speed blender, give it at least 8 to 10 minutes. The mixture may still be slightly gritty even when it looks silky-smooth, so pass it through a fine mesh sieve lined with cheesecloth to catch any remaining pecan particles. Cool to room temperature, then chill thoroughly in your fridge.

Give the base at least 3 hours to sit, then churn in your ice cream maker according to the manufacturer's instructions. In the final 5 minutes of churning, add the remaining chopped pecans right into the mix, allowing the paddle to stir the pieces in for you.

As the ice cream nears completion, carefully unroll the cake and have it ready on the counter. Scoop spoonfuls of the freshly churned but still soft ice cream all over the cake, leaving about a ½-inch border along the edge. Smooth it into as even a layer as possible. Quickly but methodically begin rolling the cake back up the same way it was unrolled—from short end to short end. Some of the ice cream may spill out from the ends, but just keep going! I promise, it will all be okay.

Wrap the towel tightly around the filled roulade, twisting the ends and placing them underneath the cake. Place on a large plate or baking sheet and stash the whole thing on a flat surface in your freezer. Let set for at least 6 to 8 hours.

When ready to serve, remove the towel and transfer to a serving platter, placing the seam-side down. Slice off the messy ends, and present with great fanfare. The true pumpkin king has arrived!

Stress less and focus on the cake, if you already have a lot of holiday prep on your plate. Skip the homemade ice cream in this case and pick up 1 or 2 pints of your favorite vegan pecan, vanilla bean, caramel, or coffee ice cream for the filling. Just be sure to soften it slightly before rolling, so that it's easier to spread. Either temper it on the counter for 10 to 15 minutes or microwave for 30 to 45 seconds, stirring thoroughly afterward. The cake itself is so impressive that no one will be able to pause for a breath between bites to ask. Your secret is safe with me!

Frozen Fraisier

MAKES 12–14 SERVINGS

Fanciful terms like mousseline, dacquoise, and gelee are casually tossed around to describe this prime example of fine French patisserie, but it needn't be daunting for the everyday home baker. It's merely a matter of stacking up airy vanilla cakes with fresh berries and fluffy mousse in the middle, finished by a mirror-like glaze of ruby red strawberry gel. It can be challenging at room temperature since all those fragile pieces want to slide apart at the barest hint of movement, but taken into the freezer, it's truly a piece of cake to bring together.

VANILLA SPONGE CAKE

1 cup plain nondairy milk
1 teaspoon apple cider vinegar
½ cup olive oil
1½ teaspoons vanilla extract
¼ teaspoon almond extract
1½ cups all-purpose flour
¾ cup granulated sugar
1 teaspoon baking powder
½ teaspoon baking soda
¼ teaspoon salt

MOUSSELINE ICE CREAM

3 cups plain nondairy milk
½ cup granulated sugar, divided
3 tablespoons tapioca starch
2 tablespoons kirsch (cherry liqueur) or brandy
1 teaspoon vanilla extract
½ cup aquafaba

TO ASSEMBLE

2 tablespoons kirsch liqueur
⅓ cup whole strawberry preserves or jam
1 pint fresh strawberries

STRAWBERRY GELEE

½ cup strawberry preserves or jam
¼ cup water
½ teaspoon agar powder

Starting with the cakes, preheat your oven to 325°F. and lightly grease 2 (9-inch) round cake pans. In a large bowl, whisk together the nondairy milk and vinegar, and let rest for 5 minutes, until slightly curdled. Add in the oil, vanilla, and almond extract and whisk vigorously to combine.

Separately, sift the flour, sugar, baking powder and soda, and salt, and combine well. Slowly incorporate the dry goods into the wet, stirring just enough to bring the batter together—a few lumps are fine. Distribute the batter equally between your prepared pans, and bake for 25 to 30 minutes, until golden brown on top and a toothpick inserted into the center comes out clean. Let cool in the pans completely.

For the ice cream, whisk together the nondairy milk, sugar, and starch in a medium saucepan over moderate heat. Make sure it's completely smooth, with no lumps of starch remaining. Bring the mixture to a steady boil. When the mixture has just started to boil and has significantly thickened, immediately remove from the heat and stir in the kirsch and vanilla. Place a piece of plastic wrap directly on the surface to prevent a skin from forming. Place in your fridge to chill for at least 3 hours before proceeding.

To complete the mousseline, place the aquafaba in your stand mixer and slowly whip to steady froth before increasing to full speed. Continue beating the mixture for up to 10 minutes, until light and fluffy. Take about half

(Continued on next page)

of the meringue and use a wide spatula to gently fold it into the cooked custard, being careful not to beat out all the bubbles. Repeat the process with the remainder, until the airy mixture is smooth and well-combined.

To begin assembly, take one cake and trim off the dark brown surface with a serrated knife. Place it in a 9-inch round springform pan and brush the kirsch evenly over the cut side. Gently heat the jam, just enough to loosen it up, and spread it evenly across the layer. Slice the strawberries in half, and place them standing up along the perimeter of the cake.

Gently spoon the fluffy mousseline mixture right on top, smoothing it out to the edges, so that it completely fills the ring of strawberries. Turn the second cake out, and carefully place it into the springform pan, on top of the strawberries and filling. Press down gently to even out the layers. Move the whole cake into the freezer, and allow at least 3 to 4 hours for it to solidify.

Finishing with the layer of gelee, blend the strawberry preserves or jam with the water, and strain to remove the seeds. Transfer the puree to a saucepan and sprinkle in the agar, whisking vigorously to combine. Make sure the mixture is entirely smooth and free of lumps before turning on the heat to medium-low. Cook, stirring constantly, until the agar has dissolved, and the mixture comes to a full boil.

Quickly pour the mixture over the entire top of the cake, tilting the pan to even it out and completely fill the space. Either return the cake to the freezer until ready to serve, or run a thin spatula around the edge of the pan to loosen. Release the sides of the springform and transfer to a serving plate. Slice, serve, and enjoy with pinky fingers out, if you feel so fancy.

Grape Galaxy Ice Cream Cake

MAKES 10–12 SERVINGS

Look to the sky on a cloudless night to see untold worlds sparkle from afar, planets circulating gently in orbit, stars shining as they smolder from within, suns and moons rising and setting, all just beyond reach. Dark, beautiful, and irresistible, outer space is said to be the final frontier, but it's entirely attainable in cake format, swirling with nebulas of sprinkles. This pioneering ice cream galaxy uses dark, juicy grapes to sweeten the expedition. The end results, finished with a pinch of imagination and childlike glee, are definitely out of this world.

CHOCOLATE COOKIE CRUST

1½ cups finely ground chocolate sandwich cookie crumbs
¼ cup vegan butter or coconut oil, melted

GRAPE SORBET

2 pounds red seedless grapes
3 tablespoons lemon juice
½ cup granulated sugar

GRAPE CREAM

1 can full-fat coconut milk
1 cup 100% concord grape juice concentrate
½ cup raw cashew pieces, soaked for 6 hours and drained

TO ASSEMBLE

1 tablespoon black cocoa powder
1 teaspoon vodka
Sprinkles (page 280, or store-bought) (optional)

To make the crust, place the ground cookies in a large bowl and drizzle the melted butter or oil on top. Stir thoroughly to moisten all the crumbs. Transfer the mixture to a 9-inch round springform pan or round silicon cake mold, and use lightly moistened fingers to firmly press it evenly on the bottom. Use the bottom of a flat measuring cup or drinking glass, lightly greased, for a smoother surface. Set aside.

For the sorbet, place the grapes and lemon juice in the bowl of your food processor and blend the grapes until pureed, although the consistency might be a bit coarse due to the skin and seeds. Never fear; those add flavor, and will be removed later on. If your food processor is on the smaller side, work in batches until you've processed all the grapes.

Transfer the grapes to a medium saucepan along with the sugar. Simmer over medium-low heat for 15 to 20 minutes, until slightly thickened and deeply fragrant. Let cool for at least 15 minutes before passing through a fine-mesh sieve, straining out the solids. Transfer the perfectly smooth puree to a bowl and chill in the fridge for at least 3 hours before churning according to the manufacturer's instructions.

For the grape cream, combine the coconut milk, grape juice concentrate, and cashews in your blender and puree on high speed, pausing to scrape down the sides with your spatula as needed, until completely smooth.

(Continued)

To assemble, whisk together the black cocoa and vodka in a small bowl and set aside. Spoon the freshly churned grape sorbet on top of the prepared crust, smoothing it down in an even layer. Drizzle the grape cream all over, followed by the cocoa mixture. Use a thin spatula or butter knife to swirl and marble all the components together, tapping the pan gently on the counter to even out the top and remove air bubbles.

Return the cake to the freezer and let chill until firmly set before serving, at least 6 hours but ideally overnight. Top with sprinkles, if desired, just prior to slicing and revealing a galaxy of grape greatness.

Lemon Meringue Baked Alaska

MAKES 10–12 SERVINGS

Fire meets ice with a flashy plume of flames in this show-stopping dessert. Instead of a traditional crust and lemon curd filling, a soft graham cake holds nearly effortless lemon sherbet. You don't need to set anything on fire to drop jaws with this stunning masterpiece; the fluffy crown of toasted eggless meringue will be unforgettable as is.

GRAHAM CAKE

¾ cup graham flour
½ cup all-purpose flour
½ cup granulated sugar
1 tablespoon ground flaxseeds
1 teaspoon baking powder
¼ teaspoon baking soda
¼ teaspoon ground cinnamon
¼ teaspoon salt
½ cup plain nondairy milk
¼ cup vegan butter or coconut oil, melted
¼ cup maple syrup
½ teaspoon vanilla extract

LEMON SHERBET

1 cup lemon marmalade
2 cups vanilla nondairy milk
½ teaspoon ground turmeric

MERINGUE

¼ cup aquafaba
⅔ cup granulated sugar
¼ teaspoon cream of tartar
1 teaspoon vanilla extract

For the cake, preheat your oven to 350°F. and lightly grease an 8-inch round cake pan. Place both flours, sugar, ground flaxseeds, baking powder and soda, cinnamon, and salt in a large bowl, whisking to combine.

Separately, mix together the nondairy milk, melted butter or oil, maple syrup, and vanilla. Stir until smooth before adding the liquid ingredients into the bowl of dry. Use a wide spatula to stir just until combined, leaving any small lumps. It's better not to risk overmixing the batter.

Transfer to your prepared cake pan, smoothing out the top with your spatula, and bake for 18 to 22 minutes, until golden brown and a toothpick inserted into the center comes out clean. Let cool completely and chill in the fridge while preparing the sherbet.

For the sherbet, simply place all the ingredients into your blender and puree on high. Blend until completely smooth, but no longer than necessary, to prevent the mixture from warming up. Pour the base into your ice cream maker and churn according to the manufacturer's instructions.

Meanwhile, line a 1-quart, 9-inch round bowl with plastic wrap or aluminum foil; set aside.

When the sherbet is done churning, spoon the soft sherbet into the bowl, smoothing out the top with your spatula. Tap the pan a few times on the counter to knock out any air bubbles. Quickly move the bowl to a flat surface in your freezer and let rest until solidly set, at least 3 hours.

For the meringue, when you're ready to assemble, pour the aquafaba into the bowl of your stand mixer with the whisk attachment installed and gradually increase the speed up to its highest setting. Once you have a steady froth going, slowly sprinkle in the sugar and cream of tartar together. Whip at full power for 5 to 7 minutes, until you achieve a sturdy meringue that stands up at firm peaks.

Pull out the cake and release it from the pan, placing it on a serving plate. Remove the sherbet dome, placing it on top, and remove the plastic or foil.

Apply the meringue all over and around the scoop of sherbet, making sure that it completely covers the filling and connects with the graham base. Either run the baking sheet under the broiler for just 1 or 2 minutes, or toast the individual servings with a kitchen torch, until the meringue is golden brown all over. Serve immediately.

Can't find or don't like lemon marmalade? Swap in orange marmalade to make a delightful **Orange Meringue Ice Cream Cake** instead. Don't be afraid to venture forth with other citrus flavors, too! If you're into jamming at home and make your own marmalade, or find an adventurous artisan, grapefruit and lime are equally zesty, refreshingly different options.

Peaches and Cream Icebox Cake

MAKES 8–10 SERVINGS

So soft, so delicate, the finest of peaches must simply be eaten ice cold, leaning over the sink to catch any errant drips, as it bursts with more sweet juice than one fruit should possibly contain. These peaches epitomize summertime revelry; unhurried, unfussy, pure and simple satisfaction. When you have more peaches than can be simply eaten straight, however, I have an equally rewarding suggestion. Inspired by the retro icebox cakes of yore that were refrigerated no-bake creations, layers of cookies, cream, and lush ripe stone fruit come together in a flash for almost effortless gratification. Sure, it takes time to chill out to the perfect frosty consistency, but some things, just like a lazy summer's day, can't be rushed.

4 large peaches (about 1½ pounds), divided
¼ cup dark brown sugar, firmly packed, or coconut sugar
¼ teaspoon ground cinnamon
¼ teaspoon ground ginger
3 (14-ounce) cans full-fat coconut milk, chilled
¼ cup granulated sugar
1 teaspoon vanilla extract
8–10 whole rectangular graham crackers
½ cup sliced almonds

Line a 9 x 5-inch loaf pan with plastic wrap or aluminum foil, leaving at least a 2-inch overhang on all sides.

Pit and thinly slice 3 of the peaches. Place the sliced peaches in a bowl with the sugar, cinnamon, and ginger, tossing gently to combine. Let sit for 15 to 20 minutes for the flavors to mingle and the fruit to slightly soften.

Meanwhile, carefully open the chilled cans of coconut milk, being sure not to shake them, and scoop off the top layer of thick coconut cream. Save the watery liquid left behind for another recipe (it's great in curries or soups!). Place the coconut cream in the bowl of your stand mixer and install the whisk attachment. Whip on high speed for about 3 minutes before slowly beginning to sprinkle in the sugar, just a little bit at a time. Continue beating the mixture for up to 10 minutes, until light and fluffy. Finally, fold in the vanilla extract; keep refrigerated until ready to use.

After 15 to 20 minutes, when the fruit is properly macerated, spread ¼ of the whipped coconut cream evenly across the bottom of your prepared loaf pan. Top that layer with sheets of graham crackers, broken into smaller pieces if needed to cover without overlapping. Drain away any excess liquid that might have come out of the peaches before distributing about ⅓ of the mixture on top. Repeat until all the components have been used up, finishing with a layer of whipped coconut cream.

Cover and stash in the freezer for at least 3 hours, but ideally closer to 12 hours, allowing the graham crackers to soften and the coconut cream to set. When ready to serve, invert the loaf pan onto a platter. Slice and pit the final peach. Remove plastic wrap or aluminum foil, and decorate the top with peach slices and sliced almonds.

Peppermint Bark Roulade

MAKES 10–12 SERVINGS

I have two words for you: Peppermint Bark. All it takes is chocolate and crushed candy canes, yet it can elicit the same level of enthusiasm as a laborious multi-tier Christmas cake.

Something about the combination of creamy chocolate slabs festooned with crunchy red and white striped mint confections seems to strike a chord with everyone, young, old, jolly, and curmudgeonly alike. It's all about the ratio and quality of ingredients that hits the sweet spot.

Plain peppermint stick ice cream is a wonderous limited edition treat, but without a chocolate crunch, something seems to be missing. Enter, the glorious peppermint bark roulade, complete with creamy candy cane ice cream, topped with crisp chunks of chopped chocolate, all wrapped up in a fudgy, tender chocolate cake. As if that wasn't enough, the whole thing is smothered in another layer of snappy dark chocolate shell, and finished with a flurry of crushed peppermint candy. It's a bite of holiday joy that's far better than anything you could wrap up with a bow.

CHOCOLATE ROLL CAKE

¼ cup aquafaba
¼ cup granulated sugar
1 cup unsweetened applesauce
¾ cup chocolate nondairy milk
¼ cup olive oil
¼ cup dark brown sugar, firmly packed
¼ cup confectioners' sugar
1 teaspoon vanilla extract
1 teaspoon apple cider vinegar
1 cup all-purpose flour
¼ cup Dutch-processed cocoa powder, plus additional for dusting
1 teaspoon baking powder
½ teaspoon baking soda
½ teaspoon xanthan gum
¼ teaspoon salt

PEPPERMINT STICK ICE CREAM

3 cups plain nondairy milk
¼ cup granulated sugar
1½ tablespoons arrowroot powder
1 cup crushed candy canes or starlight peppermint candies, divided
1 teaspoon vanilla extract

TO ASSEMBLE

½ cup (3 ounces) dark chocolate, finely chopped
½ cup Dark Chocolate Shell (page 285)
¼ cup crushed candy canes or starlight peppermint candies

Beginning with the cake, preheat your oven to 375°F and line a 10 x 15-inch jelly roll pan with parchment paper, making sure the edges are completely covered. It's important to use a sheet close to these dimensions or the cake will be too thick or thin to roll properly.

Pour the aquafaba into the bowl of your stand mixer with the whisk attachment installed and gradually increase the speed up to its highest setting. Once you have a steady froth going, slowly sprinkle in the sugar, and then whip at full power for 5 to 7 minutes, until you achieve a sturdy meringue that stands up in firm peaks.

(Continued on next page)

In a separate bowl, whisk together the applesauce, nondairy milk, oil, brown sugar, confectioners' sugar, vanilla, and vinegar. Sift together the dry ingredients until thoroughly distributed. Add this blend into the applesauce mixture, stirring lightly until just combined. Add about half of the whipped aquafaba, using a wide spatula to gently fold it in. Try to keep it light and airy, mixing just enough to combine without beating out all the air bubbles. Repeat the procedure with the remaining fluff.

Spread the batter out evenly across your prepared jelly roll pan. It may seem like a very thin layer, but fear not! It shouldn't be very tall, as that would make it impossible to roll. Smooth out the top and bake for 15 to 18 minutes, or until firm but springy to the touch. Let cool for 5 minutes in the pan.

Use the edges of the parchment paper to gently lift the cake out of the pan. Lightly dust the top with additional cocoa powder, and place a clean dish towel on top. Roll the cake lengthwise, from short end to short end, peeling away the parchment paper and wrapping in the dish towel as you go. The cake will be the most fragile at this stage so try to keep it fairly loose and handle the cake as little as possible. Cool to room temperature before transferring to the fridge to chill.

To prepare the ice cream, vigorously whisk together the nondairy milk, sugar, and arrowroot in a medium saucepan, beating thoroughly to break up any clumps. Set over moderate heat, and add in ¾ cup of the crushed peppermint candies—these will melt into the liquid, turning it deeper and deeper pink color. Don't worry; it will lighten quite a bit during the freezing process, since the air that gets folded in as it churns brightens the mixture. Bring to a boil, whisking occasionally, at which point the liquid should be considerably thickened with no solid pieces of the candy remaining. Turn off the heat and whisk in the vanilla. Cool to room temperature before chilling for at least 3 hours before proceeding.

Churn in your ice cream maker according to the manufacturer's instructions. In the final 5 minutes of churning, add the remaining crushed peppermint candies right into the mix, allowing the paddle to stir the pieces in for you.

As the ice cream nears completion, carefully unroll the cake and have it ready on the counter. Scoop spoonfuls of the freshly churned but still soft ice cream all over the cake, leaving about a ½-inch border along the edge. Smooth it into as even a layer as possible. Sprinkle evenly with the chopped chocolate. Quickly but methodically begin rolling the cake back up the same way it was unrolled. Some of the ice cream may spill out from the ends, but just keep going!

Wrap the towel tightly around the filled roulade, twisting the ends and placing them underneath the cake. Place on a large plate or baking sheet and stash the whole thing on a flat surface in your freezer. Let set for at least 6 to 8 hours.

For the final decorations, remove the towel and transfer to a serving platter, placing the seam-side down. Slice off the messy ends and pour the liquid chocolate shell in a straight line down the center, allowing it to drip down the sides. Quickly sprinkle the final handful of crushed peppermint candies on top, as the chocolate will set almost instantly. Stash back in the freezer until ready to slice and serve.

Pitaya Princess Ice Cream Cake

MAKES 6–8 SERVINGS

Prinsesstårta, otherwise known as princess cake, hails from Sweden, festooned with pastel marzipan enveloping layers of airy sponge cake, jam, pastry cream, and a thick domed layer of whipped cream. Originally dubbed the "green cake" (grön tårta) for the original green exterior it was designed with, it was renamed in honor of Prince Carl's three daughters, who were reportedly wild about the fanciful confection. Years later, all manner of soft-hued colors adorn this almond bombe, though pretty princess pink is the clear favorite among diminutive queens to be.

My frosty interpretation takes a more tropical departure, sourcing natural luminosity from exotic pitaya (dragonfruit) powder. So bright and bold that it practically vibrates on the plate, this specialty ingredient is easily found in the superfoods or raw foods section of health food shops, and of course, online. Pineapple, coconut, and mango jam meld beautifully with the rich almond foundation, ensuring a peaceable kingdom for all those who partake.

PITAYA PARADISE ICE CREAM

1 (14-ounce) can full-fat coconut milk
1 (8-ounce) can crushed pineapple in juice, undrained
½ cup granulated sugar
2 tablespoons pitaya powder (freeze-dried dragonfruit)
1 teaspoon vanilla extract

ALMOND CAKE

⅔ cup almond meal
⅔ cup white whole wheat flour
⅓ cup granulated sugar
½ teaspoon baking powder
¼ teaspoon baking soda
⅛ teaspoon salt
2 tablespoons olive oil
⅔ cup plain nondairy milk
¼ teaspoon apple cider vinegar
1 teaspoon almond extract

FILLINGS

8 ounces vegan Cream Cheese (p. 282)
½ cup confectioners' sugar
½ cup mango or apricot jam

PRETTY PINK MARZIPAN

2 cups blanched, finely ground almond flour
1 cup confectioners' sugar, plus additional for dusting
2 teaspoons pitaya powder (freeze-dried dragonfruit)
2 tablespoons aquafaba
1 teaspoon almond extract

TO ASSEMBLE

Dragees or sprinkles (optional)

For the ice cream, place all ingredients into your blender and puree on high speed. Blend for 3 to 5 minutes, until the mixture is completely smooth. Chill if not already cold before churning in your ice cream machine according to the manufacturer's instructions.

Meanwhile, line a 1-quart, 6-inch wide bowl with plastic wrap or aluminum foil; set aside. When the ice cream is done churning but still soft, spoon it into your prepared bowl, tapping it gently on the counter to release any air bubbles. Smooth out the top and place on a level surface in your freezer. Let rest for at least 3 to 4 hours, until firmly set.

(Continued)

Moving on to the cake, preheat your oven to 350°F. and generously grease a 6-inch round cake pan. Combine the almond meal, flour, sugar, baking powder, baking soda, and salt. Stir to combine and set aside.

Separately, whisk together the oil, nondairy milk, and vinegar vigorously until the mixture is slightly frothy and bubbly on the surface. Incorporate the almond extract. Slowly add in the dry mixture, whisking just until everything is combined. Pour the batter into your prepared pan and bake for 15 to 20 minutes, until a toothpick inserted into the center comes out clean. Let cool for at least 15 minutes before turning out on a wire rack to cool. Make sure it's completely cool before proceeding.

Slice the cooled cake horizontally into thirds, creating 3 even rounds. Place the first one on a serving plate.

For the filling, beat together the cream cheese and confectioners' sugar for the filling until smooth, and spread it evenly on top. Cover with the center slice of cake, and smooth the jam over that. Finish with the final layer of cake and chill until the ice cream is ready to go. Once solid, remove the dome of ice cream from the bowl, placing it on top of the cake layers, and remove the plastic or foil. Return the whole thing to the freezer while preparing the marzipan.

For the marzipan, place the almond flour, confectioners' sugar, and pitaya powder into your food processor. Pulse briefly to combine. Slowly drizzle in the aquafaba, followed by the almond extract, while continuing to pulse. Once fully incorporated, you should end up with a cohesive ball, not unlike thick cookie dough, which can be modeled and shaped like clay.

Lightly knead the dough on a nonstick silicone mat lightly dusted with additional confectioners' sugar until completely smooth. Use a rolling pin to flatten it out into as thin a sheet as possible, about ⅛-inch thick.

Pull out the stacked cake and ice cream tower and carefully drape the sheet of marzipan on top, keeping it as centered as possible. Use the silicone mat to help maneuver it more easily into place. Smooth it down the sides, patching any holes with your fingers as needed. Trim any excess away from the bottom. Decorate with dragees or sprinkles, if desired.

Return the cake to the freezer until ready to serve.

Rainbow Sherbet Cake

Sherbet, the love child of ice cream and sorbet, has always been a bit flamboyant. Tie-dyed with wild neon colors, it's not afraid to sing with fruity citrus notes at full volume. Oranges, raspberries, limes, and lemons are the most common refrains, but the best pints are those that swirl the full rainbow together for one kaleidoscopic scoop. Making sure you get a bit of each one is always the challenge, though, since it's impossible to see what might lurk beyond the top layer.

Displaying the entire citrusy, juicy range of flavors in a more natural pastel hue, sherbet has never looked cooler. This simple cake conversion employs a no-churn base, set atop a no-bake crust, so it may be even easier than the traditional approach, too.

GRAHAM CRACKER CRUST

1½ cups finely ground graham cracker crumbs (from about 12 full rectangle sheets)
6 tablespoons vegan butter or coconut oil, melted

RAINBOW SHERBET

½ cup aquafaba
¼ cup granulated sugar
⅛ teaspoon cream of tartar
2 cans coconut milk, chilled for 24 hours
¾ cup confectioners' sugar
1 tablespoon orange zest
2 teaspoons lemon zest
¼ teaspoon ground turmeric
1 tablespoon lime zest
½ teaspoon matcha
⅓ cup seedless raspberry jam

TO ASSEMBLE

Coconut Whipped Cream (page 17)
Sprinkles (page 280, or store-bought)

To make the crust, place the crumbs in a large bowl and drizzle in the melted butter, stirring thoroughly to moisten the ground cookies. Transfer the mixture to a 9-inch round springform pan or round silicon cake mold, and use lightly moistened fingers to firmly press it evenly on the bottom. Use the bottom of a flat measuring cup or drinking glass, lightly greased, for a smoother surface. Set aside.

For the sherbet, pour the aquafaba into the bowl of your stand mixer with the whisk attachment installed and gradually increase the speed up to its highest setting. Once you have a steady froth going, slowly sprinkle in the granulated sugar and cream of tartar together. Whip at full power for 5 to 7 minutes, until you achieve a sturdy meringue that stands up at firm peaks. Transfer to a large bowl and reassemble the mixer.

Carefully open the chilled cans of coconut milk, being sure not to shake them, and scoop off the top layer of thick coconut cream into your stand mixer with whisk attachment. Discard or save the watery liquid left behind for another recipe. Whip on high speed for about 3 minutes before slowly beginning to sprinkle in the confectioners' sugar, just a little bit at a time. Continue beating the mixture for up to 10 minutes, until light and fluffy.

Take about half of the meringue and use a wide spatula to gently fold it into the whipped coconut cream, being careful not to beat out all the bubbles. Repeat the process with the remainder, until the airy mixture is smooth and well-combined.

Divide the fluff into three bowls. Into the first, fold the orange zest, lemon zest, and turmeric. For the second, add the lime zest and matcha. The last gets the raspberry jam. Stir lightly, until the colors and flavors are fully incorporated.

Spoon dollops of each mixture on top of the crust at random, until all components are used. Swirl them all together using a thin spatula or butter knife, marbling but not completely mixing them. Tap the whole cake lightly on the counter to flatten down the top.

Place on a flat surface in the freezer to chill for at least 6 hours, until fully set.

Before serving, pipe or spoon coconut whipped cream around the top border and finish with a light shower of sprinkles.

I will forever have a soft spot for the classic **Orange Creamsicle**, and this cake lends itself perfectly to just such a variation. Before adding flavors, divide the base between only two bowls. Add 3 tablespoons of orange zest + ½ teaspoon turmeric to one, and ½ teaspoon vanilla extract to the other. Assemble with dollops and swirls as instructed.

Raspberry Red Velvet Ice Cream Cake

MAKES 10–12 SERVINGS

Considering the skyrocketing popularity of red velvet cake, I eagerly await any opportunity to re-imagine the classic confection, infusing it with a fresh palate of new flavors. That occasion lined up perfectly with the changing seasons, dropping the inspiration to add tart, juicy raspberries right into my mixing bowl. A summery treat with its own bold style, it beams brightly in a fire engine-red hue, thanks to entirely natural, flavorful sources. Far more than the mere whisper of cocoa and hint of vanilla, bolstered by artificial dye found in most renditions, it's an ideal blend of substance and style.

RASPBERRY RED VELVET CAKE

1¼ cups all-purpose flour
¾ cup granulated sugar
1 tablespoon natural cocoa powder
1 teaspoon baking powder
¼ teaspoon salt
4 ounces (about ⅔ cup) steamed, sliced red beets
8 ounces (about 2 cups) fresh or frozen and thawed raspberries
½ cup olive oil
1 tablespoon lemon juice
1 teaspoon vanilla extract
½ teaspoon apple cider vinegar

CREAM CHEESE ICE CREAM

1½ cups nondairy milk
1 cup confectioners' sugar
1 cup (8 ounces) vegan Cream Cheese (p. 282)
1 tablespoon lemon juice
½ teaspoon vanilla extract
⅛ teaspoon salt

TO ASSEMBLE

Coconut Whipped Cream (page 17)
Fresh raspberries
Fresh mint leaves
Sprinkles (page 280, or store-bought) (optional)

For the cake, preheat your oven to 350°F. and lightly grease a 2 (9-inch) round cake pans. In a large bowl, whisk together the flour, sugar, cocoa, baking powder, and salt. Set aside.

Place the beets, raspberries, oil, lemon juice, vanilla, and vinegar into your blender or food processor. Process for a solid 2 to 4 minutes, depending on how powerful your machine is, until completely smooth. Pass the mixture through a fine mesh strainer if any seeds or grit remains.

Pour the beet and berry mixture into the bowl of dry ingredients and mix just enough to combine. Equally distribute the batter between your prepared pans, and bake for 22 to 25 minutes, until a toothpick inserted into the center comes out clean. Cool completely before chilling in the fridge.

For the ice cream, place all the ingredients into your blender and puree until smooth. Blend no longer than necessary, to prevent the mixture from warming up. Pour into your ice cream maker and churn according to the manufacturer's instructions.

When the ice cream is almost done churning, pull out the chilled cakes and place one at the bottom of a 9-inch round springform pan. Spoon the soft ice cream on top, spreading it evenly in a single layer. Place the second round of cake on top, pressing down gently but firmly. Tap the pan a few times on the counter to knock out any air bubbles.

Quickly move the springform pan back into the freezer, and let rest on a flat surface until set, at least 3 hours.

For the final assembly, release the layered cake from the pan and transfer to a serving platter. Smooth the coconut whipped cream all over the top and sides, covering the entirety of the cake. Transfer any leftovers to a piping bag to adorn the borders if desired, and finish with fresh raspberries, mint leaves, and sprinkles, if desired. Serve immediately or keep in the freezer until ready to serve.

I try not to be too fussy about ingredients, but in this case, it's critically important that you use natural cocoa, and not Dutch-processed. Much of the color and loft of this cake is gained through the chemical reaction made possible due to the high acidity levels of the ingredients. Dutch-processed is more alkaline, and wouldn't react in quite the same way.

Viennetta

MAKES 6–8 SERVINGS

Harkening back to my earliest memories of Sunday brunch with my grandparents, there are many sights and sounds that I still hold dear. Without fail, my grandpa would burst through the garage door with great fanfare as we sat around a bowl of mixed nuts, snacking and sharing details of our lives. Brandishing brown paper bags from Gold's, our old-school traditional deli, we all knew that this was the sign that mingling had concluded, and the meal was about to begin.

After the sandwiches came my favorite part; the stunning chocolate and vanilla ice cream cake my grandma would keep hidden in the freezer, for just such an occasion. Impossibly thin shards of crisp chocolate layered across a hundred folds of soft vanilla frozen cream, straddling the line between pudding and whipped topping, there was nothing else I had ever experienced like it, and have yet to find a similar dessert.

Later in life I found out that the frozen confection of my childhood dreams was called "vienneta" and lo, it's still made to this day! Unfortunately, it's only available in Europe now, and worst still, unsurprisingly, a dairy-filled gut-bomb.

Recreating a memory is always tricky, but this shockingly simple homemade rendition quickly surpassed my expectations. Though it may not have quite as many paper-thin layers of chocolate, and my grandpa is no longer around to bring home the cold cuts, it reminds me of those sweet, simple days. If he could still join us for brunch, I'd like to think that he'd approve of my version, with a sly wink and a nod, and maybe even consider picking up a package of corned seitan for lunch, too.

½ cup aquafaba
¼ cup granulated sugar
½ teaspoon cream of tartar
1 (14-ounce) can full-fat coconut milk, chilled for 24 hours
1 cup confectioners' sugar
1 teaspoon vanilla extract
1 batch Dark Chocolate Shell (page 285)

Pour the aquafaba into the bowl of your stand mixer with the whisk attachment installed and gradually increase the speed up to its highest setting. Once you have a steady froth going, slowly sprinkle in the granulated sugar and cream of tartar together. Whip at full power for 5 to 7 minutes, until you achieve a sturdy meringue that stands up at firm peaks. Transfer to a large bowl and reassemble the mixer.

Carefully open the chilled can of coconut milk, being sure not to shake it, and scoop off the top layer of thick coconut cream. Discard or save the watery liquid left behind for another recipe. Place the coconut cream in the bowl of your stand mixer and install the whisk attachment. Whip on high speed for about 3 minutes before slowly beginning to sprinkle in the confectioners' sugar, just a little bit at a time. Continue beating the mixture for up to 10 minutes, until light and fluffy.

Take about half of the meringue and use a wide spatula to gently fold it into the whipped coconut cream, along with the vanilla, being careful not to beat out all the bubbles. Repeat the process with the remainder, until the airy mixture is smooth and well-combined.

Transfer the mixture to a piping bag fitted with a large star tip. Line an 8 x 4-inch loaf pan with parchment paper or have a silicone loaf pan of the same dimensions at the ready. Pipe a single layer of the whipped mixture over the bottom, covering it completely. Warm the chocolate shell so that it's pourable but not hot, and drizzle it over the filling. Place the loaf pan in the freezer for about 15 minutes to begin to set, and stash the piping bag in the fridge in the meantime.

Retrieve the pan and pipe another layer of whipped filling on top of the solid chocolate shell. Drizzle another layer of the chocolate shell on top. Return to the freezer, and repeat. Continue this process until you reach the top of the loaf pan, ending with a layer of the whipped mixture.

Let rest in the freezer for at least 3 hours, until solidly set, before unmolding and transferring the cake to a serving platter. Decorate with any remaining whipped topping and/or magic shell, if desired.

MELTDOWN MASTERPIECES

Having grown up with a voracious sweet tooth and a penchant for all frozen desserts, I firmly believe there is no such thing as too much ice cream. Immersing myself in a world of frosty wonders, testing and tasting, eating it for breakfast, lunch, and dessert . . . There is, however, such thing as too much ice cream to fit into the freezer. In a desperate attempt to use up my surplus in the most thrifty way possible, I stumbled into a brave new world of baking and cooking with ice cream, putting it to work in ways that will turn heads, redefining the very concept of a finished frozen dessert. Building upon the principle of ***wabi-sabi****, "nothing is perfect, nothing is permanent, and nothing is ever fully complete," as quickly as a pristine scoop can revert back to its liquid state, it can be entirely reinvented all over again.*

If you think about it, the components of a traditional custard form the backbone of countless other creations. Merely eggs, dairy, and sugar, this liquid base adds binding power, sweetness, and luscious mouthfeel, depending on the application. It's like the ultimate dessert starter, all in one, not sold in stores nor found in a boxed mix. You've already done the hard work, so you might as well relish the sweet rewards, albeit in a different format.

Some scoops are too precious to dissolve down to their essential components. I would never ask you to nuke your favorite flavor or make a monstrous multi-layered ice cream cake just to let it thaw again. You can just as easily whip up any of the bases called for and simply skip the churning step. Even more simply, if you want an instant shortcut when there's no ice cream on hand, take a peek at my notes for the Sweetened Condensed Cashew Milk (page 310). Go ahead, study up. I'll wait here while the next pint defrosts.

EKCO

Bakery-Style Blueberry Muffins

MAKES 8 LARGE MUFFINS

What makes a muffin worthy of displaying in a lofty glass-paneled bakery case? Tall domes risen well beyond the confines of a pan, crisp and crusted with sugared streusel are just the beginning. Soft and tender crumbs bear satisfying heft, clearly denser than a cupcake. A perfect muffin begins and ends here, ideally with a generous allotment of fruit somewhere in the middle. Bakery-style goes above and beyond the basic breakfast pastry and with a little know-how, are just as easy to create at home. Melted ice cream is the secret ingredient here that brings just the right degree of decadence to wholesome ripe berries and wheat flour. Don't be shy when filling the pans; everyone knows the best part of a muffin is the top.

BLUEBERRY MUFFINS

1 cup melted Triple Vanilla Frozen Custard (page 103), or store-bought vegan vanilla ice cream
1 teaspoon apple cider vinegar
2 tablespoons olive oil
2 cups white whole wheat flour
2 teaspoons baking powder
½ teaspoon baking soda
¼ cup unsweetened applesauce
1 tablespoon lemon zest
1 cup blueberries, fresh or frozen, thawed, and drained

STREUSEL TOPPING

3 tablespoons vegan butter
⅓ cup white whole wheat flour
⅓ cup granulated sugar

For the muffins, preheat your oven to 375°F. and lightly grease 8 standard muffin tins. Combine the melted ice cream and vinegar, whisking vigorously until frothy. Incorporate the oil into the milk mixture and beat until fully emulsified. Add in the flour, baking powder, baking soda, applesauce, and lemon zest, being careful not to overmix. Gently fold in the blueberries. Spoon the batter into your prepared muffin tins.

For the crumb topping, combine the butter, flour, and sugar with a pastry cutter or fork, until it resembles coarse crumbs. Sprinkle evenly over each mound of raw batter. Bake for 16 to 20 minutes, until a toothpick inserted into the center of a muffin comes out clean. Let the muffins sit for at least 10 minutes before removing them from the pan.

Cheesecake Bites

MAKES 36–48 SMALL BITES

Cheesecake, smooth and subtle, dense and creamy, lightly sweetened, subtly tangy, and soft as silken sheets, is the ultimate blank canvas. Unleash your inner artist to paint it with splashes of flavor, limited only by the confines of your imagination. I've included a few classic variations to explore, but these are just the start. Consider any jam or thick topping sauce fair game, and feel free to combine one, two, or more of these all in one rich little square. If, on the other hand, you'd like to take the purist's approach, there's nothing wrong with sticking to clean and simple straight-up cheesecake, no toppings need apply.

GRAHAM CRACKER CRUST

1 cup graham cracker crumbs
2 tablespoons vegan butter or coconut oil, melted

CHEESECAKE FILLING

2 (8-ounce) packages (2 cups) vegan Cream Cheese (page 282, or store-bought)
1¼ cups melted Triple Vanilla Frozen Custard (page 103), or store-bought vegan vanilla ice cream
2 tablespoons lemon juice
1 tablespoon cornstarch
1 teaspoon vanilla extract

OPTIONAL TOPPINGS

1 cup strawberry jam or fruit preserves
½ cup Cara-Miso Sauce (page 279) or Smoked Butterscotch Sauce (page 305)
½ cup mini chocolate chips or cacao nibs

For the crust, preheat your oven to 350°F and line a 13 x 9-inch baking dish with parchment paper or aluminum foil (leave a bit overhanging the edges to make it easier to lift out later). Lightly grease and set side.

In a large bowl, combine the crumbs and melted vegan butter or oil with a fork until evenly moistened. Press into bottom of prepared pan, using the bottom of a flat measuring cup, lightly greased, to help smooth it out.

For the filling, beat the cream cheese until softened and slowly add in the melted ice cream, stirring to incorporate. Once smooth, whisk in the lemon juice, cornstarch, and vanilla. Alternately, the filling can be combined all at once with a quick blitz in the blender. Either way, once smooth, pour over the graham cracker crust.

For a plain cheesecake, skip ahead straight to baking. If using jam, stir until smooth and drop by small spoonfuls over surface of filling. With a knife, swirl the jam gently through to create a marble effect. If using caramel or chocolate sauce, drizzle it in thin lines over the surface of the cheesecake, then swipe a knife through it in opposite directions. For chips or chunks of any sort, simply sprinkle them at random, to your heart's content.

Bake for 25 to 30 minutes or until lightly puffed and the top is no longer shiny. It should still jiggle slightly when tapped. Cool to room temperature and then chill for at least 8 hours, ideally overnight.

Lift the whole rectangle out using the parchment or foil, and slice with a very sharp knife into small squares. Serve chilled or at room temperature.

Cherry-Berry Custard Tartlettes

MAKES 6 TARTLETTES

What grows together, goes together. That ideology has guided countless classic pairings, as proven by the timeless marriage of cherries with any fresh berry you can name. Raspberries are a personal favorite, but I've been known to shake things up with blueberries, strawberries, blackberries, or any blend of the aforementioned fruits. Those dark cherries, edible rubies that hang heavily on the tree, weighed down by their own sweet juices, play very nicely with others.

PASTRY CRUST

6 tablespoons vegan butter
½ cup confectioners' sugar
1 tablespoon whole flaxseeds
2 tablespoons water
1½ cups all-purpose flour
¼ teaspoon salt

CHERRY-BERRY CUSTARD

1½ cups melted Raspberry White Chocolate Frozen Yogurt (page 73), Strawberry Shortcake Ice Cream (page 87), or store-bought vegan berry ice cream
½ pound (about 1½ cups) pitted sweet cherries, fresh or frozen and thawed
1½ tablespoons cornstarch

TO ASSEMBLE

Fresh berries and/or cherries (optional)

For the crust, preheat your oven to 350°F. and lightly grease 6 (3-inch) tart molds or jumbo muffin cups. Beat the vegan butter and sugar in your stand mixer until light and creamy. Grind the flaxseeds into a powder with a spice grinder and blend them together with the water. Add the flax mixture into your mixer and blend well. Add half of the flour, mixing until it is completely incorporated. Follow with the other half of the flour along with the salt, mixing until smooth. If the dough is still crumbly, add up to 2 additional tablespoons of water, just until the mixture sticks together. Divide the dough into 6 equal pieces and place one into each prepared tin. Press the dough up the sides of the pan using your fingers or the end of a wooden spoon, to form the tartlette shells. Bake for 12 to 15 minutes, until lightly browned. Let the tartlet shells cool completely.

To make the filling, combine the melted ice cream, pitted cherries, and cornstarch in your blender and let it rip! Puree on high speed for a solid 5 to 8 minutes, until completely smooth. Pass through a strainer if needed to remove any errant lumps.

Transfer the mixture to a saucepan and warm gently over medium-low heat, stirring frequently, taking care not to scorch the bottom. After about 2 to 4 minutes of even cooking, the mixture should thicken significantly. Once bubbles begin to lazily burst on the surface, remove the pan from the stove. Spoon the filling into the tartlet shells and chill for at least an hour before serving. Garnish the tartlets with fresh cherries and/or berries if desired.

Coconut Macaroons

MAKES 24–26 MACAROONS

Soft and chewy on the inside, crisp and golden on the outside. I don't like using such definitive superlatives, but I daresay that these are the perfect coconut macaroons.

5 cups unsweetened shredded coconut
¾ cup melted Triple Vanilla Frozen Custard (page 103), or store-bought vegan vanilla ice cream
1 teaspoon vanilla extract
¼ teaspoon salt
¼ cup aquafaba

Preheat your oven to 325°F. Line two baking sheets with parchment paper. In a medium bowl, mix together the coconut, melted ice cream, vanilla extract, and salt. Set aside.

Place the aquafaba in the bowl of your stand mixer and install the whisk attachment. Beat on medium speed until frothy, and then increase to high. Whip for 6 to 8 minutes, until stiff peaks form. Add about half of the fluffy mixture into the bowl of coconut batter, and use a wide rubber spatula to fold together. Add the remainder and continue folding gently until fully incorporated.

Using a small ice cream scoop or two spoons, form heaping tablespoons of the mixture into mounds on the prepared baking sheets, spacing about 1 inch apart. Bake for 23 to 25 minutes, rotating the pans from top to bottom and front to back halfway through, until the tops and edges are golden. Let cool on the pans for a few minutes, then transfer to a wire rack to cool completely.

The cookies keep well in an airtight container at room temperature for about a week.

Cookie Monster Magic Bars

MAKES 12–16 BARS

There are many recipe titles that provide no clues, but plenty of intrigue. "Magic Bars" fall firmly into that category. Cookie bars made in minutes, bound together with little more than a can of condensed milk. Consider it the cookie version of the classic dump cake, traditionally lavished with shredded coconut, chopped nuts, and plenty of chocolate. They come together so easily, and satisfy so effortlessly, there really is a certain sort of magic to them.

The real power of any tried-and-true recipe, however, comes from its near magical ability to bend to the will of innovation. When cravings led me to pine over every single cookie I could think of, all at once, I thought it would take a miracle to scratch that itch. Turns out it was really just a matter of some sweet sorcery, combined with a pint of ice cream.

Designed for the cookie monster that lies at the heart of every child and reasonable adult, these bars can do no wrong, as far as I'm concerned. Melted ice cream serves as the decadent glue that binds this cookie overload together, handily replacing the sticky sweetened condensed milk that is usually embedded in the formula. Best of all, you've got a cookie quartet singing sweetly in every bite—a quintet if you count the finished bar itself.

- 1¼ cups finely ground graham cracker crumbs
- ¼ cup coconut oil or vegan butter, melted
- 1 cup melted Triple Vanilla Frozen Custard (page 103), or store-bought vegan vanilla ice cream
- 1 cup semi-sweet chocolate chips
- ½ cup Faux-reos (Cream Filled Chocolate Wafer Cookies) (p. 286), roughly chopped
- ½ cup crunchy mini chocolate chip cookies, roughly chopped
- ½ cup unsalted cashews, halves and pieces

Preheat your oven to 350°F. and line an 8 × 8-inch square baking pan with aluminum foil. Lightly grease and set aside.

Combine the graham cracker crumbs and melted coconut oil or vegan butter in small bowl and mix until all the crumbs are thoroughly moistened. Transfer to your prepared pan, and firmly press it across the bottom. If you're having trouble getting the mixture to cooperate, it helps to lightly grease the bottom of a flat measuring cup and use that to get a nice, smooth layer.

Now comes the fun stuff! Pour the melted ice cream all over the crust. Sprinkle the chocolate chips, both types of chopped cookies, and cashews all over. Use your palms to press the goodies down gently but firmly.

Bake for 25 to 30 minutes or until lightly browned. Let cool completely in the pan, and then use the aluminum foil like a sling to remove the whole sheet. Slice into bars or squares as desired.

Creamed Cookies

MAKES 12–15 BIG COOKIES

In the battle for cookie supremacy, is thin and crispy the way of the future, or soft and chewy the only option? Little love is spared for another alternative: thick and cakey. As long as you fire up the oven and bake something in bite-sized form, there are no losers here. Spongy, soft, somewhere between a buttery scone and tender snack cake, creamed cookies are light on their feet, loftier than the typical Toll House affair, and dangerously easy to eat by the dozen. If you hadn't given the third wave of cookie creations a fair shake, now is the time to even the playing field.

½ cup vegan butter, melted
½ cup melted Triple Vanilla Frozen Custard (page 103), or store-bought vegan vanilla ice cream
½ cup granulated sugar
1 teaspoon vanilla extract
1½ cups all-purpose flour
½ teaspoon baking soda
¼ teaspoon salt
1½ cups semi-sweet chocolate chips (optional)

Chocolate chip cookies are hard to beat, but they're not the only game in town. Omit the morsels to make sweet and simple **Sugar Cookies**, or roll the unbaked balls in a mixture of ¼ cup granulated sugar and 2 teaspoons ground cinnamon to make warmly spiced **Snickerdoodles** instead.

Pour the melted vegan butter into a large bowl, along with the melted ice cream. While still warm, whisk in the sugar and vanilla, stirring until smooth. Add in the flour, mix lightly with a wide spatula, then add baking soda and salt. Stir just until the dough comes together before adding the chocolate chips, mixing to incorporate.

Use an ice cream scoop or large spoon to scoop about 3 tablespoons of dough per cookie, rolling them lightly between moistened palms until smooth. Place the balls onto a baking sheet lined with a silicone baking mat or piece of parchment paper, spaced about 2 inches apart. Press the tops lightly to flatten just a bit. Place the entire sheet in the fridge and chill for at least 1 hour.

When ready to proceed, preheat your oven to 350°F. Bake the cookies for about 9 to 11 minutes, straight out of the fridge, until very lightly golden brown. They may not seem done but resist the temptation to keep them in the oven, as they'll continue to cook on the sheet. Cool for 10 minutes on baking sheet before transferring to a wire rack to cool completely.

Cookies can be stored in an airtight container for up to 4 days or frozen for up to 1 month.

The flavor options here are truly limitless, which makes it hard to even begin rambling off suggestions. My only advice here is to avoid anything with chunks or crunchy inclusions, since so much of the magic in this dessert is in its luscious, perfectly smooth texture.

Flan

MAKES 6 SERVINGS

Known in Spain as flan, in Italy as crema caramella, and in France as crème renversée, the concept of a softly set, chilled custard enrobed in burnt sugar transcends cultural boundaries to find a place at the table worldwide. Lending richness, body, and flavor all in one fell swoop, any flavor of melted ice cream will shine in this creamy custard. The slightly bitter edge of a dark caramel sauce envelopes each trembling round, adding greater depth than a mere scoop could hope to achieve alone. Make no mistake, it's a snap to throw together, but this is some genuinely swoon-worthy stuff.

CARAMEL

1 cup granulated sugar
¼ cup water
¼ teaspoon apple cider vinegar

CUSTARD

3 cups plain nondairy milk
⅔ cup granulated sugar
¼ teaspoon salt
1 cup melted Triple Vanilla Frozen Custard (page 103), or store-bought vegan vanilla ice cream
1 tablespoon agar powder
2 teaspoons arrowroot powder
2 teaspoons vanilla extract

Lightly grease 6 (6-ounce) ramekins and set aside, but keep them nearby so they're easily accessible.

Beginning with the caramel layer, combine all ingredients in a small saucepan. Stir to moisten all of the sugar, but keep your spatula out from here on, to prevent crystallization. Bring to a boil over medium-high heat and cook until the mixture starts to darken around the edges, 8 to 10 minutes. Rather than stirring, gently swirl the pan to evenly color the whole mixture. This will also ensure that it doesn't burn in the corners or on the bottom of the pan. Continue to cook until the sugar turns dark amber. It should be just on the edge of burning and smoking, but not so close that it smells acrid. Once it starts to darken, it will continue to take on color very quickly, so keep a very close eye on it.

Turn off the heat and immediately pour into your prepared ramekins, equally distributing it between them. Let sit undisturbed at room temperature for the caramel to harden.

For the custard, in a medium saucepan over medium heat, vigorously whisk together the nondairy milk, sugar, salt, melted ice cream, agar, and arrowroot. Whisk frequently but gently, scraping bottom and sides of the pan as it heats. Cook until bubbles begin to break regularly on the surface and the liquid has significantly thickened. Remove from the heat and whisk in the vanilla. Carefully pour equal portions of the custard into the waiting ramekins. Tap the bottoms of the cups lightly on the counter to knock out air bubbles. Smooth out the tops with a spatula if necessary.

Let cool to room temperature before transferring to the fridge. Let rest until chilled, at least 2 hours, and up to 2 days. To serve, simply tip each custard out of its ramekin and onto its own dessert plate. If it doesn't release right away, run a thin knife around the edges and try again.

Foolproof Fudge

MAKES 32 SMALL SQUARES

Never toil over a hot stove only to suffer the injustice of grainy fudge again! The secret to the creamiest, easiest little squares of chocolate heaven is—you guessed it—melted ice cream. Two essential ingredients, three minutes of prep work, and three dozen decadent bites later, it's hard to imagine going back to the old-fashioned approach.

2 cups semi-sweet chocolate chips
¾ cup melted Melted Truffle Dark Chocolate Ice Cream (page 63), or store-bought vegan chocolate ice cream
1 cup pecans or walnuts, toasted and chopped (optional)

Line an 8 x 8-inch square baking pan with parchment paper or aluminum foil and lightly grease; set aside.

Combine the chocolate chips and melted ice cream in a microwave-safe bowl. Heat for 1 minute, stir thoroughly, and heat for another 30 to 60 seconds. Stir well until the chocolate has all melted and the mixture is completely smooth.

Mix in the toasted nuts, if using, and pour the chocolate mixture into your prepared pan. Smooth out the surface with your spatula.

Place the pan in your refrigerator and chill for at least 1 hour, until firmly set, before cutting it into squares. To hasten the process, you can place the fudge in your freezer for at least 30 minutes instead.

Store in an airtight container in the fridge for up to a week.

French Toast

MAKES 3 SERVINGS

Life is short; eat dessert first. Instead of saving the best for last, I recommend starting strong with the most important meal of the day. French toast is already an indulgent entrée, so you might as well embrace it and slice into that bread custard with no regrets. Melted ice cream creates the base in an instant, so you may be ready to dig in before the coffee even finishes brewing.

6 slices (about 1 ounce each) bread
½ cup melted Triple Vanilla Frozen Custard (page 103), or store-bought vegan vanilla ice cream
¼ cup aquafaba
1 teaspoon cornstarch
½ teaspoon ground cinnamon
¼ teaspoon salt

It's ideal if you can start with either slightly stale or lightly toasted bread, since it will be a bit firmer and hold up better to the extra moisture you'll be adding.

Whisk together the melted ice cream, aquafaba, cornstarch, cinnamon, and salt in a shallow pan, making sure that everything is well distributed.

Meanwhile, heat a large, lightly greased skillet over medium heat on the stove.

Whisk the liquid mixture once more before using, and dip your first 3 pieces of bread (or as many will fit in your skillet at one time) letting them soak for about 30 seconds. Once saturated, carefully lift the slices out with a large spatula and place them into the hot skillet. Cook for approximately 3 to 5 minutes per side, until golden brown and crisp on the outside. Transfer the toast to a plate, and repeat the process with the remaining bread. Serve with maple syrup, fresh fruit, or powdered sugar, as you see fit.

Hot Chocolate Lava Cakes

MAKES 4 SERVINGS

No dessert menu is complete without some form of molten chocolate cake prominently listed near the top. Clichéd or quintessential, it presents an existential crisis every time the option is presented. Uncreative, uninventive, it presents nothing new, and yet it's for precisely that reason that it's a guaranteed hit. I'd like to think that we can use that quality to our advantage, while still injecting a bit of new life into the old standby.

Filled not just with liquid ganache and half-baked batter, the marshmallow topping for a classic mug of hot cocoa has quietly slipped inside, ready to come pouring out with the swift stab of a fork. Everything comes down to timing here, with every second of cooling tightening the interior, so don't delay. Sprint straight from the oven to the dinner table to release the most impressive, torrential lava flow of gooey marshmallow goodness.

4 ounces (about ¾ cup) unsweetened chocolate, finely chopped
1 cup melted Melted Truffle Dark Chocolate Ice Cream (page 63), or store-bought vegan chocolate ice cream
½ cup all-purpose flour
¼ cup Dutch-processed cocoa powder, plus more for dusting
¼ teaspoon baking powder
⅛ teaspoon salt
4 large vegan marshmallows
Mini marshmallows, or Maple Marshmallow Sauce (page 299)

Preheat your oven to 425°F. Generously grease 4 (6-ounce) ramekins and dust lightly with extra cocoa powder. Tap out the excess, place the ramekins on a baking sheet, and set aside.

Gently melt the unsweetened chocolate in a microwave-safe bowl at 30-second intervals until smooth. Stir vigorously between heat intervals to ensure even melting. Set aside and let cool slightly.

Meanwhile, in a large bowl, mix the melted ice cream, flour, cocoa, baking powder, and salt. Once mostly incorporated, add in the melted chocolate and stir to combine.

Divide the batter between your prepared ramekin cups. Gently poke one large marshmallow into the center of each one, allowing the top to remain visible from the surface. If you press it all the way to the bottom, it will simply stick to the ramekin and leave a sad, empty crater in the cake.

Bake for 10 to 12 minutes, until the edges are set, but the center of cakes are still soft. The key is to leave them just slightly under-baked, like properly chewy cookies.

Gently run a butter knife or mini spatula around the edges of the ramekin to release the cakes. Invert ramekins onto plates, garnished with whipped cream or marshmallow sauce, and serve immediately.

Ice Cream Biscuits

MAKES 6–8 BISCUITS

Cream biscuits have long been a staple on southern tables, made humbly from flour, heavy cream, and the lightest kiss of sugar. Blurring the line between breakfast pastry and dinner side dish, they share many commonalities with English scones—soft, tender, with a slightly savory edge that seems to pair well with everything on the table. The trick for these featherweight rolls is to keep it simple. Melted ice cream cuts down the ingredient list to only three essentials, so there's no excuse for a barren breadbasket from here on out.

2¼ cups all-purpose flour, plus more as needed
1 tablespoon baking powder
1 cup melted Triple Vanilla Frozen Custard (page 103), or store-bought vegan vanilla ice cream
2 tablespoons vegan butter, melted (optional)

Nothing can top a perfectly buttered biscuit, although it's nice to shake up the flavors every now and then. For a taste of something different, try these bold variations . . .

Sweet & Spicy: Use melted Sweet Heat Chipotle Pecan Ice Cream (page 93) instead of vanilla and add ½ of a finely diced jalapeño pepper.

Creamed Corn: Replace 1 cup of the all-purpose flour with coarse yellow cornmeal and add ½ cup fresh corn kernels.

Bettah Cheddah: Use melted Cheddar-Style Ice Cream (page 47) and add ½ cup vegan cheddar shreds.

Preheat your oven to 425°F. In a medium bowl, stir together the flour, baking powder, and melted ice cream until the dough forms a cohesive ball. Turn the dough out onto a surface dusted with additional flour. Fold the dough in half, turn 90 degrees, and press out flat again. Fold and repeat 4 to 5 times, adding just enough flour to keep dough from sticking to your hands.

Gently roll out dough to ½-inch thickness. Using a 3-inch biscuit cutter or cookie cutter coated with flour, cut dough into biscuits. Re-roll scraps and repeat, but bear in mind that any subsequent rollings will create tougher, less tender biscuits.

Place the biscuits on a baking sheet lined with parchment paper or a silicone mat, leaving at least 1 inch between each one. Brush the tops with melted vegan butter, if desired, for a touch of extra richness. Bake for about 14 to 18 minutes, until the biscuits are evenly browned.

When the biscuits come out of the oven, you can brush them with a little more melted vegan butter, to really go all out. Let the biscuits cool for at least 10 minutes before serving.

Instant Brownie Fudge Bars

MAKES 16–24 SERVINGS

Science has proven that we're less capable of tasting the full flavor nuances of anything chilled below 32°F. I'd like to think I was simply wise beyond my years, gleefully turning sundaes into spoonable milkshakes for maximum enjoyment.

It wasn't long after gaining the privacy of my own tiny apartment kitchen that I began to tinker with some downright insane concepts, while taking my penchant for ice cream soup to the extreme. After one cycle too many in the microwave, I discovered that my luscious chocolate ice cream had "defrosted" far beyond the realm of milkshake territory, sloshing around inside its cardboard carton freely. While one could toss the liquid back into an ice cream churn and salvage the mess, I saw this as a new opportunity. A new ingredient to play with, once again, to transform into an entirely new treat.

No baking is required for these decadent treats. In fact, the end results taste even better when eaten chilled; an inadvertent homage to its frozen origins. For anyone who's ever craved a brownie denser and fudgier, just a hair lighter than pure ganache, these devilishly rich bars fill that gap. Admittedly, the squares pictured here are much too large for any reasonable human being to consume in one sitting. Just a little bit goes a long way with these deep, dark chocolate squares.

2 cups melted Melted Truffle Dark Chocolate Ice Cream (page 63), or store-bought vegan chocolate ice cream
¼ cup coconut oil
½ teaspoon salt
4 cups (about 18 ounces) finely ground Faux-reos chocolate sandwich cookie crumbs (page 286, or store-bought)
½ cup chopped walnuts or pecans, divided

Line an 8 × 8-inch square pan with aluminum foil and lightly grease; set aside.

Place the ice cream, coconut oil, and salt into a medium saucepan and set over medium heat. Allow everything to fully melt, bringing the liquid to a gentle boil. Reduce the heat to medium-low and continue cooking, whisking periodically, for about 5 minutes.

Add in the cookie crumbs and half of the nuts, stirring quickly and vigorously with a wide spatula. The resulting batter will be very thick, so don't be afraid to put some muscle into it. Transfer to your prepared pan and spread the mixture out into a smooth, even layer. Sprinkle the remaining nuts over the top and use your palms to gently press them into the surface.

Move the pan into your fridge and chill for at least 4 hours, or into your freezer for 2, before slicing into bars or squares as desired. Store in an airtight container in the fridge, for up to a week—if you can keep your hands off them that long.

Matcha Mug Cakes

MAKES 2 SERVINGS

Mug cakes are frequently ridiculed for their rubbery texture, but it's the microwave oven at fault, not the overall concept. Wattage varies greatly depending on the model, so what works perfectly in one kitchen may set off smoke alarms in the next. The air inside the microwave is at room temperature, so foods don't get brown or crispy as they would with other forms of cooking. Thus, the typical visuals of a perfectly baked cake won't apply here, making it far easier to accidentally overcook the crumb to the consistency of a wrung-out dish sponge.

Know your appliance and err on the side of caution, cooking less, rather than more, until you master the machine.

⅔ cup melted Triple Vanilla Frozen Custard (page 103), or store-bought vegan vanilla ice cream
½ cup all-purpose flour
2 teaspoons matcha powder
½ teaspoon baking powder

Mix all ingredients until smooth and divide between 2 (8-ounce) microwaveable mugs.

Cook each one individually on full power for about 2½ minutes*. It will be done when the mixture puffs up significantly and appears set in the center. To double check, insert a skewer into the middle. If it comes out clean, the mug cake is done! Let cool for at least 5 minutes before enjoying

*This recipe was tested in a 700-watt microwave. Adjust cook times accordingly for your individual wattage:

600 Watts = 2 Minutes 55 Seconds
800 Watts = 2 minutes 11 seconds
900 Watts = 1 Minutes 56 Seconds
1000 Watts = 1 Minutes 45 Seconds
1100 Watts = 1 Minutes 35 Seconds
1200 Watts = 1 Minutes 27 Seconds

Pear Frangipane Cake

MAKES 8–12 SERVINGS

Frangipane is a delicate, buttery, almond-scented, soft-set cream typically encased in pastry. Here, unencumbered by a rigid crust, it stands alone as an incredibly moist cake, merely baked in a tart form. Thinly sliced pears fan out like a proud peacock displays its tail feathers. Crisp apples would be equally attractive, and at the height of stone fruit season, peaches, apricots, and plums could add new color to this highly adaptable, nutty custard-meets-cake.

1¼ cups blanched almond flour
½ cup all-purpose flour
1 tablespoon tapioca starch
1 teaspoon baking powder
¾ cup melted Triple Vanilla Frozen Custard (page 103), or store-bought vegan vanilla ice cream
⅓ cup dark brown sugar, firmly packed
2 tablespoons olive oil
1 teaspoon almond extract
¾ teaspoon vanilla extract
2 small pears, halved, cored, and thinly sliced
2 tablespoons sliced almonds

Preheat your oven to 350°F. and lightly grease a 9-inch round tart pan with removable bottom. In a large bowl, whisk together the almond flour, all-purpose flour, tapioca starch, and baking powder. Set aside.

In a separate mixing bowl, whisk the melted ice cream, brown sugar, oil, and almond and vanilla extracts until smooth. Pour this liquid mixture into the bowl of dry ingredients, using a wide spatula to bring the two together until just combined. The resulting batter will be thick and sticky.

Spoon the batter into the prepared tart crust, smoothing out evenly. Arrange the sliced pears on top and finish with a sprinkle of sliced almonds.

Bake for 30 to 40 minutes or until a toothpick inserted into the middle of the frangipane comes out clean. Let cool for at least 15 minutes in the pan. Slice and serve warm or at room temperature.

Rum-Raisin Bread Pudding

MAKES 12–14 SERVINGS

Bread pudding is the stone soup of the dessert world. Any scraps or leftovers, pantry staples, or surplus you have on hand can be right at home in the mix. Rum-raisin is simply a natural when using up excess ice cream, since the combination was born of old-fashioned scoop shops itself. Even raisin haters will be mollified by a strong rum infusion, soaking and softening the fruit into juicy, jammy pearls. Strong spices go particularly well if you'd like to branch out a bit, so don't be afraid to play with something like Gingerbread Ice Cream (page 177), Eggnog Ice Cream (page 185), or Sweet Heat Chipotle Pecan Ice Cream (page 93) instead, just for starters. As I said, anything goes here.

RUM-RAISIN BREAD PUDDING

- **¾ pound sourdough or French bread, cut into ¾-inch cubes**
- **3 cups melted Triple Vanilla Frozen Custard (page 103)**
- **⅓ cup dark rum**
- **2 tablespoons ground flaxseeds**
- **1 teaspoon ground cinnamon**
- **1 cup raisins, soaked in hot water for 30 minutes and thoroughly drained**

RUM-RAISIN SAUCE

- **½ cup vegan butter**
- **½ cup dark brown sugar, firmly packed, or coconut sugar**
- **½ cup raisins**
- **⅓ cup dark rum**
- **⅓ cup plain nondairy milk**
- **1 teaspoon vanilla extract**

For the bread pudding, preheat your oven to 350°F and lightly grease a deep dish 9-inch square baking pan, 9 x 13-inch baking pan, or 3-quart casserole dish. Spread the bread out in an even layer on an ungreased baking sheet and toast for 8 to 10 minutes, just to crisp them up a bit.

In a large bowl, whisk together the melted ice cream, rum, flaxseeds, and cinnamon. Once smooth, add in the toasted bread cubes along with the soaked and drained raisins. Stir to thoroughly combine. Transfer into your prepared pan, making sure the raisins are well distributed throughout. Press down on the surface with your spatula to ease the pieces into a more or less even layer. Bake for 45 to 50 minutes, until golden brown all over.

Meanwhile, for the sauce, melt the butter with the sugar in a small saucepan over medium low heat. Whisk thoroughly and heat on low for 1 minute, just until the sugar has dissolved.

Place the raisins, rum, nondairy milk, and vanilla in your blender and puree on high speed until completely smooth, 5 to 8 minutes. With the motor still running, slowly stream the melted butter mixture in to emulsify, much like you would for a salad dressing. Let cool for at least 5 minutes.

Serve the bread pudding warm or at room temperature with warm rum-raisin sauce drizzled over each portion. Serve the extra sauce on the side.

We could spend all day tossing around ideas for modifications; I have yet to find one displeasing variation, no matter how many times I find myself scrounging together odds and ends for a last-minute dessert. A few of my favorite combinations are as follows:

Sugared Plum: Replace the raisins with chopped prunes (dried plums) and finish with a generous sprinkle of turbinado sugar on top before baking.

Lime in the Coconut: Use the coconut cream base from page 203 instead of vanilla and add 2 teaspoons finely grated lime zest. Omit the cinnamon. After baking, sprinkle ½ cup toasted shredded coconut on top.

Chocolate-Cherry: Replace the raisins with dried cherries and use Melted Truffle Dark Chocolate Ice Cream (page 63) instead of vanilla. Mix in 3 ounces (½ cup) finely chopped bittersweet chocolate. Top the finished pudding with a light sprinkle of cocoa powder before serving, if desired.

Salted Caramel Blondies

MAKES 12–16 SERVINGS

Describing a blondie as merely a brownie without chocolate does the treat a severe disservice. Soft, chewy squares that highlight the subtle molasses notes of brown sugar deliver all the satisfaction of chocolate chip cookies without any extraneous distractions. Upping the ante with velvety caramel ice cream draws out those dark and alluring toffee notes. The only thing that would make these stellar bars even better is an extra scoop of caramel ice cream on top; no chocolate need apply.

6 tablespoons melted vegan butter or coconut oil
⅔ cup dark brown sugar, firmly packed
½ cup melted Kalamata Caramel Ice Cream without the Kalamata Almond Brittle (page 58), or store-bought vegan caramel ice cream
1 teaspoon vanilla extract
1 cup all-purpose flour
¼ teaspoon baking powder
¼ teaspoon salt
½ cup walnuts or pecans, toasted and chopped
Flaky or coarse sea salt, to garnish

Preheat your oven to 350°F. and lightly grease an 8 x 8-inch baking dish.

In a medium bowl, whisk together the melted butter or oil, brown sugar, and melted ice cream, beating until the sugar is dissolved. Stir in the vanilla.

In a separate bowl, whisk together the flour, baking powder, and salt. Add the nuts and toss to coat with the flour.

Pour the liquid ingredients into the bowl of dry goods and stir just until combined. Be careful not to overmix, which will yield tough cookies. A few lumps in the batter are perfectly fine.

Transfer the batter to your prepared pan and use your spatula to smooth down the top into an even layer. Bake for 24 to 28 minutes, or until golden brown and the edges pull away from the pan slightly. Let the blondies cool completely before topping with sea salt if desired and cutting into bars.

Strawberry Cream Pie

MAKES 6–8 SERVINGS

It was an average day, punctuated by chores and assignments, including a considerable grocery shopping expedition. Distracted by all the to-dos and a rapidly shrinking timeline, something was bound to get overlooked. Unfortunately, it was the ice cream. By the time it was discovered, tucked into the fridge, not the freezer, it had fully liquified into a pale white puddle. Loathe to think that such a precious treat would be wasted because of a careless mistake, my thoughts turned to the possibilities of a little kitchen alchemy.

This humble pie requires a mere seven ingredients, from crust to filling, thanks to the magic of melted ice cream. Strawberries and cream truly shine together in this brilliantly simple ode to spring. The only baking required is a brief flash in the oven to set the crust, but this can be further simplified with a ready-made rendition. Even more impressive than this recipe's effortlessly delicious outcome is its versatility, easily adaptable for any season. Swap out the berries for just about any fresh fruit that's ripe and ready, such as peaches or apricots in the summer, pumpkin puree in the fall, baked apples or pears in the winter; the potential for different flavors is practically endless.

VANILLA COOKIE CRUST

5 tablespoons melted vegan butter or coconut oil

1½ cups finely ground Va'Nilla Wafer cookie crumbs (page 311, or store-bought)

STRAWBERRY CREAM FILLING

1 pound fresh strawberries, washed, hulled, and roughly sliced

1½ tablespoons lime juice

1 teaspoon lemon zest

1½ teaspoons agar powder

2 cups melted Triple Vanilla Frozen Custard (page 103), or store-bought vegan vanilla ice cream

For the crust, preheat your oven to 350°F. Combine the melted butter or coconut oil with the cookie crumbs in a large bowl, stirring thoroughly to completely moisten every last crumb. Transfer the mixture to a 9-inch pie pan and use your hands to press it evenly across the bottom and up the sides. Bake for 10 to 15 minutes, until golden brown. Let cool while you move on to the filling.

For the filling, toss all ingredients into your blender. Puree until mostly but not entirely smooth, leaving a few small chunks of berries intact. If you'd prefer a silkier texture, continue blending until no lumps remain, and pass the pink mixture through a fine mesh sieve, discarding the seeds. Transfer the mixture to a medium saucepan and set over moderate heat. Whisk frequently as it warms up, cooking until it comes to a full boil. Continue stirring vigorously for a full 2 minutes and then pour the hot filling into your prepared crust.

Tap the pan lightly on the counter to release any air bubbles, and let cool to room temperature. Only then is it safe to transfer to the fridge to continue cooling. Don't rush this process, since an agar gel that's cooled too quickly will weep and become watery later on.

Once fully chilled and solidified, slice and serve with additional fresh berries if desired—or, additional scoops of ice cream!

TOPPERS, SAUCES, SIDES, AND STAPLES

Top this. If the umpteen components woven into the more elaborate ice cream concoctions are not enough, still more options remain to be relished. Certain core staples are necessary to round out any decent collection of ice cream recipes, lest a single craving go unaddressed. Can you imagine sidling up to the counter at your local parlor, only to be denied a basic human right, like fudge sauce or rainbow sprinkles?

Naturally, these separate components are worthy additions to other, less chilly desserts as well. You'll never regret having extra strawberry jam on hand, and no reasonable human would turn up their nose at a stack of homemade wafer cookies. Stock your pantry, fill your cookie jar, and prepare your fridge; these are the essential staples and utter whimsies that will elevate your dishes to the next level.

Apple Butter

MAKE ABOUT 1 QUART

Apple butter, a humble spiced preserve, has nothing to do with any dairy additives, contrary to what the name might suggest. Naturally vegan, it's easy to find in just about any grocery store. Unfortunately, like most other mass-produced jams and jellies, it's typically composed of more sugar than fruit. Seeking an option focused on flavor rather than pure sweetness, I decided to take things into my own hands. The process is easy enough for a complete beginner to master on the first try, even if you've never considered jamming before. Just make sure you have plenty of time before you light up your stove because it's not exactly a "quick fix" recipe.

6 cups unsweetened applesauce
12 ounces (1½ cups) frozen no-sugar added apple juice concentrate, thawed
2 tablespoons ground cinnamon
1 teaspoon ground allspice
½ teaspoon ground cloves
½ teaspoon salt

Combine all the ingredients in a large, heavy saucepan over medium heat on the stove. Whisk thoroughly to incorporate all the spices without any clumps remaining and bring to a boil. Reduce the heat to low, keeping the mixture at a gentle simmer. Continue to cook, uncovered, stirring periodically to make sure that nothing sticks to the bottom of the pan. Be patient as it will take anywhere from 2 to 4 hours to properly reduce by about half, to a thick, spreadable, jammy consistency. When finished, it will be considerably darker in color and coat the back of a spoon richly.

Let cool for at least 30 minutes before packing into glass jars and sealing tightly. When completely cool, store in the fridge for up to 2 weeks. This apple butter is low in acidity and thus difficult to properly can without extensive equipment, so it isn't shelf stable. That just means you need to slather it on thick and eat it faster, which shouldn't be too much trouble!

Apples aren't the only fresh autumnal delights to harvest from the orchard. Go ahead and pump-kin it up! Convert this seasonal schmear into **Pumpkin Butter** by trading the apple sauce for 1 (14-ounce) can of pumpkin puree. Swap the allspice for nutmeg to get that classic freshly baked pumpkin pie flavor.

Berry Gummy Bears

MAKES ABOUT 200 GUMMY BEARS

Berry good things are in store when you shop nature's candy store for the "bear" essentials of this chewy childhood treat. Gummy bears typically get their bouncy bite from gelatin, but these natural cuties are purely plant-based! Whole fruits and juices, unsullied by artificial extracts or colors, burst with fresh flavors the average fruit snack can only dream of.

½ cup blueberries or chopped strawberries, fresh or frozen and thawed
¾ cup 100% unsweetened apple juice
¼ cup maple syrup
1 tablespoon lemon juice
1½ tablespoons agar powder
1 teaspoon tapioca starch

This basic formula bear-ly scratches the surface of all the potential flavorings for your bouncy confections! Here are a few more of my favorites, but any fruit purees or juices can work just as brilliantly.

Sour Bears: Pucker up for some serious sour power by tossing the finished bears in a mixture of ½ cup confectioners' sugar and 2 teaspoons citric acid. Citric acid is a powder available in specialty cake shops and online.

Pumpkin Spice Bears: Replace the berries with pumpkin puree and add 1½ teaspoons pumpkin spice.

Banana Bread Bears: Replace the berries with very thoroughly mashed banana and add 1 teaspoon ground cinnamon.

Have about 4 sheets of silicone gummy bear molds (or a comparable shape) at the ready. Each sheet should have about 50 cavities for standard, ½-inch bears. Alternately, you can line an 8 x 8-inch square baking pan with foil and plan to simply cut out gummy squares. Just be sure to lightly grease the foil before proceeding.

Place all the ingredients in your blender and thoroughly puree for a full 5 to 8 minutes until completely smooth. Transfer to a small saucepan and set over medium heat. Stir gently but consistently; you should start to feel the mixture thicken almost instantly. Continue scraping the bottom and sides of the pan as you stir to prevent sticking or burning, until the mixture is sticky but spoonable. It will be so dense that it doesn't quite come to a boil, but should bubble up around the edges quite a bit.

Smooth the mixture into your molds as quickly as possible, as the candy sets up very quickly. Let stand at room temperature until fully set, at least 20 to 30 minutes. Pop the bears out of the molds and trim away any excess, if necessary. Store in an airtight container in the fridge for up to a week.

Cara-Miso (Miso Caramel) Sauce

MAKES ABOUT 1 CUP

Caramel is best with a pinch of salt, so when you add in a hit of miso paste, you'll create a deeply umami taste sensation. Naturally, this versatile syrup finds itself most at home atop luscious scoops of ice cream, but don't limit yourself to frozen desserts alone. Try it drizzled on top of pancakes, swirled into brownie batter, or as a dip for fresh strawberries, too.

1 cup granulated sugar
¼ cup water
¾ cup full-fat coconut milk
3 tablespoons sweet white miso paste
3 tablespoons vegan butter or coconut oil
¼ teaspoon salt

Combine the sugar and water in medium-sized saucepan, then set over moderate heat. Resist the urge to stir, but rather, gently swirl the pan in a circular motion to mix the contents.

Meanwhile, mix a few tablespoons of coconut milk with the miso paste. Whisk vigorously to thoroughly incorporate the miso. Make sure that there are no remaining lumps before stirring in the rest of the coconut milk and set aside.

Continue to cook the sugar mixture, swirling occasionally, until it turns deep amber in color, but do not allow it to begin smoking or smelling burnt. You want to cook it to a fairly dark shade to give it the most flavor, but if it smells burnt, it's already too late and you must start again. Once it begins to color, it will progress very quickly, so do not walk away.

Once deeply colored, very carefully pour in the coconut milk along with the butter or coconut oil. The mixture is likely to sputter and bubble up, so you may want to stand to the side while making this addition, and it's not a bad idea to wear long sleeves to cover your arms, just in case. The mixture may seize and crystallize slightly, but don't worry, it's easy to fix. Continue to cook the syrup over gentle heat until any crystals are dissolved, and the mixture is completely smooth again. Stir in the salt and turn off the heat.

Let cool completely before using or storing in a glass jar.

Confetti Quin Sprinkles

MAKES ABOUT 1½ POUNDS SPRINKLES

Everyone loves them, but few people even know their proper name. Those large, flat sprinkles that can be found in every color and shape under the sun, from simple circles to elaborate dinosaurs, Christmas trees, or peace signs—they're not merely "sprinkles," but in fact a specific type known as "quins." Though the origin and meaning of this word is rather fuzzy, these edible confetti are often even better than a cherry on top. Easily adapted to fit any special occasion, just a pinch of well-placed quins can brighten up a sweet treat like nothing else. My homemade edible confetti is constructed much like rolled fondant cut into tiny pieces, so patience is the most important ingredient here, as they take a decent amount of time to fully dry before use.

1 (10-ounce) bag vegan miniature marshmallows
2 tablespoons water
4 cups (1 pound) confectioners' sugar, plus additional as needed
Food coloring, as needed
Edible luster dust (optional)

Dust a clean kitchen counter or large cutting board with powdered sugar. Be prepared to devote some space to this, because things could get messy.

Place the marshmallows and the water in a large microwave-safe bowl. Microwave on high for 1 minute, until the marshmallows have puffed up. Stir the marshmallows with a rubber spatula until they are melted and smooth. If some unmelted marshmallow pieces remain, return to the microwave for 30 to 45 seconds, until the marshmallow mixture is entirely smooth and free of lumps.

Add the confectioners' sugar, stirring until the sugar is mostly incorporated and it becomes impossible to stir anymore. It will be sticky and lumpy, but never fear! It gets better from here.

Transfer the marshmallow-sugar mixture out onto the prepared work surface and sprinkle a bit more confectioners' sugar on top. Dust your hands with powdered sugar and begin to knead the fondant mixture like bread dough, until it smooths out and loses its stickiness.

Once the sugar dough is smooth, divide it into pieces for as many different colors as you want. Roll the pieces into balls, and then flatten the balls into disks. Work with one at a time to prevent transferring hues between the pieces. You might want to wear plastic gloves if you're worried about temporary staining.

Add your desired amount of coloring or flavoring to the center of each disk. Start with a modest amount, since you can always add more, but never take it away. Fold the disk in half so that the color is enclosed in the center. Knead the ball of dough, until the color is slowly incorporated and becomes uniform through and through. Adjust the hue now if you want it to be more vibrant.

Use a rolling pin to flatten the dough to about 1/16-inch. Use a pasta roller if you have one, because thinness is essential! Use a round piping tip to stamp out circles, allowing them to stack up inside the cone until it's full. Gently place them in a small dish and toss with luster dust, if desired.

Knead together the scraps, re-roll, and repeat.

Cream Cheese

MAKES ABOUT 2 CUPS

Slightly salty, slightly sweet, cream cheese is one of the most versatile spreads around, and an essential ingredient in my kitchen. Since it plays such a crucial role in desserts like cheesecake, quality really counts. Go the extra mile to make your own from scratch and instantly elevate your creations to the next level or enjoy it simply as a spread that will make even the average bagel sing.

Kombucha is an unconventional addition that you won't find in most recipes, but I've found that this fermented tea gives my schmear a perfectly tangy flavor. Seek out the most neutral variety available, such as an "original" flavor or a citrus blend.

1 cup raw cashews
½ cup slivered almonds
1 tablespoon apple cider vinegar
1 tablespoon lemon juice
1 tablespoon white miso paste
¼ teaspoon salt
½ cup kombucha

Place the cashews and almonds in a medium saucepan along with enough water to cover. Bring to a boil and simmer for 15 minutes. The nuts should have swollen a bit from absorption and have a more tender, "al dente" bite. Drain thoroughly and transfer to a high-powered blender or food processor.

Add in the vinegar, lemon juice, miso, and salt. Begin blending on low to break down the nuts, using the tamper to continue pushing the mixture into the blades, pausing periodically to scrape down the sides of the canister with a spatula. Once it becomes a crumbly, coarse meal, begin slowly streaming in the kombucha with the motor running. Turn up the speed to high and continue to puree, until completely smooth. Allow enough time for the blender or food processor to do its magic. Depending on your machine, it could take anywhere from 5 to 15 minutes to achieve the ideal, silky-smooth texture.

Transfer to an airtight container and store in the fridge for up to 5 days. Kombucha is a living, fermented ingredient, so the cream cheese will continue to get tangier the longer it sits. Plan accordingly if you want to either downplay or highlight this distinctive flavor in your food or desserts.

Don't feel like baking this homemade delicacy into another dessert? Transform your basic cream cheese into a fancy flavored spread by blending up any of the following:

Garlic & Herb: Add 1 clove finely minced garlic, ¼ cup minced fresh parsley, 1 minced scallion, and ¼ teaspoon dried thyme.

Italian Tomato: Add ¼ cup finely minced sundried tomatoes, 1 tablespoon tomato paste, 2 tablespoons fresh minced basil, ½ teaspoon dried oregano, and ¼ teaspoon dried thyme.

Spicy Queso: Add 3 tablespoons nutritional yeast and 1 diced chipotle canned in adobo sauce.

Strawberry: Add ¼ cup seedless strawberry jam or preserves.

Maple Brown Sugar: Add 3 tablespoons dark brown sugar, firmly packed, 1 tablespoon maple syrup, and ¼ teaspoon ground cinnamon.

Lemon Poppy Seed: Add 2 tablespoons lemon zest, ¼ cup confectioners' sugar, and 1 tablespoon poppy seeds.

Dark Chocolate Shell

MAKES ABOUT 1¼ CUPS

Defying all ordinarily accepted states of matter, this magical shell is a truly wizardly sweet sauce that starts out as a liquid and instantly transforms into a solid the moment it hits frosty ice cream. Ideal for enrobing frozen desserts in a thin sheath of flawless, hard-crack cacao, it's an equally enchanting topper on any solo scoop. Few things are more satisfying than watching the shining coat quickly chill down to a matte glaze, ready to shatter with a sharp whack with the back of your spoon. It an experience that every child, or child at heart, should revel in.

⅓ cup coconut oil
1 cup (6 ounces) semi-sweet chocolate chips, or a bar cut into chunks
½ teaspoon salt

Place all ingredients in a heat-safe bowl and microwave for 60 seconds. Stir thoroughly before microwaving for another 30 to 60 seconds, pausing at 15 second intervals to stir thoroughly until the chocolate has completely melted and the mixture is smooth.

Let it cool to room temperature, or for at least 10 minutes, before using.

This recipe can easily be doubled, tripled, or even quadrupled if you're planning a big ice cream social. Just store the sauce in an airtight container in the fridge, for up to 6 weeks. It will solidify from the cold but is easily revived. Gently warm it by microwaving at 15-second intervals and stirring well until it's pourable again.

Don't just stop at chocolate! It's a foolproof classic, but far from the final word on finishing glazes. There's a boldly flavored, wildly colorful world of different hard crack coatings to drizzle on your frozen creations.

Peanut Butter Shell: Replace the chocolate with 1 cup peanut butter, creamy or crunchy, depending on your preference, and add 1 tablespoon maple syrup.

Gingerbread Shell: Replace the chocolate with 1 cup creamy speculoos spread and add 1 tablespoon molasses, 1½ teaspoons ground ginger, and 1 teaspoon ground cinnamon.

White Chocolate Shell: Replace the chocolate with ¾ cup melted, food-grade cocoa butter and add 1 teaspoon vanilla paste or extract.

Birthday Cake Shell: Prepare as for white chocolate magic shell, and add 1 tablespoon ground freeze-dried strawberries and 2 to 3 tablespoons rainbow sprinkles.

Faux-reos (Cream Filled Chocolate Wafer Cookies)

MAKES 50–60 WAFERS; 25–30 SANDWICH COOKIES

Sure, while the Oreo® cookie is "accidentally" vegan, darned tasty as is, and readily available worldwide, making your own from scratch is next-level sandwich cookie mastery. Dark as night, black and Dutched cocoa powders work in concert to unlock a world of chocolate flavor not found in the originals. Crisp yet tender wafers come together with a smear of cream filling in the middle, applied with a deft hand to suit your personal preference, even if you opt for double-stuffed, triple-stuffed, or beyond.

For the final flourish, make a big impression with embossed rolling pins to give the wafers that classic Oreo® texture. Alternately, get creative with what you have on hand, such as large rubber stamps (never used with ink, please!), a potato masher, or the edge of a squiggly, spiraled, twisted-looking cookie cutter to press random patterns into the unbaked dough.

CHOCOLATE WAFER COOKIES

1 cup vegan butter
1 cup granulated sugar
½ cup Dutch processed cocoa
¼ cup black cocoa powder
2 cups all-purpose flour
½ teaspoon baking powder
¼ teaspoon salt
¼ cup aquafaba
1 teaspoon vanilla extract

CREAM FILLING

1 cup vegan butter
4 cups confectioners' sugar
1 teaspoon vanilla extract
2 teaspoons aquafaba

For the cookies, use your stand mixer with the paddle attachment installed to thoroughly cream the vegan butter and sugar together. Continue mixing until homogenous, light, and fluffy. Scrape down the sides of the bowl with your spatula before adding both cocoa powders next. Beat vigorously again until fully incorporated.

In a separate bowl, sift the flour, baking powder, and salt, stirring well to combine. Add about half of these dry ingredients into the mixing bowl, processing it until fully incorporated. Pour in the aquafaba and vanilla, along with the remaining flour mixture. Continue to mix until it forms into a smooth, homogeneous dough. Form the dough into a ball, flatten it out a bit, wrap in plastic, and chill for at least 1 hour before proceeding.

After the dough has had time to rest in the refrigerator, preheat your oven to 325°F. and line 2 baking sheets with silicone baking mats. Set aside.

On a lightly floured surface, roll out the dough to about ¼- to ⅛-inch thick. Use an embossing rolling pin (or any of the alternative methods outlined above) to create a decorative texture on the surface. Take a 2- to 2½-inch round cookie cutter and punch out the cookies, and place them on the prepared baking sheets. Brush the excess flour off the cookies, but don't go crazy if it still has a light coating; most of it will bake off.

Bake for about 13 to 16 minutes. It's tough to judge when these cookies are done because they're so dark to begin with, but the edges should be firm, and the centers soft and slightly puffed up.

Cool completely on a wire rack before filling, eating, or using in further baking exploits.

To make the filling, whip together the vegan butter, confectioners' sugar, vanilla, and aquafaba in your stand mixer, starting at a low speed. Once incorporated, turn up the speed to high, and beat for 2 to 5 minutes, until light and fluffy.

Spoon, pipe, or spread the filling as desired on the back of a single wafer and sandwich with a second on top. Repeat until all cookies are used.

Store in an airtight container at room temperature for up to 4 days, or in the fridge for up to a week. Prior to sandwiching, the wafer cookies can be stored in the freezer for up to 3 months.

Graham Crackers

MAKES ABOUT 30–40 SQUARES, OR 15–20 RECTANGLES

Graham crackers are the building blocks of many a dessert, which is quite ironic because they were originally designed as an austere addition to a highly restrictive regimen, designed to cut down on rampant desire and other excesses. Reverend Sylvester Graham would likely be horrified by the sugary turn these originally bland wafer planks have taken, but the general public is all the better for it. Now a simple biscuit worthy of solo consumption, the only trouble is finding an option that doesn't contain honey. Scout out store brands for some "accidentally vegan" gems or get busy making an even better version from scratch. These won't cure you of any dietary evils, but they will instantly elevate your cheesecake crusts, pie crusts, or simple s'mores to new culinary heights.

- ½ cup vegan butter
- 1 cup dark brown sugar, firmly packed
- 1 cup graham flour
- 1¼ cups all-purpose flour
- ½ teaspoon baking soda
- ½ teaspoon ground cinnamon
- ¼ teaspoon salt
- ¼ cup agave nectar or maple syrup
- 1 teaspoon vanilla extract

In your stand mixer, cream together the butter and sugar thoroughly, until fluffy and homogeneous.

Separately, sift together the flours, baking soda, cinnamon, and salt, before adding them all into the bowl of the mixer. Start on low speed and begin to gently incorporate into the butter and sugar mixture. Add in the agave or syrup and vanilla and continue mixing until the dough comes together. Be sure to scrape down the sides of the bowl with your spatula periodically.

Once smooth and cohesive, pat the dough out lightly into a flat round, and divide it in two. Wrap up each half in plastic wrap, and chill for at least 2 hours. If you can spare the time, I recommend letting it rest overnight for the least sticky, most easily workable dough.

When you're ready to proceed, preheat your oven to 350°F and line two baking sheets with parchment paper or silicone baking mats.

Roll out one half of the dough at a time on a lightly floured, clean surface, to about ⅛- to ¼-inch thick. Use a fluted pastry wheel or plain pizza cutter to slice the graham cracker shapes into either 2½-inch squares for s'mores or ice cream sandwiches, or 2½ x 5-inch rectangles to match the traditional dimensions. Carefully transfer the shapes with a flat spatula over to your prepared baking sheet and use a fork to evenly prick the cookies all over. Repeat with the second half of the dough. Afterward, gather up the scraps, re-roll, and repeat once more.

Bake for 11 to 14 minutes for the squares, 13 to 16 minutes for the rectangles, until very lightly golden brown around the edges and no longer shiny on top. Let cool completely on the sheets. Store in an airtight container at room temperature.

Homemade Marshmallows

MAKES 48–60 MARSHMALLOWS

After almost 15 years of experimentation and about 100 pounds of sugar down the drain, I finally did it. I finally made real, fluffy, squishy, bouncy, vegan marshmallows. No gelatin, and no corn syrup for that matter, either. I'm so happy, I could drink myself silly with melty mallow-y hot chocolate, and now you can, too!

1½ cups aquafaba, divided
½ teaspoon cream of tartar
2 teaspoon xanthan gum
2 cups granulated sugar
2 teaspoons agar powder
½ cup water
1 vanilla bean, split and scraped
1 teaspoon vanilla extract
½ cup tapioca or potato starch

Lightly grease a 13 x 9-inch baking dish and set aside.

Place 1 cup of the aquafaba and cream of tartar in your stand mixer with the whisk attachment installed and beat to stiff peaks. Slowly sift in the xanthan gum while the motor is running, until completely incorporated. Pause when the mixture is thick and fluffy.

Meanwhile, combine the sugar and agar in a medium saucepan with the remaining ½ cup aquafaba, water, vanilla bean seeds, and extract. Stir once to moisten all the sugar and then keep your spatula out of it! Gently swirl the pan from this point forward to prevent the mixture from crystalizing. Bring to a boil and cook until it reaches 250°F.

Turn the mixer up to high speed and very carefully stream the sugar syrup in. Beat for 1 minute longer before quickly transferring the sticky fluff to your prepared baking dish. Work quickly as it will begin to set as soon as it cools.

Let rest at room temperature for 30 minutes before wrapping the whole tray in plastic and refrigerating for at least 4 hours, or ideally overnight. When thoroughly chilled, turn out the massive mallow onto a clean counter coated generously with tapioca or potato starch. Use kitchen shears or a very sharp knife coated with more starch to slice small cubes. Toss each once in the starch to coat, to prevent them from sticking to one another.

Stored in an airtight container in the fridge, the marshmallows will keep for at least 5 days, though they will grow progressively softer and stickier.

Honey Syrup

MAKES ABOUT 1¼ CUPS

When plain old agave just won't do, this bee-free "honey" imposter is close enough to actual flower nectar that hive dwellers might confuse it with their own work. Even if you have no plans to use it in or on your ice cream, it's a delicious condiment to have on hand for tea, pancakes, or scones.

1½ cups granulated sugar
½ cup water
¼ cup maple syrup
1 teaspoon lemon juice
⅓ cup dried, untreated rose petals, or 1 cup fresh
¼ teaspoon orange blossom water
¼ teaspoon vanilla extract

In a medium saucepan, combine the sugar, water, maple syrup, and lemon juice, and bring to a boil. Reduce the heat so that the mixture maintains a gentle simmer for 10 minutes.

Meanwhile, if using fresh rose petals, thoroughly rinse and dry them, being careful to remove any rotten or green sections.

Remove the pan from the stove and add in the rose petals. Stir to incorporate, cover, and let steep for 45 to 60 minutes.

Strain out the spent petals (or just fish them out with a fork if they're easily removed) and finally mix in the orange blossom water and vanilla. Transfer to a glass jar and let cool completely before covering. Store in a dark place at room temperature.

The syrup will keep almost indefinitely but will begin to lose its delicate floral flavor after 6 months.

Hot Fudge Sauce

MAKES ABOUT 2 CUPS

There's no shame in taking shortcuts and I'm all for making life easier with some store-bought staples, but one thing I just can't endorse is bottled hot fudge sauce. Sure, there are some genuinely decadent, carefully crafted options of the highest caliber out on boutique shelves, but the sticker shock is more than my wallet can bear. For pennies on the dollar and just a few minutes of your time, you'll be richly rewarded for making such a deceptively simple final flourish. Satisfying enough to spoon up solo, the quality of your cocoa defines the full-bodied flavor, so don't skimp on quality here.

1 cup Dutch-processed cocoa powder
1 cup granulated sugar
½ teaspoon salt
¾ cup plain nondairy milk
½ cup vegan butter
1½ teaspoons vanilla extract

In a medium saucepan, whisk together the cocoa powder, sugar, and salt before turning on the heat or adding any liquid. This should help break up any lumps. Slowly add the nondairy milk, a little bit at a time, while whisking continuously. Once smooth, turn on the heat to medium low.

Cut the vegan butter into tablespoon-sized chunks and add them to the saucepan. Cook gently, continuing to stir, until the butter melts and everything is combined. Bring just to the brink of a boil and immediately turn off the heat. Whisk in the vanilla last.

The sauce will continue to thicken as it cools; let stand for at least 30 minutes before serving. Transfer leftovers to a glass jar and store in the refrigerator for up to 2 weeks. It will become firm once chilled, so when ready to use, simply reheat in a saucepan over medium-low heat or microwave for 15 to 45 seconds.

It's hard to go wrong with simple molten chocolate, but sometimes it's nice to spice things up, too. Here are a few of my favorite variations:

Mexican Hot Fudge Sauce: Add ½ teaspoon ground cinnamon, ⅛ teaspoon chili powder, and ⅛ teaspoon cayenne pepper.

Peppermint Crunch Hot Fudge Sauce: Add ½ teaspoon peppermint extract and 3 tablespoons cacao nibs.

Dark Mocha Hot Fudge Sauce: Add 2 teaspoons instant coffee powder or granules.

Tropical Citrus Hot Fudge Sauce: Replace the nondairy milk with full-fat coconut milk, swap the vegan butter for coconut oil, and add 1 teaspoon orange zest.

Ladyfingers

MAKES ABOUT 2 DOZEN

More like miniature snack cakes than cookies, ladyfingers are spongy little sweets that are rarely eaten solo but are indispensable components of many classic desserts. Eggs proliferate in packaged options, as no vegan manufacturers have yet stepped up to make their own ready-made renditions. Never fear! I promise, they're even easier than pie to whip up at home.

⅓ cup aquafaba
½ cup granulated sugar
1 cup all-purpose flour
3 tablespoons potato starch
1 teaspoon baking powder
½ teaspoon vanilla extract
½ teaspoon lemon zest (optional)
2 tablespoons confectioners' sugar

Preheat your oven to 350°F. and line two baking sheets with silicon baking mats or pieces of parchment paper.

Place the aquafaba into the bowl of your stand mixer and install the whisk attachment. Whip on medium speed until frothy, and slowly begin to sprinkle in the granulated sugar. Increase the speed to high and continue to whip for about 5 to 7 minutes, until soft peaks form.

Separately, sift together the flour, starch, and baking powder, mixing to evenly distribute all the dry ingredients. Add about half of the dry ingredients into the bowl of fluff, and gently use a large spatula to fold it in, being careful not to beat out all the bubbles. Incorporate the remainder of the dry goods along with the vanilla and lemon zest, if using. The resulting batter should be fairly thick, but still airy at the same time.

Spoon the batter into a piping bag fitted with a large, round tip (about ½-inch) and pipe 3-inch long strips onto your prepared sheets, spacing each about 1 inch apart.

Sprinkle a light coat of confectioners' sugar over the cookies with a sifter or fine mesh strainer, and bake for 9 to 12 minutes, until the cookies no longer appear shiny and are just barely browned around the edges.

Maple Marshmallow Sauce

MAKES ABOUT 1 CUP

Everyone knows that the best part of a s'mores or a crispy rice treat is the gooey marshmallow goodness holding it all together, so let's cut to the chase. Sticky, sweet, fluffy, and creamy, this sugar rush in a jar deserve a place on every sundae bar. Accented with the woodsy smokiness of maple syrup and ambrosial botanical notes of vanilla, this version is more than mere child's play. All grown up with an unexpected wealth of complexity, there's no shame in spooning it into your morning mug of coffee, too.

⅔ cup aquafaba
½ cup + 2 tablespoons granulated sugar, divided
¼ teaspoon cream of tartar
⅓ cup maple syrup
1 teaspoon vanilla extract

To begin, install the whisk attachment in your stand mixer and place the aquafaba in the bowl. Beat briefly with 2 tablespoons of the sugar and cream of tartar until foamy. Increase to high speed and continue to whip until the mixture achieves peaks. If you have a splatter guard, you may want to take a moment to attach it now.

Meanwhile, in a saucepan, combine the remaining ½ cup sugar and maple syrup. Set over medium heat and bring to a full, rolling boil.

Resume beating the aquafaba mixture on medium-high speed and in a slow, steady stream, pour the hot liquid syrup into the bowl. Try to aim for the center of the bowl, away from the sides, to reduce the amount of potential splash and splatter.

Increase the speed and continue to whip on high for 5 minutes, until bright white and fluffy, but still soft and pourable in consistency. Add the vanilla extract and beat for 1 more minute.

Serve right away, or store in an airtight container in the fridge for up to 1 week, or in the freezer for 2 months. If frozen, thaw for about an hour in the refrigerator before using.

Maraschino Cherries

MAKES 1 PINT

The literal cherry on top was never a prize when I was growing up. The taste reminded me only of cough syrup, saccharine and artificial, dripping with day-glow red dye. Discovering fresh cherries spun my whole world around, opening my eyes up to the incredible range of vibrant, highly nuanced, and distinctive varieties out there. Making amends with the maligned maraschino cherry takes considerable effort, but it turns out that starting fresh is the best way to redeem this relationship, too. Sour cherries, tiny, tart, and thin-skinned, are the only kind suitable for such treatment, especially since they're too acidic to eat out of hand. Stalk the farmers markets around late July and when you spot them, don't hesitate; they'll be gone next week.

½ cup pomegranate juice
½ cup granulated sugar
2 tablespoons lemon juice
1 pint sour cherries, pitted (stemmed if desired)
1 cup maraschino liqueur, kirsch, or amaretto

In a medium saucepan over medium heat, combine the pomegranate juice, sugar, and lemon juice. Bring to a boil, allowing the sugar to completely dissolve before adding the cherries and liqueur of choice.

Reduce the heat to medium low, keeping the liquid at a gentle simmer for 10 minutes. Remove the pan from the stove, cover, and let cool completely, slowly infusing the cherries in the process. The cherries are ready to enjoy right away, but get better with a bit of age. Store in an airtight container in the fridge for up to 6 months.

Orange Marmalade

Makes about 5 cups

Homemade marmalade is the crowning jewel atop any breakfast spread, shimmering in the sunshine like a genuine pot of gold. Bathe your whole kitchen with the aromatic perfume of fresh citrus with every new batch, as restorative as a walk in the orange groves themselves. There's a fine line between bitter and sweet, so I've carefully calibrated the balance between zest and sugar. It's a labor of love to remove the harshly astringent pith, but always worth the effort. While you can always buy marmalade for a quick fix, it may be tough to go back after making it from scratch.

4 pounds (about 8–10) medium oranges, thoroughly scrubbed and dried
2½ cups water
½ cup lemon juice
5 cups granulated sugar

Add a whole new dimension of flavor to really bring your jam to the next level. Consider adding any or all of the following along with your fruit: 2 tablespoons fresh ginger, finely grated; 1 vanilla bean, split and seeds scraped; 1 tablespoon lemon zest; 1 tablespoon orange blossom or rose water; 1 teaspoon ground black pepper.

Use a very sharp paring knife to slice away the outer orange peels, removing only the brightly colored zest. Leave behind the white pith, which is very bitter. If necessary, go back over your cut peels and shave away any pith that remains. Slice the clean zest into thin, short ribbons, and set aside.

Returning now to the naked oranges, remove the thick layer of white pith left behind. Thinly slice the fruits about ¼-inch thick, membrane and all, removing any seeds you might encounter.

Combine the zest, innards, water, and lemon juice in a large heavy pot and bring to a boil.

Meanwhile, stash a small plate in the freezer to chill. This will help determine when the marmalade is thick enough to set properly. Have 3 pint-sized jars, or 1 quart and 1 half-pint jar, cleaned and set nearby the stove.

Reduce the heat to a simmer and cook, stirring frequently, until the peels are translucent, and the liquid has reduced by at least ¾. Be patient, as this may take as long as 60 minutes. Add the sugar and continue to cook for another 45 to 55 minutes, until the liquid has almost completely evaporated. To test the consistency, spoon a dollop onto the chilled plate, let it sit for a minute, and drag a spoon through the mixture. When properly set, the marmalade will hold a clean path behind the spoon.

Remove from the heat, divide between the waiting jars, and seal immediately. Can the marmalade for long-term storage or keep in the refrigerator for quick consumption. Even if not traditionally canned, it will keep in the fridge for at least 4 to 6 months due to the high sugar content, if you can keep your spoon out of it that long, of course.

Smoked Butterscotch Sauce

MAKES ¾ CUP

Not to be confused with caramel sauce, this sticky golden nectar bears the warm undertones of molasses embedded in brown sugar, rather than harsher edge of burnt sugar granules. This makes it sweeter by default, but provides an accommodating base for more savory, salty contrasts as well. Earthy, woodsy, and intense, a hint of liquid smoke elevates this simple staple into something you might just crack open at midnight and eat with a spoon while no one's looking. If you'd rather stick with the basics for a more kid-friendly topper, go ahead and omit the liquid smoke and alcohol—but trust me, it's worth the risk to try something different.

¼ cup vegan butter
½ cup dark brown sugar, firmly packed
½ cup full-fat coconut milk
¼ teaspoon salt
1 tablespoon scotch or bourbon
1 teaspoon vanilla extract
¼ teaspoon liquid smoke

Get this saucy party started by melting the vegan butter in a medium saucepan over medium heat. Add the brown sugar, coconut milk, and salt, stirring with a rubber spatula until well blended. Bring the mixture to a full, rolling boil, scraping down the sides occasionally, and continue to boil it for about 4 to 5 minutes, until smooth and slightly thickened. The butterscotch will continue to thicken considerably as it cools, so it's important to not over-boil it or you'll end up with chewy caramel candies rather than a pourable sauce. There are worse things, of course, but it's harder to serve those over ice cream!

Remove the mixture from the stove before stirring in the scotch or bourbon, vanilla, and liquid smoke. Stir thoroughly to incorporate.

Cool to room temperature and store in a glass jar. In the fridge, it will keep for up to 3 weeks.

Warm gently in the microwave, heating at intervals of 15 seconds, to serve.

Speculoos Spread

MAKES 1 GENEROUS CUP

Gaining popularity in the states well before the cookie itself, the best way to describe speculoos is to imagine if peanut butter were made of cookies rather than nuts. Velvety smooth, mildly flavored, and sweet as frosting, you'd be hard pressed to include it as part of a balanced breakfast. Something about the commercial variety just never struck my fancy, striking me as both waxy and pasty at the same time, with too little flavor payoff to make the consistency worth suffering through. Sure, my homemade rendition has a bit more grit and crunch to it, but I like to think of that as much-needed character in a textural wasteland. Plus, avoiding all the questionable oils and stabilizers is a nice added bonus.

5 ounces speculoos cookies (about 1¼ cups finely ground)
2 tablespoons vegan cream cheese
1 tablespoon maple syrup or light agave nectar
¼ cup vegan butter or coconut oil, melted

Lightly smash the cookies into smaller pieces to make them easier to break down before placing them in your food processor. Pulse until they are very fine crumbs. Add the cream cheese and syrup, pulse to combine, and then allow the motor to run. Slowly stream in the butter or coconut oil. After incorporating all of the oil, pause to scrape down the sides of the bowl, and then puree for about 2 to 3 minutes more to make sure the mixture is fully emulsified and smooth.

Store in an airtight container at room temperature for up to a week, or in the fridge for up to 3 weeks. Once chilled, the spread will solidify, but softens up nicely after just a few seconds in the microwave.

Can't find authentic speculoos cookies to begin with? Try substituting graham crackers instead, with an extra 1 teaspoon ground cinnamon added into the mix.

Strawberry Jam

MAKES ABOUT 4 CUPS

This brilliantly simple formula doesn't need any pectin, starch, or agar to set and works just as well for blackberries, blueberries, or raspberries. If you've got more room in the pot, make the most of your harvest and double up to deal with summer's bounty.

4 cups strawberries, fresh or frozen and thawed, roughly chopped
3 cups granulated sugar
2 tablespoons lemon juice
1 teaspoon vanilla extract

Make your jam seedless by passing the puree through a fine mesh strainer. Discard the solids and proceed with the recipe as written.

Place the berries in a large saucepan over high heat, mashing them roughly with a sturdy wooden spoon or potato masher as they begin to warm. Add the sugar and lemon juice, stirring roughly to incorporate while continuing to break down the fruit. Bring to a full rolling boil and cook for 10 to 15 minutes, stirring constantly.

When the jam is ready, it should reach about 220°F. On a candy thermometer, or use the old-fashioned "spoon test": dip a cold metal spoon into the hot jam. Immediately lift it out and away from the steam and turn it horizontally. At the beginning of the cooking process, the liquid will drip off like a light syrup. The jam is done when the drops are very thick and run together before falling off the spoon.

Stir in the vanilla, ladle into glass jars, and seal immediately. Let cool completely before using.

Super Seedy Granola Crunch

MAKES 4 CUPS

Granola preferences are as personal and definitive as an individual's fashion sense. Do your tastes skew towards austere oats, or something more indulgent, akin to dessert for breakfast? Are you a spicy, or more of a plain Jane? My favorite blends all yield thick, hearty clusters, teeming with toasted seeds, a gentle hint of cinnamon whispering sweet nothings in every spoonful. Distinctive yet adaptable for any occasion, this essential blend will never steer you wrong.

2¼ cups old-fashioned rolled oats, divided
2 tablespoons whole flaxseeds
⅔ cup crispy quinoa or rice cereal
¼ cup pepitas (shelled pumpkin seeds)
¼ cup sunflower seeds
2 tablespoons chia seeds
2 tablespoons hemp seeds
1 teaspoon ground cinnamon
½ teaspoon salt
½ cup maple syrup
¼ cup coconut oil, melted

For a **Simplified Seedy Granola**, feel free to cut down on the variety of inclusions and double up on the good stuff. Increase the pepitas to ½ cup, omit the sunflower seed, substitute additional whole flaxseeds instead of the chia, and simply omit the hemp.

Preheat your oven to 300°F. and line a baking sheet with parchment paper; set aside.

Begin by placing ¼ cup of the oats and all the flaxseeds into your blender or food processor, grinding them into a fine flour. This will help bind everything together and make those crisp, crunchy clusters.

Transfer the powdered blend into a large bowl and add in the quinoa or rice cereal, pepitas, sunflower seeds, chia seeds, hemp seeds, cinnamon, and salt. Stir thoroughly to combine.

In a separate bowl, whisk together the maple syrup and oil before pouring the liquid ingredients into the bowl of dry. Mix vigorously to coat and moisten all the cereals and seeds, forming small, moist clumps.

Spread the granola out in an even layer on your prepared baking sheet and slide it into the oven. Bake for 40 to 45 minutes, rotating and stirring halfway through, until lightly browned and fragrant. Let cool completely and gently break the granola into bite-sized clusters. Store in an airtight container at room temperature for up to 2 weeks.

Sweetened Condensed Cashew Milk

MAKES 1½ CUPS

Stack the culinary deck in your favor with this ace in your pocket. It may seem like a frivolous curiosity until you have it on hand and experience firsthand just how much it can do. A neutral base of raw cashews provides a versatile foundation for the more subtle buttery sweetness to shine through. As a standalone sauce, the viscous white syrup clings tenaciously to any dessert like liquefied vanilla frosting. Used as an ingredient for baking or confectionary exploits, it works just as well as the conventional canned dairy. Most importantly for my needs, it works as a 1-to-1 swap for melted ice cream in any of the previous Meltdown Masterpieces (page 237), if you can't bear to thaw out a precious pint.

¾ cup raw cashews, soaked for 6 hours
½ cup granulated sugar
½ cup water
2 tablespoons vegan butter, melted
¼ teaspoon vanilla extract
⅛ teaspoon salt

Thoroughly drain the cashews before placing them in your blender, along with the remaining ingredients. Blend on high speed for 6 to 8 minutes, until completely smooth. Cashews should be entirely pureed, and sugar dissolved. The resulting cream should be about the consistency of creamy yet sticky pancake batter.

Store in an airtight container in the fridge for up to 2 weeks.

Va'Nilla Wafers

MAKES 24–36 WAFER COOKIES

Stick with real vanilla, bold and ambrosial, to easily whip up a wafer cookie so good, it could never have come out of a box.

¼ cup vegan butter
¼ cup vegan Cream Cheese (page 282, or store-bought)
½ cup granulated sugar
¼ cup dark brown sugar, firmly packed
1⅓ cups all-purpose flour
½ teaspoon baking powder
¼ teaspoon salt
2 teaspoons vanilla extract

Preheat your oven to 325°F. and line two baking sheets with silicone baking sheets or parchment paper. Set aside.

In your stand mixer, thoroughly cream together the vegan butter, cream cheese, and both sugars, so that the mixture is fluffy and homogeneous. Scrape down the sides of the mixing bowl with a spatula as needed, to incorporate all the ingredients.

Whisk together the flour, baking powder, and salt in a separate bowl before adding all the dry goods into the stand mixer. Begin mixing on the lowest speed so that the flour doesn't fly out and dust the entire kitchen. Add in the vanilla last, and continue mixing until you've created a smooth, cohesive dough.

Scoop out about 2 teaspoons of dough per cookie, and roll into a ball between the palms of your hands. Place them at least 1 inch apart and flatten each ball out to about ¼-inch thickness. Bake for 16 to 20 minutes, until golden brown all over. Remove the baking mats or parchment from the hot baking sheets and cool completely.

Store in an airtight container at room temperature for up to 1 week.

Waffle Cones

MAKES APPROXIMATELY 20–24 SMALL WAFFLE CONES

Remember walking into an ice cream shop for the first time as a kid and being struck by the singular, unmistakable aroma of fresh waffle cones? Warm and buttery, with a hint of burnt sugar, it's the sign of a dedicated artisan at work. More than mere edible containers, tender-crisp waffle cones are stellar treats in their own rights. The Dutch have the right idea by sandwiching two flat rounds with a firm caramel core, creating stroopwaffels. *Alternately, rolled into cylinders, they can be used as the foundation for cannolis, or when wrapped even more tightly, dipped in chocolate to make spectacular pirouette cookies.*

Made on a dedicated ice cream cone maker or pizzelle iron, the biggest roadblock in this recipe is simply acquiring the proper equipment. If you're not one for unitaskers in the kitchen, however, you still have options! I've had fairly good results playing with an electric panini press, too. Beyond that, the batter is just a pour-and-stir affair, ready to turn into crisp cones with just a minute or two on the hot iron.

2 cups all-purpose flour
½ cup granulated sugar
2 tablespoons ground flaxseeds
½ teaspoon baking soda
¼ teaspoon ground cinnamon
6 tablespoons vegan butter or coconut oil, melted
⅔ cup water
1 teaspoon vanilla extract

Homemade cones almost always have holes at the bottom, varying from small pin-prick openings to rather gaping canyons. To prevent extreme drippage while eating your ice cream, plug up the bottom by filling it with a whole vegan marshmallow and/or melted chocolate, allowed to dry and harden.

Begin heating your pizzelle maker first because the batter comes together very fast. Sift together the flour, sugar, ground flaxseeds, baking soda, and cinnamon in a large bowl, whisking lightly to combine. Mix the melted butter or coconut oil, water, and vanilla briefly in a separate bowl before pouring into the dry ingredients. Stir just enough to bring the batter together without any lumps.

Very lightly grease each side of the pizzelle iron. I like to use a small cookie scoop to ensure even sizes of all of my wafer cookies, but you can also just measure out about 1 tablespoon of batter per cone. Try placing it slightly off-center on the iron, just above the middle, because the action of pressing the top iron down tends to spread it outwards. After securing the lid (usually there's a latch, which I recommend employing for the thinnest, most even wafers) bake for about 30 to 60 seconds, until golden brown. Quickly pry the cookies loose with a thin metal spatula and transfer to your wire rack. Though floppy at first, they will continue to crisp up as they cool.

Carefully wrap the hot, flexible cookie around a waffle cone roller or metal cream horn mold, creating a cone shape. Place the cookie on a flat surface with the seam down, holding it closed, until cool and hardened. Slide the cone off the mold and transfer to a wire rack. Repeat this process for the remaining batter.

Wet Nuts

MAKE 1 CUP

Truth be told, my primary motivation for reviving this antiquated ice cream topping was simply immaturity. My juvenile impulses wanted the opportunity to offer a generous spoonful of sweet wet nuts with a straight face, just to see the reaction. Lucky for you, they're far more delicious than the depraved title may sound! Traditionally made with corn syrup and walnuts, my rendition is all grown up with maple syrup and pecans instead, even if the name remains as childish as ever. Feel free to call it a "toasted pecan sauce" if that makes you more comfortable.

⅓ cup maple syrup
3 tablespoons dark brown sugar, firmly packed, or coconut sugar
1 teaspoon vanilla extract
¼ teaspoon salt
1 cup toasted pecans, roughly chopped

Bring the maple syrup, brown sugar, vanilla extract, and salt to a boil in a medium saucepan over moderate heat. Once the sugar has fully dissolved, stir in pecans and simmer for about 3 minutes, until the syrup thickly coats the nuts. Let cool and serve, or transfer to a glass jar with an airtight lid. Store in the refrigerator for up to 1 month.

Conversion Charts

Metric and Imperial Conversions

(These conversions are rounded for convenience)

Ingredient	Cups/Tablespoons/ Teaspoons	Ounces	Grams/Milliliters
Butter	1 cup/ 16 tablespoons/ 2 sticks	8 ounces	230 grams
Cheese, shredded	1 cup	4 ounces	110 grams
Cream cheese	1 tablespoon	0.5 ounce	14.5 grams
Cornstarch	1 tablespoon	0.3 ounce	8 grams
Flour, all-purpose	1 cup/1 tablespoon	4.5 ounces/0.3 ounce	125 grams/8 grams
Flour, whole wheat	1 cup	4 ounces	120 grams
Fruit, dried	1 cup	4 ounces	120 grams
Fruits or veggies, chopped	1 cup	5 to 7 ounces	145 to 200 grams
Fruits or veggies, pureed	1 cup	8.5 ounces	245 grams
Honey, maple syrup, or corn syrup	1 tablespoon	0.75 ounce	20 grams
Liquids: milk, water, or juice	1 cup	8 fluid ounces	240 milliliters
Oats	1 cup	5.5 ounces	150 grams
Salt	1 teaspoon	0.2 ounce	6 grams
Spices: cinnamon, cloves, ginger, or nutmeg (ground)	1 teaspoon	0.2 ounce	5 milliliters
Sugar, brown, firmly packed	1 cup	7 ounces	200 grams
Sugar, white	1 cup/1 tablespoon	7 ounces/0.5 ounce	200 grams/12.5 grams
Vanilla extract	1 teaspoon	0.2 ounce	4 grams

Index